CASES IN PUBLIC RELATIONS MANAGEMENT

RAYMOND SIMON

Utica College of Syracuse University

FRANK WINSTON WYLIE

California State University, Long Beach

NTC Business Books

a division of *NTC Publishing Group* • Lincolnwood, Illinois USA

To Judy, Lyn, and our students: your challenges and successes, sharing and support impart so much happiness.

Library of Congress Cataloging-in-Publication Data

Simon, Raymond.
   Cases in public relations management / Raymond Simon, Frank W. Wylie.
     p.   cm.
   ISBN 0-8442-3374-9
   1. Public relations—Management—Case studies.   I. Wylie, Frank W. II. Title.
HD59.S4567 1993
659.2—dc20
                     93-9214
                     CIP

Published by NTC Business Books, a division of NTC Publishing Group
4255 West Touhy Avenue
Lincolnwood (Chicago), Illinois 60646-1975, U.S.A.

3 4 5 6 7 8 9 ML 9 8 7 6 5 4 3 2 1

CONTENTS

1 UNIT — Business Organizations

UNIT 3   Counseling Firms and Agencies

UNIT 4   Personal/Personnel Concerns

Cases in Public Relations Management has evolved from an earlier work *Public Relations Management: A Casebook,* which, in three editions was used by teachers and students in more than 100 colleges and universities in the United States and abroad, and in one- and two-day corporate and nonprofit organizational workshops. Its main purpose remains the same as that of its predecessors: to provide a teaching and learning resource for upper-level and graduate courses in public relations and for practitioner seminars and workshops.

The basic premise of this case book postulates that those who go through the experience of dealing with cases in real life public relations settings and situations will better be able to cope with the rigorous challenges of public relations practice. Realistic cases, developed from actual situations which faced practitioners, provide students with the opportunity to come to grips with the kind of problems they will face when they enter the field. Taking advantage of that opportunity is dependent on understanding the following crucial elements of the case method of instruction and of this case book:

• In case study classes the professor does not "instruct" but serves mainly as a moderator who guides discussion among class members, probes for reasons behind class responses, at times adds some new details to case fact patterns, and seldom if ever provides "answers" to case situations. Because there is no one correct "answer" to the situations and problems in the cases in this book, students learn in time to consider wise and unwise "options" and to be prepared to defend their choices. As one professor told her class early in the term: "Don't look to me for the right answers because I won't be around after you graduate and encounter situations and problems. Each of you brings to class discussion a different set of skills and each of you will discover that there are a series of right and wrong ways to address and deal with situations of each case. Let the time you spend in the class be the time for you to develop your own unique skills through clear thinking about public relations problems."

• Because the facts set forth in the cases are so important, it is imperative that students absorb case fact patterns *prior* to class meetings. Whether teachers permit or prohibit open books in class, the need to know the case fact pattern before discussion ensues is essential for adequate class participation and understanding the principles behind public relations management. You can color the face red of the student who is unable to respond when asked to "please summarize the case facts."

• Virtually all the cases in this book either present flaws or faults in public relations judgment, actions, reactions, statements, and activities, or else set forth situations in which students are required to state what they would do and why they chose those actions. Role-playing is often used and students are frequently asked to respond to a situation with the exact words they would use and then to defend their remarks.

• Interaction among public relations, managerial and media people is what distinguishes the cases and the classes using this book. It is expected that through class discussions of the situations and people in the cases, students will hone their insights, perceptions, thought processes, and interpersonnel skills as they analyze how the public relations people in the cases act and interact. Finally, it is hoped that such discussions will teach students important insights about themselves and about their colleagues.

To enable those using this book to sharpen their perceptions, insights, and judgments we have assembled a wide variety of cases grouped within four categories as listed in the Contents section. We have developed 28 new cases—23 full and five mini cases—and updated and improved the 17 cases from the previous edition. The cases deal with public relations people at all levels of management and of career development. They examine practical and ethical situations and problems, and their scope ranges from the very personal problems of a young intern to the impersonal problems of large corporate and counseling organizations.

The cases present a set of facts relating to situations that faced practitioners who had to deal with these facts in handling a particular public relations problem or set of problems. People described in the cases make statements and respond in certain ways to remarks made by others in the cases. Decisions are made and actions taken. It is expected that students will act as a group in going through the process of analyzing and considering each case and exchanging ideas about the case situations and the people in them. At times students will be asked to play the roles of participants in dealing with an unfolding situation in which they are placed. Those playing roles in these situations will be required to make statements, engage in conversations, and either take action or state what action they intend to take in handling a specific set of public relations or personal problems.

As the class goes through each case discussion, students will begin to come to grips with the very real problems faced by those who play the main roles in the cases. Class members should, in effect, try to see the case through the eyes and mind of those involved, and to note and comment about the validity and soundness of assumptions which have been made and actions which have been taken. In the end analysis, both the cases and simulations should serve as catalytic agents. To be most effective they should trigger among the class members a series of comments which will usually trigger other responses from the participants. The class will discover that someone has seen an important nuance which others have overlooked; that someone will question a case item which has been taken for granted; that someone has a good "answer" which is totally at variance with other "answers." It is our hope that those participating in the discussion will find that the cases and discussions will have helped to clarify each student's thinking and will provide valuable public relations and personal lessons for the future.

At various points throughout this book of cases we have included "Reprint for Discussion,": articles, interviews, talks, and comments by leading public relations practitioners and by those writing and reporting about the American public relations scene. The reprints are generally not as long or as involved as the cases and are meant to serve as alternative focal points for discussion or for written reaction assignments. Some teachers prefer to assign reprint reading in advance and some prefer to bring a reprint to class attention following a discussion of the case. As with the cases, the reprints are meant to serve as catalytic agents for student discussion and exchange of ideas and thinking about public relations concepts and practices.

Finally, we want to express our warm appreciation to those who have provided the material and data for the cases in this book and for those who graciously granted us reprint permission. A special note of deep appreciation is extended to our wives and families for constant encouragement, support, and forebearance, and to NTC Business Books editors Anne Knudsen and Karen Shaw for their skillful and most helpful editing.

. . .

We decided to begin this book of cases with an excerpt from a lecture by Harold Burson, rather than with a case, because we believe that the substance of Burson's remarks sets the scene for the cases by providing an overall framework for the roles of public relations. Burson is the founder and chairman of the Burson-Marsteller public relations counseling firm.

His thoughts about the roles public relations should play in today's society are presented in the Overview for your analysis and discussion.

Raymond Simon
Professor Emeritus of
  Public Relations
Utica College of Syracuse
  University
Utica, N.Y.

Frank Winston Wylie
Professor Emeritus of
  Journalism
California State
  University, Long Beach
Long Beach, CA

Available to instructors, trainers, and seminar leaders is the accompanying *Case Analysis Manual* (ISBN: 0-8442-3373-0). Please contact:

NTC Publishing Group
4255 West Touhy Ave.
Lincolnwood
IL 60646
(708) 679-5500

FOUR MAIN ROLES OF PUBLIC RELATIONS*

Harold Burson

. . . Who will speak for the corporation as a social institution?

Who will help it anticipate social change?

Who will help it shape policies and practices that respond to the will of a democratic society?

And who will make sure that it lives up to its own stated standards and ideals?

I first started thinking seriously about those questions when I was invited by Columbia University to deliver their first Garrett Lecture on Public Policy and Social Responsibility. I was honored then—as I am today—because Paul Garrett, first vice president of public relations at General Motors, endowed the Garrett Chair of Corporate Social Responsibility at Columbia's Graduate School of Business.

In that lecture, I observed that public relations professionals fulfill a role for the corporation that can be divided into four parts.

First, they serve as a sensor of social change. They perceive those rumblings at the heart of society that augur good or ill for their organizations.

To succeed in this role, they must possess a sensitive

Excerpted from the inaugural lecture in the Harold Burson Distinguished Lecture Series at Utica College of Syracuse University. Reprinted with permission of Mr. Burson.

antenna and excellent analytical skills. That's because every issue starts in a small way. Some melt away, and some snowball.

Women's liberation is an example of the issue that would not go away. The genesis of women's lib was implicit in Betty Friedan's book, *The Feminine Mystique*. But it didn't get too much attention at first in the boardrooms of male-dominated corporations.

Neither did Rachel Carson's *Silent Spring*. It was either ignored or ridiculed by the managements of some of our larger chemical companies. Indeed, some mounted communications campaigns to discredit the environmental notions expressed in *Silent Spring*.

But those first small voices on equal opportunity and pollution were joined by others. And, with the help of television, they grew to thunderous roars in legislatures across the land.

It's my belief that public relations professionals must detect those issues that are potentially explosive and help management prepare for their onslaught and their impact.

The second role of the public relations professional is that of corporate conscience. In his influential essay written 150 years ago, Henry David Thoreau wrote:

> It is truly enough said that a corporation has no conscience; but a corporation of conscientious men is a corporation with a conscience.

Those are powerful words, and ones which the public relations professional should always bear in mind. But please don't misunderstand.

I don't mean that the public relations professional is by nature either more sensitive, more ethical, or more dedicated to the public interest than executives with different titles. These qualities may exist in others, but they are not basic to their job description. They are—or they should be—basic to the job description of public relations officers.

The third major role is that of communicator. Public relations people must be verbal—that is, they must be able to write well. And they must be articulate—that is, they must be able to speak well. I say this because their first line of communications may be internal—to the individuals inside the company.

An individual, for example, who is a good sensor of social change but a poor communicator will surely fail. The reverse is also true. It's quite possible to write well-crafted messages that don't respond to reality.

Many people, including many in public relations, think communications is the main public relations role. Most likely, they think that way because they have spent a lot of time mastering communications skills and very little time honing their social judgments. Communications is not the one main role; it is one of four important roles.

The fourth role of public relations is to serve as a corporate monitor—to make sure corporate policies and programs match public expectations.

I'm tempted to use the word "ombudsman" here. Obviously the public relations officer can't be an ombudsman in the strict sense of the word, but I do think the spirit of the ombudsman should pervade his job.

Of course this is not possible unless the chief executive, who has a lot of other things to do, understands the necessity for this role and supports it to the hilt. And this, I think, is perhaps the best reason for the senior public relations officer to report to the highest level of management, the chief executive officer. Access is essential.

Interestingly, a number of newspapers around the country have experimented with this idea. They have appointed a respected reporter to serve as an ombudsman who calls public attention to lapses in journalistic ethics and responsibilities.

I think we must ask ourselves: Do corporations have less public responsibility than newspapers? I tend to doubt it. I don't think corporations need to go "public" with all their mistakes. But I do think they need to have them audited and aired—at least internally—in a healthy manner, and the public relations professional is the logical person by temperament and training to take a major role in this process.

Those, then, are the four main roles as I view them. The public relations professional must be:

- the corporate sensor of social change

- the corporate conscience

- the corporate communicator, and

- the corporate monitor.

I do believe that professional public relations, which began with the pejorative PR, has gained in stature and has a socially useful role to perform.

I do believe that role is guaranteed—indeed, licensed—by the First Amendment, and that it will increase in value with the passage of time.

In that context, I can say I have but one regret. I wish I were sitting where you students are sitting. I wish I were beginning my career.

Because I believe that the best is yet to come.

And I believe that those of you who rise to the challenge will one day look back on your careers with the same sense of gratification that I feel today.

EMBARGO CONFRONTATION AT JONUS CORPORATION*

Two months ago, on June 16, the Jonus Corporation, a major manufacturer of computer hardware, held a special preview for trade, science, and business magazines. The concept of this preview was that information and product pictures would be given to the magazines early enough to meet their printing deadlines. In exchange, the magazines attending this preview had agreed to hold the materials until the specified release date of September 1 for a new notebook computer and September 15 for the other products.

The major new product, a $5 \times 7''$ notebook computer with built-in scanning capability, had a separate release date from the other products because the Jonus public relations director, Jack Quinn, thought the company would secure more media coverage that way. The advance magazine preview enabled the magazines to use the new product materials and pictures at the same time as the newspapers, radio, and TV. This was particularly important to Quinn, who coordinated the preview, because the trade magazines are the bibles in the computer business. The magazines paid all expenses for their editors and reporters, and Quinn was very pleased

*All names, places, and dates in this case are disguised.

by their enthusiastic comments about the new products and by the preview event.

On Wednesday, August 15, the Jonus Corporation held a national meeting in New York with financial analysts. The firm's top executives and key PR staff members arrived on the company jet the day before. In addition to general sessions, the analysts had an opportunity for one-on-one interviews. It was a busy and convivial occasion. The analysts wanted their exclusives, and the company was anxious to get all the exposure it could for its new products, reorganization, and improved profit margins. It was also an ideal time to showcase the top executives, especially the chairman and CEO, William Bradford Boynton, 63, who was two years away from the company's mandatory retirement age. A lawyer by profession, he had been with Jonus's legal firm, had joined the corporation as executive vice president, and had been named CEO five years ago.

Generally speaking, Boynton was heartily disliked by both the press and the staff of Jonus. He was not overly popular with the analysts either. Those who knew him better and had more occasion to interact with him, liked him less. They saw him as arrogant, egocentric, and mean, a man with a great sense of his own importance and authority. At Jonus, there were only two basic choices: Boynton's way and the wrong way. Increasingly ignoring channels, he called sudden meetings to announce his decisions and enforced his will by authority and a fierce temper.

The meeting with the analysts started with a long, lavish cocktail party followed by a dinner. Except during the last half hour of the cocktail party and the dinner, the interviews continued, and a few were held afterward. At all times, public relations people manned the pressroom, and both financial and technical experts were available to field any questions. It was a pleasant, productive event.

Boynton Calls a Meeting

Slightly after 10:30 p.m., Jack Quinn got a call to go to the CEO's suite. As a 20-year public relations veteran with the company, Quinn was wary, concerned. Boynton was the most unpredictable of the four chairmen the 43-year-old Quinn had known. As he went to the chairman's suite, he wondered what the meeting might be about. Who was Boynton going to attack, and why? Was it a real problem or had the evening and hospitality just progressed too far? It could be anything, but he knew that the more you work in public relations, the more you learn that there is always something new. This late, sudden meeting was certainly a first.

Quinn was a dedicated optimist. He worked hard, planned ahead, and tried to anticipate all the problems that could come along. Although he had been with the company for two decades, he had quit and been hired back twice. The first time, he received a substantial raise. The second time he was promised, and got, a promotion. The years had given him a sense of confidence in his own abilities as a public relations director. He was making $75,000 plus bonus and options. Given a relatively free hand with the corporation's public relations department, he reported to the vice president of public affairs, Martin Simonis, 57, an experienced, capable, registered lobbyist who worked mainly on government affairs in Washington.

While each day would bring something new, especially with unpredictable Chairman Boynton, Quinn never doubted that he had the ability to handle the problems that came along. His wife, two college-age sons, and his 20 associates in the public relations department knew how he felt. As he once stated, "There's no assurance that I'll have the same job at the end of the day, but if you're willing to stand up for your beliefs, you must be willing to give up the job to protect your integrity." He felt there was nothing sanctimonious about this; it was just the way he felt about public relations.

As he entered the CEO's suite that night, Quinn quickly noticed that all of the top executives had been summoned. Some seemed to have had more than enough to drink. No one seemed to know why they'd been called together. The room was packed, tense. Conversation was nervous. Then Boynton, standing at the front of the room, called for quiet. It was to be one of the shortest, sharpest meetings ever at Jonus.

"You're probably all wondering why I called you together tonight," said Boynton. "Well, this evening I was talking to Roger Stevenson—I assume most of you know he's the publisher of one of the country's most prestigious consumer magazines—and he told me that he will give us the cover of his magazine if we let him have the pictures of our prize new notebook computer on August 25th.

"He needs an answer tomorrow morning, and I promised to give it to him. It sounds like I have a pretty good deal, wouldn't you say?"

The room was deathly still. These executives had seen Boynton in action, and they knew also that Boynton liked to be the one who straightened things out, made the world work. Twenty seconds passed.

Quinn, who was standing in the rear of the room, took a quick look at Simonis and saw that he was staring at the ceiling. It was obvious to Quinn that Simonis didn't intend to say anything. Almost impulsively, and a bit louder than he had intended, Quinn spoke up.

"That's immoral," he said.

The words hung in the air. As in an old western movie, everyone moved to the sides of the room, leaving Boynton and Quinn facing each other.

"Are you calling me immoral?" a flushed Boynton said, raising his voice.

"No, I'm not calling you immoral," Quinn replied. "I'm just saying that anyone who would do that is immoral. Two months ago we established the release date, met with the magazines, and secured their agreement to hold to it. It would be immoral for us to break our own agreement with them."

Boynton, still flushed and seeming ready to explode, said nothing for ten seconds. "Well," he finally said, "we don't have to decide this tonight. If any of you have some more thoughts about this, see me in the morning. This meeting is over."

Boynton turned swiftly and strode into the other room. The exodus was quiet, orderly, and quick.

Some Second Thoughts

As soon as Quinn got back to his hotel room he did two things. First he replayed in his mind the scene that had just ended, then he worked out what options were available to him.

Quinn had always felt that an intelligent person ought to learn lessons from life's experiences. So the first question he asked himself was: How did I handle myself? Perhaps I simply should have said nothing at that particular time, avoided a public confrontation, and spoke to Boynton later.

Yet, on second thought, perhaps I was right in speaking up, but maybe I should have phrased it differently. Did I come on too strong? But what should I have said, and why say it that way? If I'm going to second-guess myself, I had better have intelligent alternative remarks, right?

The thought then occurred to Quinn that it might have been wiser to phrase his objection in practical rather than philosophical terms. For example, he thought, why didn't I point out that "hold for" dates would be history once Jonus gave the exclusive to Stevenson?

Finally, Quinn thought, why be so introspective? He was a realist enough to recognize he couldn't retract what he said, and so he set to work considering the options open to him that night and the next morning and explored the pros and cons of each option.

Reprint for Discussion

USA TODAY Articles on Toyota Embargo *
James R. Healey

. . . .

**T100 Product of
Research, Strife**

Toyota's 1993 T100 pickup, on sale Nov. 12, is the product of years of internal debate and second-guessing at Japan's mightiest automaker.

The beginning was a low-profile trip to the USA by T100's chief engineer, Shigeo Asai, in October 1986. Then, and during subsequent trips, he photographed folks using their big pickups—farmers throwing bales, families crammed into the pickup cabs wheeling through parking lots, beefy construction workers unloading equally beefy gear and cowboy-hatted dudes posturing down the road.

That was a necessary prelude because creating—even conceiving—a big pickup was difficult for Japanese designers. There is no such thing in Japan. Pickups there are small to fit crowded streets. And they are regarded strictly as work vehicles. Japanese don't commute or cruise in trucks.

Toyota's U.S. designers, more familiar with big pickups, were tied up with other projects and had no time to work on the T100.

A team was formed in 1987 to create a pickup to intercept compact-truck owners moving up to Detroit's big honkers. Simple idea, complicated process—and one that took strong lobbying by U.S. Toyota officials. For T100 to live:

  • T100 proponents—mainly U.S. dealers and Toyota's U.S. marketing arm— had to overcome Toyota's internal resistance to building a vehicle tailored so exclusively for just one market, North America.

Toyota now figures it also can sell the T100 in the Middle East, Australia and other roomy locales.

- Backers had to reassure some gun-shy Japanese managers worried about the political fallout when a Japanese automaker finally invaded Detroit's highest-profit niche.

- U.S. managers had to fight to get Japan to make the truck big enough for U.S.-size loads.

- To price T100 close to U.S. competitors, Toyota had to omit costly features such as safety air bags and a V-8 engine. T100 uses a V-6.

As T100 dragged on, the plans became an open secret in the USA. Magazines began running spy photos of T100 trucks undergoing testing. Impatient U.S. dealers began screaming. Excited U.S. suppliers began bragging that they were good enough to sell axles, radiators and batteries to Toyota.

Despite all that, Japanese officials maintained an attitude of "What truck?"

Finally, James Olson, a Toyota public-relations vice president in the USA, confirmed the truck's existence June 17. A few days later, auto writers received invitations to a T100 preview in Oregon the last week of July.

Why the Embargo Was Broken

You are reading about Toyota's important new T100 big pickup truck three months early.

The truck won't be out until November, and stories about it aren't supposed to be, either.

USA TODAY and other news organizations got to see and drive the T100 late last month in return for agreeing to publish nothing until Nov. 10. Such agreements are usual.

The preview was timed so that influential magazines

such as *Car and Driver, Motor Trend,* and *Sport Truck* could prepare major features for editions out in early November.

USA TODAY is breaking the embargo because information about the truck has become common knowledge. Detroit automakers have obtained copies of Toyota's fact kit and have begun discussing Toyota's truck in detail with reporters and insiders.

Also, trade weekly *Automotive News* published five photos and a cover story on the T100 early last week.

That magazine, because of a dispute with Toyota, was not invited to the July preview. It got photos from an unidentified person at the preview and scraped up other details from anonymous sources. Strictly speaking, *Automotive News* broke no embargo. It did not attend the event and thus never promised to wait.

"Ordinarily, we honor our news embargoes," says *USA TODAY* editor Peter Prichard. "But once news is out in the media marketplace, we see no reason to suppress it."

Toyota says those who violate the embargo will be banned from future previews and that publishing the information now isn't fair.

Why do publications such as *USA TODAY* attend embargoed previews? Because editors and reporters get information that—while they can't publish it—lets them avoid incorrect speculation that often precedes new models. Sometimes, embargoed previews are the only way to get intricate details about products. Toyota's Fred Hammond notes, "It's almost impossible to get the chief engineer on a new model over from Japan more than once, so we try to do one event for all journalists. We assume there will be integrity among journalists about honoring the embargo."

P&G, NEWS LEAKS, AND
THE WALL STREET JOURNAL (A)

On Monday and Tuesday, June 10 and 11, 1991, *The Wall Street Journal* (*WSJ*) carried two articles concerning Procter & Gamble (P&G), the $27 billion consumer products giant headquartered in Cincinnati, Ohio. Both articles were written by Alecia Swasy of the *WSJ*'s Pittsburgh bureau and carried her by-line.

The lead of Swasy's June 10 article, which ran to 5 column inches on page B5, stated that "B. Jurgen Hintz, executive vice president at Procter & Gamble Co., has resigned under pressure after failing to fix the company's troubled food business."

The rest of the article dealt with Hintz's place in the top tier of P&G and how his departure might relate to the three-person race to succeed 61-year-old Edwin L. Artzt as the next chief executive officer of P&G.

The June 11 article, which also ran on an inside page, totaled 15 column inches and was headlined: P&G May Soon Peddle Something New: Pieces of Its Food and Beverage Division.

Referring to unnamed current and former P&G managers as her sources, Swasy stated in her lead that the company "may carve up its troubled food and beverage division and sell off some of the pieces." Citrus Hill orange juice was described in the article as one of the "unprofitable" brands; Crisco shortening and Fisher

Nuts were termed "laggards"; and Crush soft drinks and Duncan Hines chewy cookies were described as P&G "blunders."

As regards B. Jurgen Hintz, Swasy stated that the company confirmed that he will leave P&G, and she added that "it's unclear when the management change was made. Company officials late Sunday denied that any news release on a change was pending." Swasy cited "insiders" as saying that in recent months the CEO, Edwin Artzt, termed the food business as the worst managed part of the company.

Two months after the two articles by Alecia Swasy ran in the *WSJ*, the paper on Monday, August 12, carried a page-one story updating its P&G coverage. Written by staff reporter James S. Hirsch, the 26-column-inch story stated that in an attempt to track the source of news leaks to the *WSJ*, P&G had persuaded county authorities to investigate. Acting on a complaint from P&G, wrote Hirsch, the authorities used a grand-jury subpoena to obtain from Cincinnati Bell records of telephone conversations between area residents and the *WSJ*'s Pittsburgh office and also calls made between Cincinnati and the Pittsburgh residence of Alecia Swasy. Hirsch said that a special investigator in the city's fraud squad division confirmed that the subpoena was obtained three weeks earlier.

According to Hirsch, the *WSJ* learned about the investigation of the leaks on August 8 when a former P&G manager called the paper to report he had been questioned for an hour by the Cincinnati fraud squad, who told him they had records of his calls to the *WSJ* office and Swasy's home. Hirsch quoted a P&G spokeswoman as follows:

> Cincinnati police are investigating criminal charges regarding the disclosure of highly confidential and proprietary information. It involves the unauthorized disclosure of business secrets,

and that presents a potential violation of Ohio criminal law.

According to Hirsch, the spokeswoman declined to confirm that *WSJ* was the publication involved.

A spokeswoman for Cincinnati Bell was cited by Hirsch as stating that the company, responding to the subpoena, turned over to the police printouts of long-distance calls from the Cincinnati area. Pointing out that the First Amendment and many state laws, including those in Ohio, protect reporters from disclosing the names of confidential sources, Hirsch stated: "P&G's move in effect has been to obtain the help of local authorities to bypass these protections through the use of prosecutorial subpoena power."

The *WSJ* story reported that attorneys for the paper demanded that the telephone company cease releasing to authorities records of telephone calls to *WSJ* reporters. In addition, the attorneys objected to the phone company's compliance with the subpoena without having given notice to the publisher.

According to Gary Armstrong, identified in the story as the special investigator in the city's fraud division, both P&G and the Cincinnati authorities claim that an Ohio statute bars anyone from giving away "articles representing trade secrets."

The *WSJ* story cited some legal experts as contending that they knew of no cases where the Ohio criminal law had been used to identify news sources. A specialist in First Amendment cases was quoted as saying such use of the Ohio law "smacks of outright censorship by imposing on people the prerequisite of silence."

P&G Issues Press Release

The *WSJ*'s long front-page story of Monday, August 12, brought forth a press release from P&G that was distributed to news organizations later that day.

"Recent news articles suggest highly confidential and proprietary company business information has been disclosed to people outside the company," said the release, adding that the management's "fiduciary responsibility to our shareholders" required the company to go to the police. Stating that the investigation does not violate the First Amendment rights of news reporters, the company release said that "no news media outlet is being asked to turn over any names or any information. The investigation is focused on individuals who may be violating the law."

The paper's response in its issue of Tuesday, August 13, cited in a story by reporter Hirsch on page 3 and in an editorial on page 16, was to counterpunch.

"We don't believe that we or our sources have violated any law," responded Paul E. Steiger, *WSJ*'s managing editor, in its Tuesday story. "We fear that P&G is trying to intimidate current and former employees from talking to reporters. We're appalled that prosecutors and police in Cincinnati would participate in such an effort, which we believe violates the First Amendment as well as Ohio law."

The *WSJ* editorial, headed "What Possessed P&G?", led off with this paragraph: "The marketing behemoth, Procter & Gamble, churns out Crest, Tide, Folger's, Pringles and dozens of other wholesome products. But on learning they've been prying around in our telephone records, we felt like the butt of the joke about another of their products: Want a Hawaiian Punch? Sure. KAPOW!"

The editorial termed P&G's release "a stuffy little statement protesting it only wanted lawbreakers brought to justice. We understand that P&G swings a big stick in Cincinnati, of course, and maybe the local law can, like Pampers, be stretched to cover the leak. It's not funny, though, to the folks being hassled by the cops."

The editorial's concluding suggestion was that P&G ought to be "grown up enough to recognize there's something sinister in pawing around in other people's phone records, and in suborning law-enforcement powers to pursue petty disputes."

Hirsch's story on August 13 ran to 17 column inches on page 3. In addition to citing the managing editor's statement, it also reported that the Queen City chapter of the Society of Professional Journalists had sent a letter to P&G chairman Edwin L. Artzt. In it the chapter said "your complaint has prompted a prosecutorial and police fishing expedition that amounts to censorship before the fact and could lead to further abuse of the First Amendment by other companies also disgruntled by news media coverage."

Hirsch noted in his story that P&G cited a second Ohio statute that prohibits only current employees from disclosing "confidential" company information. He reported he had asked a P&G spokesman why employee news leaks weren't handled internally, and in response the spokesman had said: "We did conduct an internal investigation and were unable to determine who was disclosing company business secrets. At that point we turned the matter over to the Cincinnati police."

Tuesday brought with it the entrance of the *New York Times* in coverage of P&G's imbroglio with the *WSJ*. Randall Rothenberg's 22-column-inch story led off with a recap of the main points of Monday's *WSJ* story, then said that several First Amendment and property law experts think the case seemed to "represent an attempt to broaden the concept of trade secrets in a way that could hinder whistle-blowers or even prevent employees from having routine discussions with reporters."

Rothenberg cited Terry Gaines, first assistant county prosecutor, as saying the subpoena issued by the grand jury was "not very broad," but he refused to comment further on the investigation. The *NYT* writer stated that Cyndy Cantoni, Cincinnati Bell media relations manager, said the telephone company could not confirm whether it was involved in an investigation, but it's company policy to comply when authorities present it with subpoenas for customer records.

Sydney McHugh, a spokeswoman for P&G, was cited as declaring "We can't discuss the nature of the business secrets." Rothenberg also reported elements of the written statement sent to news organizations the previous day by P&G.

On Wednesday, August 14, the *WSJ* ran a relatively short, 6-column-inch story on the P&G telephone record search, stating that the active phase of the investigation seemed ended and that no criminal charges were expected.

According to the story by Hirsch, Inspector Armstrong declined to comment on the results, and Gaines, the county assistant prosecutor, said he was not familiar with the progress of the police investigation. Hirsch said a P&G spokesperson reaffirmed the company's support of the First Amendment, stating the press "has the right to pursue information, but we have the right to protect proprietary information."

WSJ Reveals Scope of Telephone Search

In a story on page A3 of the *WSJ* on Thursday, August 15, Hirsch revealed the sweeping scope of the telephone record search carried out to track the news leaks concerning P&G.

Hirsch's story, which carried a Cincinnati dateline, cited the June 17 subpoena issued by the Hamilton County Common Pleas Court and said that it provided Cincinnati law-enforcement authorities with access to the telephone records of hundreds of thousands of Ohio residents.

Hirsch said that the court ordered the telephone company to identify all 513 area code numbers that dialed the home or office telephone number of reporter Alecia Swasy between March 1 and June 15. Wrote Hirsch:

> That meant the phone company had to search through some 655,297 home and business tele-

phone lines and at least 35 million toll calls made in that period. The territory involved in the search, which was done by computer, covered close to 2,400 square miles and all or part of four southern Ohio counties.

Hirsch said he asked a P&G spokesman about the scope of the subpoena, and he replied: "This investigation is being conducted by the Cincinnati police department, not P&G. You need to contact the police department about the subpoena."

According to Hirsch, the county prosecutor, Arthur Ney, declined to comment. His office said neither Ney nor anyone on his staff would comment on the case. Hirsch said the fraud squad official handling the police investigation was not available.

Noting that P&G had said it went to the authorities only after a failed internal attempt to identify the sources for the *WSJ* stories, Hirsch observed that the subpoena was issued just four working days after the second article appeared. That, he said, raises questions about how thorough the company's investigation had been. He then quoted a P&G spokesman as saying: "All I can tell you is we conducted an internal investigation and it uncovered nothing."

Giving the last word to the *WSJ*, Hirsch cited the following statement from Paul E. Steiger, the paper's managing editor:

> We're astonished that P&G would encourage, and the Cincinnati police and prosecutors and Cincinnati Bell permit, this invasion of the privacy of more than 450,000 people. Using a subpoena to chill press coverage is wrong; using one to review millions of telephone calls is ludicrous.

In the closing weeks of August the trade publication of the newspaper field, *Editor & Publisher* (*E&P*) ran two long stories by Mark Fitzgerald summarizing for *E&P* readers details about the conflict between P&G and the *WSJ*. The first full-page story was carried in the August 17 issue and the second in the August 24 issue.

"Journalists and First Amendment experts condemned the use of law enforcement authorities to conduct a hunt for the source of news leaks about Procter & Gamble to *The Wall Street Journal*," read Fitzgerald's August 17 lead.

"Procter & Gamble's police-assisted dragnet for the source of news leaks has turned up empty, the Cincinnati-based company concedes," read Fitzgerald's August 24 lead.

Both stories contained most of the details of the dispute and comments pro and con already cited in this case study. Fitzgerald also added some information and comments from his own telephone interviews.

P&G, NEWS LEAKS, AND
THE WALL STREET JOURNAL (B)

In September the case came to a quick ending. First on the media scene was a long story by Timothy Egan that appeared on page 18 of the National section of the *New York Times* of Sunday, September 1. The headline, "Vast Influence of Procter & Gamble Revives Old Questions in Cincinnati," captured the major thrust of the story. It was doubly emphasized by a large picture of the twin tower building of P&G that accompanied the story.

Egan cited the electronic search carried out at the behest of P&G and then raised these questions: "Who but Procter & Gamble, critics said, could get such help from the police? If a sandwich shop made a similar request, would the police search records from 803,000 business and home phones, as they did in this case, to investigate a misdemeanor?"

Egan quoted Tyrone Yates, a member of the Cincinnati City Council, as declaring "It is outrageous that a local corporation can use our police department like it's their own private detective force."

According to Egan, a civic soul-searching and backlash developed in the aftermath of the telephone search investigation. He cited the following comment from an editorial that ran in the *Cincinnati Post* two weeks earlier:

The use of taxpayer money to invade the privacy of just about every person in the region is, at best, heavy-handed. After years of working to improve its reputation as a corporate bully, this incident paints that picture all over again.

Egan reported that two subpoenas had been issued, one on June 17 and the other on June 24, ordering the telephone company to turn over the numbers of all people in two area codes, 513 in Ohio and 606 in neighboring Kentucky. He added the information that Gary Armstrong, the police detective who conducted the investigation, works part-time for P&G. Armstrong, added Egan, did not return phone calls for comment.

Egan quoted P&G's chairman and chief executive, Edwin L. Artzt, as stating, "There is no impropriety here but I am concerned about the appearance. We have not influenced this investigation in any way."

Robert L. Wehling, the company's vice president for public affairs, was quoted by Egan as follows: "We try, in the best sense of the word, to be a responsible, involved corporate citizen. But we also have a self-interest. If we are going to keep good people here, we have to do everything we can to enhance the quality of life."

Amplifying this point, Wehling told Egan that about 2,000 of the company's employees are involved in community service, and company executives are active on arts, education, and municipal improvement committees.

In concluding his long piece, Egan quoted Gerald Newfarmer, Cincinnati city manager, as declaring:

This is not a town run by P&G. But the company made a bad mistake, using a crazy Ohio law. I hope the law is court-tested and thrown out. And I hope P&G never makes such a mistake again.

On Thursday, September 5, four days after the above-cited story ran, the *WSJ* in a short story on page

A3 reported that P&G admitted it had made a mistake initiating its telephone search. The headline read: "P&G Admits 'Error' in Effort to Trace Leaks."

A slightly longer Associated Press (AP) story, datelined Cincinnati, September 5, ran in the *New York Times* on page A18 on Friday, September 6. The headline read: "Procter & Gamble Says It Was Wrong to Have Phone Calls Traced."

The source for both stories was a letter from P&G chairman Edwin L. Artzt sent on Wednesday to all employees. In his letter, according to excerpts from it reported in the AP and *WSJ* stories, the chairman said that P&G "made an error in judgment" three months ago when it got Cincinnati authorities to trace hundreds of thousands of telephone calls in a effort to trace news leaks.

"We thought we were doing the right thing because we had a clear legal right to seek the assistance of the authorities to investigate potential leaks of confidential company information," wrote Artzt, stating further that the disclosures entailed serious breaches of security, such as the release of capital spending figures.

The chairman stated that the decision to search out telephone calls led to such unanticipated results as "public controversy" and "reactions in the press that reflected negatively on the company."

"This has been an embarrassing experience for the company and a difficult time for our employees," Artzt said. "We created a problem that was larger than the one we were trying to solve."

The AP story quoted Artzt as advising employees: "Let's now put this issue behind us." The *WSJ* quoted him as urging employees to be "even more diligent in protecting the security of the company's confidential information."

The two stories differed in how they identified the Cincinnati police investigator who headed the search. The AP called him "a Cincinnati police officer who is also a P&G employee." The *WSJ* called him "a Cincinnati policeman who moonlights for P&G."

The AP story said that Sydney McHugh, a spokeswoman for the company, stated that the letter from Artzt had been sent to all Cincinnati employees, plant managers, and sales market managers in the United States and communications managers outside the country. She said the company has 94,000 employees around the world.

. . . .

Some Last Words by William Safire

In an op ed page commentary in the *New York Times* on Thursday, September 5, the veteran political columnist William Safire was unsparing in his appraisal of the way Edwin L. Artzt handled the news leak following publication in the *WSJ* of the two articles by Alecia Swasy.

Safire said that Artzt has brought "shame" on the company: has been "stonewalling" reporters for weeks; and has been "issuing written peeps through minions about 'no impropriety here.' "

Safire wrote that he called Artzt, and in his return call the P&G chief admitted "we made an error in judgment . . . we regret it . . . we were just plain wrong."

Artzt was cited by Safire as saying "there's no question we had a legal right to seek the assistance of the authorities, but we really made an error in pursuing that option, particularly to filing the complaint that led to a search of telephone records. We deplore the idea of invading people's privacy and interfering with freedom of the press. I went to journalism school myself."

Raising the question concerning the legal dimension of the situation, Safire cited Artzt as responding that "This is not an issue of ethics. I do not feel our action was unethical or improper. We shouldn't have done it, that's all; sometimes it isn't easy to see all the implications of a decision."

Safire's response was simply stated: "He still doesn't get it." As Safire saw it, Artzt's viewpoint is "limited to acknowledgment of a public relations blunder. He sees his misuse of local cops to plug leaks as an error only because it led to bad press, and may cause customers to switch from Crest to a toothpaste made by a company that isn't snooping through telephone records."

Safire concluded by advising P&G to save itself headaches later by making full disclosure now and showing its publics that "it understands that abuse of power and invasion of privacy are not mere errors of judgment, regrettably inappropriate—but are unethical, bad, improper, wrong."

Reprint for Discussion

CEO Must Weigh Legal and Public Relations Approaches*

Douglas A. Cooper

With growing frequency, people or businesses faced with a crisis find themselves turning to two consultants: lawyers and those engaged in public relations. The potential for a serious problem arises, however, because these two consultants bring different approaches to the problems which the decision-maker or crisis management team will face.

The often competing and adversarial approaches to problem solving used by public relations professionals and lawyers can have a paralyzing effect on the decision-making process. The decision-maker must balance the legal and public relations concerns during a crisis. If used properly, these two consultants can play significant roles in helping an organization survive a crisis.

It is strongly recommended that when faced with a crisis in which legal issues may play a role, however remote, the decision-maker should bring a lawyer onto the crisis management team. This does not mean just any lawyer, but one experienced in dealing with questions laced with public relations concerns. Some examples of these types of issues are any major land use or development debates, municipal or private labor negotiations, and political referenda where both proponents and opponents may have to analyze the possibility of legal action.

Douglas A. Cooper is an attorney at law for Cooper & Cooper, New Rochelle, N.Y.

*Copyright January 1992. Reprinted with permission of the *Public Relations Journal,* published by the Public Relations Society of America, New York, N.Y. The article by Douglas Cooper appeared in the January issue of the Journal.

Lawyers Focus on Litigation

To balance legal and public relations concerns, it is essential to understand why lawyers and public relations consultants so often have different views of the proper approach to a problem.

The most volatile, and potentially most dangerous area of the law with which a decision-maker can become involved is litigation. A good lawyer always considers the threat or existence of a lawsuit. Much of a lawyer's advice is designed to avoid litigation, position the client for the strongest litigation posture possible if a lawsuit is to commence, or to tightly control events after a lawsuit has begun. Since the law is not static but can be applied differently in the face of changing facts, the facts of a particular matter become critically important.

Legal results vary depending on the facts of each case. Facts, for the most part, are created by spoken or written words. Therefore, the last thing that an attorney wants to do is to lose control of the words that are used as litigation threatens or explodes. That's why the attorney will often insist that his client remain *publicly* silent in a crisis. Words are to be used only in the controlled environment of the litigation procedure. From the attorney's point of view, if the case is won, it does not matter what the public thinks. In reality, this may or may not be so. It is this uncertainty which is dangerous to those managing a crisis.

Court of Public Opinion Is Key

The public relations practitioner, on the other hand, is trained to *publicly* persuade the undecided, to *publicly* shake the resolve of the opposition and to educate the public with words. Litigation is, at best, an annoying distraction. At worst, it is a curse conjured by the "evil sorcerers of the bar."

From the public relations consultant's point of view, if the public is persuaded of the rightness of the decision-maker's goals, the power of public opinion will pull all else with it—including the courts of both public and judicial opinion. However, this too may or may not be so. And again, it is this uncertainty which is dangerous to the crisis management team.

· ·

Tension Blooms over Words

It is in words and their application that the inherent tension between lawyers and public relations consultants is expressed. Every word used to persuade the public is a word which may be used to persuade a judge. The conclusions reached by both, and hence the consequences, may be very different. While it is rare to find a public relations consultant trained in the law, it is no less rare to find an attorney who is able to combine his knowledge of the law with the sensitivity to understand public opinion.

The clash of the two professions is illustrated in the following examples using actual events.

A real estate developer proposes to a municipality the development of a large parcel of property in an environmentally sensitive area. The municipality is in desperate need of the anticipated tax revenue and supports the project. A large number of people in the vicinity of the parcel oppose the project because of its direct impact on their neighborhoods. A large number of people oppose the project on environmental grounds. A large number of union members support the project for the jobs which the construction will create. This is a real estate developer's Mount St. Helens ready to explode. This situation has crisis written all over it.

The public relations consultant sees one issue—seriously divided public opinion. His training tells him to go public. The tools of the public relations consultant in this effort are public words.

This, of course, is anathema to the environmental lawyer. Every word is a potential boomerang hurtling in a deadly arc back to the developer. To the attorney, the environmental approvals must be obtained at any cost. Since a war of public relations words might create evidence that can be used by the opposition in a lawsuit to delay environmental approvals, the attorney advises silence.

Each specialist suffers from professional tunnel vision. Viewed strictly as a public relations issue, if the public does not support the development, the political commitment from the municipality will not be forthcoming. This spells doom for the project even if it is approved by the state and federal environmental agencies which are concerned. On the other hand, if the environmental reviews are negative, all the political support in the world will not save the project.

. . . .

**Include
Attorney Early**

The decision-maker/real estate developer is faced with two very different and conflicting approaches to his problems. Each consultant is addressing valid concerns. Neither is correct in his approach because neither understands the validity of the other's position, and neither addresses the other's issues.

The lesson from this example is that the decision-maker has two options. He can listen to the separate views of his legal specialist, inexperienced in public relations issues, and his corporate public relations consultant. He must then balance the consultant's predispositions. Alternatively, he can rely on someone with an ability to reconcile public relations and legal approaches to issues. Bringing the public relations–oriented attorney in early lets the decision-maker chart his course with a fuller awareness of potential problems.

Another "crisis" example which involves the interplay of law and public relations further demonstrates the importance of a legal overview with an understanding of the public relations consequences.

A disaffected, lame-duck majority of a city's governing body suspends (suspension being a statutory precondition to firing) the head of another branch of the government. This creates a crisis for the suspended official, who retains an attorney to set aside the suspension. Because of a legal question concerning the legality of the suspension, the court enjoins the lame-duck officials from taking any further steps—including firing—until a hearing is held. This creates a crisis for the lame-duck group. These officials realize that if the firing does not occur before their terms end, robbing them of their majority, their actions will not only expose them to political criticism but will fall short of their goal—the removal of the official.

The lame ducks then commit two foolish acts: they fire the official in violation of the court order to make certain that the deed is done before their terms of office expire, and they make known their intention to hire a replacement official. If accomplished, this would put the incoming majority in the difficult position of having to fire—perhaps in breach of contract—the new official. The first act gives a potential public relations advantage to the suspended official. The second act warns of a future action which could seriously complicate the crisis for the suspended official.

The attorney hired by the suspended official was retained to handle the legal issues. But in addition, he understood the very separate but related political overtones. He understood the potential public relations advantage to be gained from the lame ducks' contempt of court. More importantly, he appreciated that a success in court might be pointless if the lame ducks hired the replacement. The new governing majority would be faced with the difficult choice of having to fire the new official, thereby exposing the city to a costly lawsuit for breach of contract, or submitting to the tactics of the lame ducks.

Therefore, in order to manage the suspended official's crisis, it was important to make certain that any prospective replacement official knew of the lawsuit, and that the lame duck's actions, including their hiring of him, could be declared illegal. Therefore, a replacement would be jeopardizing his political and economic future by accepting the position.

If the press picked up the threat to the replacement, it could be used to persuade any replacement not to accept the appointment. With no one hired before the expiration of the lame ducks' terms, an enormous problem would be eliminated.

This issue is much more one of public relations than

of law, but a lawyer is well-positioned to quickly understand its significance. In this example, the attorney, cognizant of the public relations implications, coordinated all of the efforts on behalf of the suspended official. The press, already aware of the contempt of court aspect, was made aware of the impact of that contempt on the "job security" of any replacement. When the story was published, no replacement would take the offered job because the risk was obvious. The terms of office expired. The lame-duck majority lost its power and the issue was disposed of favorably to the suspended official. Judgment about all of the issues, not some of them, saved a career.

If the lame ducks had hired an attorney with a sense of public relations, he would have undoubtedly advised them to expedite and appeal from the temporary stay rather than committing contempt and not to reveal the strategy of hiring a replacement. The suspended official's crisis became a crisis for the lame ducks. They failed in their efforts and violated a court order in the process.

Contrary to the suspension described above, the law and public relations often do not co-exist peacefully. The decision-maker must carefully weigh the often conflicting opinions of these two professions when they are called upon for advice.

This does not mean that attorneys are the next generation of public relations professionals. But, since the key is to appreciate the often subtle emphases which must be given to the courts of public and judicial opinion, an attorney should be part of the "crisis" team when legal issues bear even indirectly on the problem.

NEW PRODUCT INTRODUCTION AT EAGER INSTRUMENTS* (A)

Eager Instruments, Inc., was a relatively small but growing maker of control systems, with headquarters and plant in Fort Worth, Texas, and an employee force of 3,000. The firm had been founded by Morris Schwartz and a small executive group of 12 experienced scientists, and within a short time it ranked seventh in volume of sales in its field.

Although its annual sales volume represented only 5 percent of total sales volume in the control systems field (which was dominated by three to five "giants" in the industry), Eager had built up a considerable reputation among the scientists and engineers who used Eager control equipment. Eager instrument controls, each of which ranged in price from $50,000 to $200,000, were used to control radar antenna acquisitions for space flights, petrochemical plant processes, and calculation of scientific experiments. Purchase decisions for such equipment were generally made by line scientists or engineers who used the equipment, but recently a new line of Eager equipment had enabled the firm to move into the business accounting field where purchase decisions were made by top management personnel. Originally privately owned, Eager had gone public when it

---

*All names, places, and dates in this case are disguised.

was found necessary to seek new sources of operating funds. Its stock was traded on the New York Stock Exchange.

Schwartz, 44, was a dynamic instrument control expert who had made his early reputation in the space instrument field shortly after graduation from Cal Tech, had briefly served as department head of math at Purdue, and then started his company with an original investment of $100,000.

Denise O'Reilly, 38, had been hired by Schwartz as vice president of marketing. A Phi Beta Kappa who had majored in philosophy and minored in physics at Stanford, O'Reilly had been director of marketing for a major firm in the electronics field before joining Eager.

Working almost from scratch, O'Reilly had built up a ten-person marketing department when Douglas Freeman was hired by Schwartz as director of advertising and public relations. Freeman, 35, had worked for several years as a writer for an advertising trade journal, then ad director of *Instrument Journal*, and finally, before joining Eager, as advertising and public relations manager for another instrument equipment company.

When he hired Freeman, Schwartz explained that he would report and be responsible to O'Reilly in respect to budgetary and administrative matters, but he would be expected to counsel Schwartz on public relations matters. "We're so busy we don't have time for fancy organizational charts, but this is where you fit in," Schwartz said, and he sketched the chart in Exhibit 4–1.

In looking at the chart Freeman noted at once that he had a direct line relationship to both Schwartz and O'Reilly, and he assumed that meant that he would be responsible to both and under their direct control. He felt it would be advantageous for him to have a direct line to the president on public relations matters. However, he was uneasy about the fact that because he was also linked to O'Reilly on a direct line he might well find himself in the middle if Schwartz and O'Reilly differed on a public relations issue or situation. He thought briefly about expressing his misgivings, but he decided he would be wiser not to say anything at the moment and see how matters worked out.

In actuality, they worked out well. O'Reilly quickly made it known to Freeman that she expected Freeman to handle advertising and public relations without much direct supervision; O'Reilly also said she was too busy with other marketing problems to get involved in Freeman's functions. Though Schwartz was extremely busy, Freeman had no difficulty in reaching him and getting his support and cooperation when it was needed. A much more demanding person than O'Reilly, Schwartz nonetheless respected Freeman's expertise in public relations and generally deferred to Freeman's advice and counsel. By September 1990, when discussions were initiated on the introduction of the new Gamma 4 line, Freeman was administering an active three-person department with a total budget of $950,000: $600,000 for advertising and $350,000 for public relations. Both budget items were incorporated into the general marketing department budget administered by O'Reilly.

O'Reilly and Freeman were first told about the new Gamma 4 line at a meeting with Schwartz held early in September 1990. Schwartz told them this would be a new generation of instrument controls that would combine both scientific and business capabilities, would represent an entirely new design, and resulted from the firm's extensive research and development program. Schwartz said that initially the line would consist of at least three large instrument control systems: the Gamma 4-1, costing from $250,000 to $1 million; the Gamma 4-2, costing from $200,000 to $500,000; and the Gamma 4-3, costing from $50,000 to $200,000.

"We can announce the line any way we want," Schwartz told O'Reilly and Freeman. "From a production point of view, there's no reason to introduce one over the other, but we do expect to get into production on all three models by March 1991. From that point on we'll be able to deliver the Gamma 4-1 and the Gamma 4-3 by the fourth quarter of 1991 and the Gamma 4-2 by June 1992. You two figure out how you want to release the announcement about the line and let me know. I'll go along with any reasonable decision you make."

In the ensuing discussion between O'Reilly and Freeman, the former said she favored announcing all three elements of the new line at a press conference in New York City sometime in March.

"If we announce all three at the same time, we're sure to make a bigger splash," she argued. "We'd get a major news break. Further, we wouldn't have to hold back information or dodge questions about what's coming up next, as we'd have to do if we announce the line one element at a time. Finally, I know we could get Schwartz to make the announcement of all three at one major press conference, but I'm not sure we could get him to do it more than once."

"That's all true," Freeman said, "but if we announce the elements separately we stand a good chance of making a big splash on the first and still getting further story breaks when we announce the other two elements of the line. Second, we won't be able to promise delivery on Gamma 4-2 for 15 months from March 1991, and that's an awfully long spread between announcement and delivery date. Besides, if we announce the entire new line at one time, customers might stop buying our present line because they would see that the new one is an improved one at a lower price."

"But that would apply any way you announced the line," O'Reilly said.

"Well, I haven't had time to think this out thoroughly, but I'd suggest we break the news about the Gamma 4-1 first with a press conference in New York City. We won't be able to show the actual hardware, but we could get mock-ups made; I'd put together a press kit with release matter and pics; and Schwartz and you could be available to make the actual announcement and handle questions. We could break the story some time in March, and after we see what kind of coverage we get, we could make plans for the other two elements in the line."

"Well," replied O'Reilly, "I still don't like it, but it's your baby, really, so handle it any way you want. Just keep me informed as you go along."

"Oh, by the way," O'Reilly added, "I'm not up on the prompt disclosure rules of the Security and Exchange Commission and the New York Stock Exchange, so I'd appreciate it if you'd check these out and let me know how they apply. Both of us are also members of PRSA, so that's a consideration we should keep in mind."

"I don't know much about prompt disclosure either," Freeman admitted, "but I'm sure that's not really involved here, so I wouldn't worry about it."

"Okay, if you say so," O'Reilly replied. "Just remember to keep me informed."

After O'Reilly left, Freeman read through the provisions of the PRSA code and bylaws dealing with standards of professional practice, particularly as they relate to financial relations (See the Appendix for the PRSA code and bylaw provisions). He also scanned some material in his files dealing with regulations and guidelines of the Securities and Exchange Commission (SEC) and the major stock exchanges governing prompt and accurate disclosure of information that could materially affect security values or have an influence on investment decisions.

Freeman jotted down the following rough notes summarizing pertinent excerpts from the financial disclosure material in his files:

> SEC and major market exchange guidelines require that publicly held companies should reveal promptly and accurately information that might

affect in a material way the value of securities or influence investment decisions.

Guideline not entirely clear about what kind of specific information is material.

Among corporate developments mentioned as calling for prompt and accurate disclosure are those involving new products, cited as either "major new products" or as "a significant new product or products."

Seems to be general agreement that information is considered material if it is considered to be essential to an investor's informed decision-making process.

SEC and the exchanges recognize there may be valid business reasons for a delayed disclosure. Example: one authority says disclosure may be delayed where disclosure would endanger a company's goals or provide information helpful to a competitor.

However, the presumption should always be in favor of disclosure because there are only a few circumstances where disclosures might be withheld, says same authority. Quote from *The Amex Company Guide:* "The circumstances where disclosure can be withheld are limited and constitute an infrequent exception to the normal requirement of immediate prompt disclosure. Thus, in cases of doubt, the presumption must always be in favor of disclosure."

After reviewing the above notes, Freeman decided that it would probably be wise to have another talk with O'Reilly.

Exhibit 4-1

**Partial Organization
Chart**

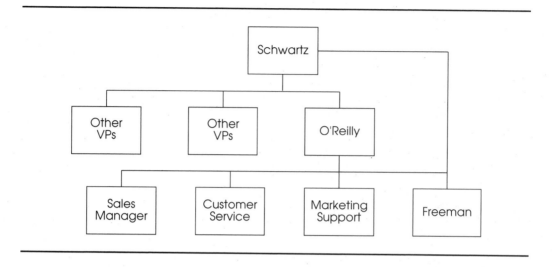

NEW PRODUCT INTRODUCTION AT EAGER INSTRUMENTS* (B)

After his second talk with O'Reilly (See "New Product Introduction at Eager Instruments (A)") Freeman decided to go ahead with his plans to announce the Gamma 4-1 at a press conference in New York City. He set the date for March 14 and informed Schwartz and O'Reilly. They agreed to be on hand, accompanied by a technical man, to handle the announcement and answer questions from the press. He then contracted with one of New York City's finest eating establishments for a continental breakfast, meeting room, cocktails, and lunch for a hundred people.

Freeman's staff put together a press kit consisting of (1) a general and a scientific press release about the Gamma 4-1, describing its special features, citing it as "the first in a new generation of Eager Instruments control systems," citing its cost and fourth quarter of 1991 delivery date; (2) three still shots of the Gamma 4-1 and its auxiliary equipment; (3) a general brochure about the company; and (4) a special brochure about the Gamma 4-1.

On March 7, Freeman's staff sent out press conference invitations to a hundred representatives of the daily press, wire services, news and trade magazines,

---

* All names, places, and dates in this case are disguised.

and the financial community. The invitation letter appears in Exhibit 5–1.

On March 8 Freeman left for New York City. When he arrived he contacted, both in person and by telephone calls, those on the press conference list in whom he had particular interest from a publicity point of view. Freeman was particularly interested in talking to contacts on the business desks of *Newsweek* and *Time* magazines.

He had initiated talks several months before with the Fort Worth bureau staffers of both publications, with the aim of interesting them in doing a profile of Eager Instruments as a young, aggressive company bucking the giants in its field. The bureau staffers had indicated that their business desks were definitely interested in the story, but neither publication had printed it yet.

Freeman's *Newsweek* contact informed him that the story, by coincidence, was running in the issue due out on the newsstands the day he called (March 9), and the *Time* man said the story was scheduled to run in the issue due out on the newsstands the day before the scheduled press conference. When Freeman called his home office March 9, he relayed the information to Schwartz, and the latter was highly pleased to learn that the company was getting such "excellent news breaks." O'Reilly, who was in on the conference-type call, also praised Freeman for his advance work, but said she was worried that the stories in the news magazines might backfire.

"Backfire?" repeated Freeman.

"Well," said O'Reilly, "how would you feel if you were with *The Wall Street Journal* and you found upon reading *Newsweek* or *Time* that they had an advance story on a press conference to which you had been invited but which hadn't yet been held?"

Freeman, aware that Schwartz was listening in, said that the *Newsweek* and *Time* stories were general profiles and not really about the Gamma 4-1. He did admit, however, that when he had talked to both publications' bureau people two weeks previously he had given them some data about the Gamma 4-1; he expected they wouldn't feature it but would rather feature the "rising young company versus the Goliaths" aspect of the story.

"Let's cut this," Schwartz interrupted. "We're busy here, and you must be also. The important thing is that we'll be getting into *Newsweek* and *Time* and that doesn't happen to us every day. We'll see you the night of the 13th, Doug. So long, and good job."

The March 14 Press Conference

Approximately seventy people showed up for the press conference on March 14. Fifty-five were accredited media people, and the others were company representatives, friends, and financial specialists. Following coffee and Danish pastry at 10:00 a.m., President Schwartz spoke about the company and the new model. He was followed by O'Reilly.

In the question-and-answer period, one of the trade press representatives asked O'Reilly to amplify the statement in the press release that the Gamma 4-1 was "the first in a new generation of Eager Instruments control systems."

"Well," said O'Reilly, "we expect several systems to evolve in the Gamma 4 series ultimately."

"Several?" said the trade press rep.

"Several, three to five," Schwartz broke in, and the matter was dropped at this point. The conference broke up on schedule for cocktails and lunch at 12:30.

Freeman, O'Reilly, and Schwartz were very pleased when they checked the evening and morning papers following the conference. *The Wall Street Journal* ran a 400-word inside page story; the *New York Times* ran a 350-word story on its first business page; the AP sent out a 125-word story; and the *New York Post* ran a 100-word story among its business pages. UPI carried nothing, *Newsweek* ran a full-page story in its business section that led off with several paragraphs about the new David among the Goliaths, five paragraphs about the Gamma 4-1, and four paragraphs about President Schwartz, the young dynamo from out of the West.

Time carried nothing about Eager Instruments, and when Freeman returned to Fort Worth, the *Time* bureau woman there told him that the story had unfortunately been cut out at the last minute in favor of a late-breaking story about another company. The *Time* woman said the story itself was not completely dead, but she wasn't certain when or if it would be run.

Both Schwartz and O'Reilly were very disappointed about the failure to get into *Time,* but they agreed that this was something out of Freeman's control. They were extremely pleased when Freeman, about a month after the press conference, showed them clippings and stories that had appeared in numerous major newspapers and in various trade publications that were important to the company. They were especially pleased with a one-page story with a picture of Schwartz that appeared in *Business Week* one week after the press conference, and with a four-column, quarter-page *New York Times* profile on Schwartz that appeared two Sundays after the press conference.

The story resulted from a ten-minute interview with a *New York Times* staffer that Freeman had arranged after the press conference proper. It included not only material about Schwartz as a personality, but also material about the company, its newest product, and its future potential.

"You know," said Schwartz pointing to the clippings and stories, "all this looks impressive, but just what does it all mean? We spent $14,000 just for the press conference itself, and of course we spent much more when you consider travel time, hotel expenses, and the hidden time costs of those of us who spent valuable time away from the office to participate in the conference. Well, did we get our money's worth? Just how do you measure and prove what it's all been worth to Eager Instruments?"

Neither O'Reilly nor Freeman had a ready answer, and as Schwartz didn't press the matter they simply let it die right there. Freeman, though, wondered what he might have said to Schwartz, or whether he should have expressed his thoughts in a memo to be sent to Schwartz later.

With announcement of the Gamma 4-1 out of the way, Freeman and O'Reilly discussed plans to announce the Gamma 4-2 and the Gamma 4-3. Both agreed that the Gamma 4-3, the smallest member of the line, had the same nine-month delivery date as the Gamma 4-1 and, as it was also the smallest of the line, it wouldn't be worth a major press conference. The alternative, both agreed, was a press release, and so announcement of the Gamma 4-3 was made by mailing a press release on August 2. Although coverage was not at all comparable to that given to the first of the line, Eager got some very good space with the third member of the line. The two staffers then prepared to handle announcement of the middle of the line. The only firm last-minute date they had was January 5, when brochures would be in the hands of the firm's salesforce, who would be making their calls with data on the Gamma 4-2 from that date on. Freeman suggested another major press conference to be held in New York City in December.

"Very few press conferences are held in December," he reasoned, "and as we've got some good solid information we could make a good splash without too much fear of competition."

O'Reilly agreed with Freeman and suggested that Freeman talk to Schwartz. However, when Freeman brought up the subject, the president rejected the suggestion immediately.

"That's out," Schwartz said. "I'm tired, I've covered

too much ground already this year, and I don't want to get on another plane until some time next year."

Freeman and O'Reilly then concluded that they ought to hold the press conference without Schwartz, but when they raised this suggestion the president rejected it also. Although the president gave no reason other than the one he had already stated, Freeman got the impression that Schwartz felt that if anyone was going to handle announcements at a major press conference it should be the president.

Listing the alternatives, Freeman figured that there were only two: (1) send the announcement through the mail as had been done with the Gamma 4-3, or (2) have Freeman make a trip to New York and hand-plant the story with various media people. Freeman also figured this was as good a time as any to bring up another matter he had been mulling over.

"It seems to me," he said to O'Reilly, "it would be worth it if we opened a New York office and put a person in it to cover announcements of this kind. As we grow, there's an increasing need also to have a regular New York City–based person on our public relations staff."

"We'd have to build a solid case, and I'm not so sure we have one," O'Reilly replied. "We have a need for another professional in your department and there's money in the budget for one, but setting up an office in New York is another matter. I'd have to be convinced it's needed, and I'd have to convince Schwartz that it's needed and would be economically justified.

"If you think you'd like to make a case for a New York City office, just let me know and I'll set up a meeting with Schwartz and you can make a personal presentation. Either that, or you can put your ideas down on paper in a memorandum."

Freeman said he'd think about it, and the two then went on with discussion of handling the announcement of the Gamma 4-2.

Exhibit 5-1
**Press Conference
Invitation**

EAGER INSTRUMENTS, INC
1410 Raymond Avenue
Forth Worth, TX 76102

(Salutation)

7 March 1991

On Tuesday, March 14, Eager Instruments will announce a major new family of instrument controls which we believe will be of significant interest to your readers.

The new Eager line features a unique design concept and represents the first such announcement since the Monitor 340. Eager President Morris Schwartz and other officers of the company will be present to answer your questions.

We hope you will be able to attend our press conference. It is scheduled for 10:00 a.m. Tuesday, March 14, at La Place, 45 East 54th Street, New York. A continental breakfast will be served prior to the meeting. Cocktails and lunch will follow the conference.

An indication of your plans to attend the conference on the enclosed reply card would be appreciated.

Very truly yours,
EAGER INSTRUMENTS, INC.

Douglas Freeman
Assistant to the President

Reprint For Discussion

Publicizing and Promoting The Civil War*

Owen Comora

In September of 1989, Jack McNulty and George Pruette of General Motors assigned Owen Comora Associates to build audience recognition for both *The Civil War* and General Motors' association with the series. The press and public response to that effort is without precedent in my more than 30 years of experience in television publicity/promotion. Though I've created and implemented hundreds of successful campaigns for critical and ratings hits such as *Jesus of Nazareth, Holocaust,* and *Shogun,* nothing like the intensity of interest generated by *The Civil War* has ever crossed my path. Even weeks after the program had aired, newspapers, magazines, and TV talk shows are still clamoring for interviews on the series.

Why has *The Civil War* become such a phenomenon? There are many reasons, and they are perhaps best left to historians and sociologists.

But why did so many of the nation's magazines, newspapers, syndicates, and TV and radio network talk shows respond so enthusiastically in advance of the air date? Why was it one of the most talked-about series before it ever reached the nation's TV screens? I feel more qualified to address those questions. And in my answers you may find some publicity/promotion concepts which can be translated into local station promotion.

There are really no secrets to the success of our efforts. Ours was a campaign fought down in the trenches, developed over many long hours and constantly devoted to detail and follow-up work. We took advantage of every opportu-

---

* Reprinted with permission of Owen Comora, president of Owen Comora Associates, from the *Advertising & Promotion Exchange Newsletter* of the Public Broadcasting Service.

nity to tell *The Civil War* story to any member of the print or electronic press who would listen—and most of them did!

We knew way back in September (1989) that we had an outstanding documentary. But how would we tell the world about it?

First, Ken Burns promised that he could deliver finished cassettes of the entire series some time in early spring. This would give us the rare opportunity to pitch the long-lead national and regional magazines and be able to deliver *The Civil War* cassettes with related press materials for advance reviews.

Last December, we wrote individual pitch letters to every national consumer magazine we could think of as well as regional and city magazines in areas which were directly affected by the Civil War. Those letters were followed up by telephone calls. Each interested editor was offered a complete set of cassettes for review purposes (over 60 of them responded favorably). They were also offered interviews with Burns and other principals associated with the program.

While we were developing materials for our four separate and distinctly different press kits, we felt it was extremely important to enlist the support of the PBS stations. A strong presence at the Dallas Mega-meeting was essential. Many of you attended that meeting and our special luncheon for *The Civil War*. Ken Burns's talk, Shelby Foote's appearance, the screening of a show segment, and the promotional materials distributed at the luncheon won your enthusiastic support.

When you returned to your stations, there were two copies of a special PI directors press kit waiting for you. Another completely different kit was sent to all PBS program guide editors. This one contained different features, black and white photos, and color slides for PTV station program guide cover consideration.

In addition, via satellite, we fed to all program directors and promotion managers an 11–minute preview tape of *The Civil War*. It was produced at General Motors' expense and given to you to play at your preview parties. These tapes also proved valuable to us when we pitched the radio and television talk shows.

We offered (via a PBS DACS) several pages of promotion ideas for PI directors to "plug-in" locally to *The Civil War*. From comments we heard, many of you found those suggestions helpful.

At the same time, we mailed approximately 600 4 × 5 transparencies to our private list of some 250 newspaper TV supplement editors. These kits were serviced on an "exclusive-to-you-in-your-city" basis along with nightly program descriptions and a special feature story. They were delivered weeks earlier than usual with a letter explaining the importance of the program. We stressed the fact that supplement editors would only get one "shot" at *The Civil War* for cover consideration. They would have plenty of time later, we added, to run the commercial network series' art which would be premiering during the same week.

It is important to point out that, other than a collage photo created for the GM educational component and borrowed by us as a color mailer, there was no color photography available for *The Civil War*. Matthew Brady's black and white art was excellent, but color photography had not been invented yet.

Since we needed a large supply of color to satisfy the many needs of newspapers and magazines, we decided to utilize the actual paintings displayed in the series. By cropping most of them to a vertical format, we found that we were able to build a large and excellent selection of color art for our many color requirements. (Because of regional sensitivities, we decided to provide the newspapers in the South with paintings featuring southern generals and themes.) Those mailings were followed up by phone calls to supplement editors in the top 40 markets. We offered them interviews, additional art, video cassettes, and more features.

Our campaign paid huge dividends and *The Civil War,*

in spite of enormous commercial network competition, won most of the nation's newspaper TV supplement covers that week.

We determined early on that for the Los Angeles press tour, we would give complete cassette sets of *The Civil War* to all of the television editors who indicated that they would attend the PBS portion of the tour. They were mailed a press kit with the cassettes approximately two weeks before they left for the L.A. meetings.

As a result, most of those editors had seen at least one or two hours of the series before they arrived at The Century Plaza in Los Angeles. When I entered the hotel, I was immediately accosted by several veteran critics who could not contain their admiration for Ken Burns's series. The press conference with Burns and Foote was one the most productive I've ever attended (and that includes over 20 years of network, cable, syndicate, and PBS press tours).

Our national press kit was then mailed to some 600 newspaper, syndicate, and wire service editors as well as to TV and radio talk show talent coordinators. We ordered 100 extra kits for special requests and needed every one of them (and then some). Each kit contained seven black-and-white photos (including a nine-head photo quiz), six features, the nightly storyline breakdown, bios of all the principals, a credit sheet, and a story concerning GM "Mark of Excellence" presentations.

The press kit mailing was followed by weekly reminder mailings to the general press ("A Writer's Challenge," "Civil War Facts," "The Voices of *The Civil War*," a feature on Shelby Foote, etc.). Additional national mailings were sent to women's page editors ("Women of the Civil War") and to photo page editors ("Civil War Photography"). Many special press packets were created for national publications requiring exclusive photos and story angles.

In all, over 260 full sets of *The Civil War* cassettes were delivered with press kit materials to magazines, newspapers, syndicates, and important columnists and talk show hosts.

After the mailings were delivered, our "grunt" work began in dead earnest. Follow-up phone calls were made to all of the key critics and to the talent coordinators at the radio and television talk shows.* To list the individual struggles with the major publications and TV shows would require more time than either you or I would care to spend. Happily, we won more skirmishes than we lost (we had the ammunition)!

Within weeks of the premiere date, our campaign had taken on a life of its own. Reviews and interviews we had set some six months before were starting to appear in print. They were all raves! A barrage of special requests began pouring in from all over the country (and Canada, too). Editors wanted interviews with Burns, Foote, and principal writer Geoffrey Ward. Soon we felt like order-takers. ("We'll try to fit you in to Mr. Burns's busy interview schedule.")

PI directors needed more press kits, more art, more of everything to take care of their program guide and local, smaller newspaper needs. Keeping up with the special requests required hiring temporary help in addition to our full-time employees (who often worked overtime).

At this writing, almost a month has passed since *The Civil War* ended. Requests for television appearances, interviews, and background information on *The Civil War* are still coming in.

Hard as it is to believe, it's almost time to start gearing up for the January and July repeat telecasts!

---

* Paraphrasing the real estate cannon, the three most important activities in any television program publicity campaign are:
  1. Follow up
  2. Follow up
  3. Follow up

BUDGET CUTS AND LAYOFFS AT SINGLETON* (A)

The Singleton Corporation, located in a southeastern state, is a large, diversified manufacturing company that not only creates and manufactures products, but also franchises retailers. As a result, it is both a supplier and a coordinator and has the intricate and infinite problems of both. Its organization follows a traditional pattern in most aspects.

Singleton in 1992 had its headquarters and chief manufacturing facility in Ruxton, a suburb located 15 miles from a city of 150,000, and had a second plant in a city of 100,000 in another state. There were 7,321 employees at Ruxton and 2,340 at the smaller facility. A total of 5,000 of the Ruxton employees were hourly workers in the plant and members of a strong international union. A different, more militant local of the same union represented 2,000 workers at the second facility. The unemployment level in both states was 7.5 percent.

Reporting to James Sontel, the CEO and president, were: Bill Stevens, vice president of manufacturing; Jack Mayhew, vice president of sales; Helen Goss, vice president of administration and procurement; Steve George, director of quality control; Jim Hunter, director

---

* All names, places, and dates in this case are disguised.

of futures planning; and Janet Williams, director of public relations. Reporting to the sales vice president were: Roger Griffith, assistant vice president of franchise sales; John Garvey, assistant vice president of supplier sales; and Peter Abrams, director of advertising and marketing.

Because of the recession, Singleton, like many other manufacturers, found that sales were reduced, retail customers were ordering less, and the manufacturing customers were ordering not only less but in rather unpredictable patterns. As Sontel observed, "It's the most unusual market we ever had and it's almost impossible to project plans, sales, and earnings. And, most certainly, California's issuance of IOUs instead of checks and massive layoffs by all the *Fortune* 500 firms in every state have made people jittery. The unemployment lines include people at every level, from laborer to top management employees."

Morale at Singleton had always been very high. The company had good labor relations, and it was a pleasant, friendly, secure place to work. There was little turnover in personnel, and the manufacturing salaries went a long way in this generally rural area. For the past year, however, uneasiness rippled through the conversations in the community as society's general economic malaise began to infiltrate people's thinking, especially among the younger and low seniority workers.

Sontel's top executives were well aware that third-quarter figures at Singleton had all been down, but they had been through problem times before and Singleton had always managed to stay ahead of the rest of the area companies. It was a matter of record and pride that Singleton had never had layoffs. Thus, Sontel's subsequent remarks at his weekly staff meeting on Monday, November 23, came as a shock to the executives gathered around the conference table in his office.

"I've been reviewing the preliminary figures for the last quarter and for the entire year, and we're in for a difficult time," Sontel said. "We have to make cuts in the budget, holdbacks in every area, and institute lay-offs. I want each of you to tell me what you can do to reduce costs and increase revenues. I'm setting a target reduction of 7 percent of the personnel budget for each department, and I expect you to meet it." Sontel paused, and it became clear he was waiting for a response from the executives.

Stevens, vice president of manufacturing and the senior executive, spoke first. "Well, as you know, Jim, we run a very tight shop in the manufacturing end, and we've already trimmed all the expenses that we could. But I'll look again and see what we can come up with. I'll let you know by tomorrow noon, if that's okay."

"That's a good start, Bill," said Sontel, "but I want you all to know that cuts *must* be made, and I want to know when and where you plan to make them. If your plans for cost savings don't achieve the figures that we need, 7 percent for now, then I will institute an across-the-board cut and in that way make the decisions for you. Time is crucial. Those who will be laid off will be leaving two weeks from Friday. You know that we've never laid anyone off before, and you also know that we provide a superb set of separation benefits: job place-ment, severance pay, double vacation, transfers where possible, relocation expenses, and continuation of health and insurance benefits for 90 days, company paid."

"I'll have our suggested cuts by mid-afternoon to-day, based on the 7 percent level," said Helen Goss, vice president of administration.

Jack Mayhew, vice president of sales, spoke next. "It's a tough market out there and we have to fight to get every sale, to sign up each new franchise, and to try to hang on to our old accounts. I'm really not sure just how we can cut and still maintain the income level we have now, but we'll have some figures tomorrow noon."

Sontel nodded, said nothing. Almost as an afterthought, Mayhew then said: "By the way, are these layoffs or a permanent downsizing?"

Sontel replied quickly, raising his voice a level: "They're what we have to do now. If we can, we'll hire everyone back when things get better. But it may well be that none of them will ever come back. I can't promise you anything on re-employment."

Steve George, director of quality control, commented, "Our reputation is based on the high quality of our product, and I hesitate to do anything that might hurt us in that regard. We're a small staff anyway. I'll make a thorough review and get back to you tomorrow."

Jim Hunter, director of futures planning, said, "Our total staff is just four people, but if it's necessary I can cut one."

Janet Williams, public relations director, commented, "Jim, the way that we handle the announcement of layoffs and cost reductions is very important, in fact, vital, and I'd like to talk with you right after this meeting to discuss the approach that I think we should take. As to budget and personnel reductions, we'll get it done even though I'm short-staffed now."

The director of advertising and marketing, Peter Abrams, interjected, "I agree with Jack. It's almost impossible to cut costs and increase revenues at the same time."

Sontel, cutting in, said sharply, "We have no choice; neither do you. From a profit standpoint, savings are better. They don't get taxed. But we have to make that employee reduction now, and this may not be the last cut."

Abrams continued, "I'll want to talk with Jack and learn what products he thinks can stand a reduction in advertising and marketing support. Then, I'll see where we can make the necessary and affordable cuts. My guess is it will be mostly in media, because that's where the big money is."

Each executive present at the meeting—Griffith

and Garvey were out of town—had now spoken. Sontel wrapped it up.

"I'm sorry it has to happen this way," he said. "The market and economic trends indicate that we have no choice. Make sure I have your figures before noon tomorrow, and they have to equal 7 percent." He looked at Williams. "Janet, I'll see you in half an hour in my office."

When Williams returned to her office she knew that she had little time to think through and prepare to present to Sontel a plan of action for handling the bombshell he had detonated at the meeting of his top executives. The first thing she did was to tell her secretary to hold all incoming telephone calls so she wouldn't be distracted while she worked on the outlines of a plan she could present to Sontel.

This challenge, she thought to herself, is one of the toughest I've had in the 14 years I've been in the field. She knew that in those years she had learned quite a lot about the difference between proactive and reactive public relations. In her four years at Singleton she had been able to effect quite a bit of positive change. The company had moved from a reclusive one to an active participant in its plant communities. Its communication with employees had always been good, but now was a bit more organized, better planned, more interactive. Media relations were excellent locally, good nationally. Shareholder relations were positive. The stock paid good dividends and had appreciated steadily.

The public relations staff, though small, was well qualified. Williams believed that the only smart approach was to hire the best, tell them what you wanted, and give them a reasonably free hand in achieving objectives. Excluding herself, she had six professional and two clerical staff members. That number would soon decrease, but Williams had decided to deal with that problem after she met with the CEO. Her immediate first step, she decided, was to set down on paper and in rough form what she perceived to be key factors bearing on the situation facing the company. Here is how she perceived these elements:

Timing crucial . . . Only Sontel and top execs know what Sontel disclosed at the meeting . . . Specifics unknown, other than the 7 percent target figure . . . Dollar figures important, if can get them from finance . . . Positives we can stress, negatives we need be aware of . . . Who makes announcements? . . . When and where? . . . Coordination with other facility . . . Only a weekly in Ruxton; a.m. daily in city and p.m. daily in other facility city . . . TV in both cities . . . National press . . . Internal publications . . . Backup plan if untimely leak . . . Other aspects I haven't considered?

As Williams reflected about the last item her intercom buzzed. The secretary reminded Williams that she was due in Sontel's office in three minutes and that his secretary had called a short time ago to inform Williams that Sontel had scheduled another top staff meeting for the next day at 5:00 p.m.

BUDGET CUTS AND LAYOFFS AT SINGLETON* (B)

Janet Williams was ushered into James Sontel's inner office as soon as she showed up on time for her meeting with the CEO.

"Well, Janet," he said, "you've always been able to get across all the good news in a way that has helped this company a great deal. Now how are you going to tell the bad news and make people like it?"

"We can't," Janet replied. "Many people are going to get hurt, and they won't like it. The community has high unemployment now and cuts at the largest employer will have a very negative effect here and in our plant city. But what we can do is tell our story quickly and honestly. By making the announcement today we can control the story. If we wait, there will be leaks and lots of rumors and misunderstanding."

Sontel broke in, fidgeting a bit as he did when he was uncomfortable. "But we can't announce today. We don't even know who is going and who is staying. There are too many loose ends."

Janet spoke quietly and forcefully. "You said the 7 percent is set in stone. We can announce that, and explain why Singleton is now forced to do this. There's nothing nice or neat about a layoff, and everyone knows

---

*All names, places, and dates in this case are disguised.

that's just a pretty word for 'firing.' If we act now, it's our story. If we delay, the story belongs to the media, and I guarantee it won't come out the way we'd like it."

"Aren't we supposed to tell our employees first?" Sontel said. "That's what you've always said, and it's worked well that way."

"That's the ideal," Williams replied. "But as soon as we tell them, the story leaks out everywhere. In this case, we have to tell them and the media at the same time—the sooner the better."

"How do we do that?" asked a puzzled Sontel. "And what about our other plant and its employees, our stockholders, and city officials? How can *you* coordinate all that?"

"That's my job," said Williams. "It can be done. The important thing is that we issue a statement. Because you've always made the important statements about Singleton, I believe that you should make this one, too. We'll point out that the steps we are taking are necessary and prudent, and we'll emphasize that we have never had a layoff before and regret deeply that it is necessary now. People understand that things are tough, that a lot of people are unemployed, that it may get worse before it gets better. The main thing is that we have to tell our story honestly, completely, and do it within the hour. Otherwise the rumors will start and the story will be muddled."

Sontel's face hardened as he said, "You've guided us well before, but you're really hanging me out on a limb now. Let me see your statement as soon as it's completed. I also want to know how you're going to tell the employees at the same time you tell the media. If I heard you correctly, you said we should announce within the hour. That leaves you little time, so you had better get with it immediately."

Janet returned quickly to her office.

BUDGET CUTS AND LAYOFFS AT SINGLETON* (C)

Monday, November 23, 1992, was the longest, busiest, most trying day of Janet Williams' entire public relations career. The day had started with the normally scheduled top executive staff meeting, and it didn't come to an end until Williams returned to her home at 9:50 that night. Although she was completely bushed, Williams knew that she still had work to accomplish. She hoped that at the age of 37 she had enough stamina to deal with the task facing her.

That task, she knew, was not an easy one. She had built a public relations staff of solid pros who were all well qualified and making a substantial contribution to the Singleton Corporation. There was so much work that the department could well be justified in adding another professional, but some of the overload was taken care of by the occasional use of public relations freelancers on a project basis. Now Williams was being asked to drop one of the six professionals. She couldn't lay off one of the clerical employees, because doing so would not meet the 7 percent target set by the CEO. Williams had to report her decision tomorrow, and so at 10:00 that evening she reviewed the individuals who comprised the professional public relations staff at Singleton.

---

*All names, places, and dates in this case are disguised.

1 ✱ Howard Craig, 37, handled media relations and was very good at it. He had started his career on a small daily newspaper, gone on to the Associated Press, and later became assistant managing editor of the daily newspaper in the city of 150,000 which was 15 miles from Ruxton. Craig, who had joined Singleton seven years ago, was single and had a significant relationship with the daughter of the daily newspaper publisher.

Maria Rector, 45, headed internal public relations. The company publications won awards every year in national competitions and were a major source of interaction with the employees. The publications were forums, not preaching organs for management, and were well regarded by top executives. Rector, who had been in the department five years, was a widow whose son had just completed his first year of medical school.

Sam McGovern, 59, was an old hand in the financial relations world and had been with Singleton 18 years. He'd worked on the business side for three newspapers, did a tour with *Financial World* magazine, and then came to Singleton via one of the *Fortune* 100 because he really wanted to come back to his home state. He had superb relationships with both the financial analysts and the financial media. He had once told Williams he expected to be with the company until he reached 65. His three married daughters lived in other states.

Glenn Hoover, 54, an excellent writer and communicator, had joined Singleton seven years ago when the company had gone on the New York Stock Exchange. Prior to that time one person had handled both financial and shareholder relations, but Williams felt that was now inadvisable. Hoover had 10 years of midwestern newspaper experience before he got into financial relations. He was married and had two children, ages 20 and 18, in college. He had an MBA from Wharton.

2 ✱ Kimberly Mentor, 47, handled public affairs. Prior to joining the company 12 years ago, she had worked at the state capitol as an assistant to the chair of the labor com-

mittee. Excellent at dealing with government agencies, Mentor seemed to be welcomed on both sides of the aisle. She was married to a prominent attorney who was a senior partner in the most prestigious law firm in the state.

Roland Watson, 34, community relations manager, had joined the company five years ago. He had graduated from local schools and the area college. Watson knew a great number of people and had established close working relationships with all parts of the community, particularly the black community in which he had spent his formative years. Watson was married and had four young children. Williams had learned last month that Watson's wife had been diagnosed as having inoperable, terminal cancer.

Janet Williams had a high degree of personal and professional respect for all six members of her staff, but she knew she had to let one of them go. The problem was, which one should it be?

It's All In How You Look At It*

You're the public relations director of a large, multi-city corporation with 4,000 employees. The company is attempting a financial restructuring to obtain relief from a debt burden incurred as the result of a leveraged buy-out during the exuberant '80s.

You and the human resources director are summoned to a meeting with Chester Cautious, your CEO. A frustrated Cautious explains that the company's lenders and investors will not agree to a financial restructuring unless the company eliminates those assets which are providing a below-average return on investment.

During the next 24 months, the company will have to sell two divisions, close three facilities employing a total of 400 people, and reduce the remaining head count by 500 through attrition, early retirement and layoffs.

Cautious is concerned about the effect of these actions on employee morale, future sales, vendor relations, shareholder relations and community relations. He asks you to prepare a comprehensive communications program while the director of human resources works up the details of the reduction in forces.

As you prepare to leave, Cautious says, "I'll also want you to develop a schedule for the release of the bad news. It should take the form of a 24-month cold tablet—releasing just the amount of bad news that employees can absorb at any one time. They won't be so devastated if they don't see the whole picture. What they don't know can't hurt them or us!"

You hesitate only a moment before saying, "Mr. Cautious I . . ."

*Copyright July 1991. Reprinted by permission of the *Public Relations Journal,* published by the Public Relations Society of America, New York, N.Y.

One of six hypothetical cases in an article entitled "What's Right?" The authors, Richard Truitt and Davis Young, noted that all of the ethical questions in the six cases would be discussed at the November annual national conference of the Public Relations Society of America. Truitt is managing partner, Truitt & Arnold, New York City, and Young is president, Edward Howard & Co., Cleveland.

THE PRINCETON DENTAL RESOURCE CENTER

It is not often that advertising and public relations involving one company co-exist in the same issue of a major daily newspaper. But that's exactly what happened to the M&M/Mars candy company in the *New York Times (NYT)* of Wednesday, April 15, 1992.

The advertising, as with virtually all advertising, was paid for by the company and ran as a full-page ad on page A13. The art consisted mainly of wrappers of various Mars products, including its chocolate bars. The copy was built on the line, "Bringing America Change." It tied the concept of change to a refund program run by the company and bringing monetary change into the pockets of consumers who mail in refund coupons and certificates. (At the time the cost of a full-page *NYT* ad was about $50,000.)

The public relations involving M&M/Mars appeared in a story by Barry Meier that ran for 10 inches on the front page and was carried over another 30 inches on page 6 of the Business section. Headed "Dubious Theory: Chocolate a Cavity Fighter," the story centered mainly on a research report carried in a newsletter published by the Princeton Dental Resource Center of Princeton, New Jersey. The page-one part of the story carried an excerpt from the newsletter measuring two columns wide and two-and-a-half inches deep.

Lead paragraph of the excerpt read: "As the old

adage goes, an apple a day may keep the doctor away, but several recent studies indicate that a piece of chocolate a day may keep plaque bacteria—key players in the cavity process—at bay."

The first three paragraphs of the *NYT* story noted that thousands of dentists have received newsletters from the Princeton Dental Resource Center asking them to pass along the newsletter to patients. Included in the newsletters, noted the story, had been advice to patients that snacking on chocolate bars in moderation might even inhibit cavities.

Stating that many dentists passing along the newsletter were unaware that the Princeton center "was financed by the M&M/Mars candy company," the story said that "the publications make no mention of the connection. And researchers and consumer experts are angry."

Michael Jacobson, executive director of the Center for Science in the Public Interest, a consumer advocacy group, was quoted by Meier as stating "This sounds like the most brazen way of doing things that I have ever heard of." Meier also wrote that "dentists say the new attempts to turn chocolate into a friend of the tooth go too far."

According to Meier, the scientist on whose report the Princeton group's newsletter relied mainly for its allegations concerning chocolate's anti-cavity powers said his work had been "mischaracterized." Meier identified the scientist as Dr. Lawrence Wolinsky of the University of California at Los Angeles.

Samuel Ostrow, described in the *NYT* story as a spokesman for the Princeton group, denied there was any mischaracterization of Dr. Wolinsky's study. The *NYT* also said that Hans Fiuczynski, external relations director for the M&M/Mars division of Mars, Inc., rejected any suggestion that the company tried to influence the group's publications.

According to Fiuczynski, the company established the Princeton Dental Resource Center in Princeton,

N.J., in 1987 as a private foundation. Drs. Marilyn C. Miller and Thomas F. Truhe, two dentists, run the Princeton group, according to the *NYT* story.

Fiuczynski was further cited by the story as stating, "We have never made any secret about it being funded by M&M." According to the story, Fiuczynski said that Mars had contributed about $1 million each year to the group and that amount represented at least 90 percent of the financing.

Citing Fiuczynski further, the *NYT* story reported him as saying that Mars was concerned that if it placed its name on the Princeton newsletter this might deter other companies from financing the newsletter. "And additional sponsors might not be thrilled with the idea that Mars gets all the credit," he added.

In citing the reaction of dentists, the *NYT* story said a dentist in New York, Dr. Stanley Sirgutz, became suspicious about the newsletter's backing when he read in it the favorable reference to snacking and chocolate. Dr. John Gardner, a Missouri dentist, was quoted as saying, "I feel totally misled." Dr. Patrick Carroll, an Arkansas dentist, said he was not bothered by Mars's involvement.

According to the *NYT*, several dentists believed that the Princeton Dental Resource Center was affiliated with Princeton University, and that much of the research reported in its publications was accurate.

Readers of *Jack O'Dwyer's Newsletter,* a weekly publication of the public relations field, were informed of the *NYT* story in a report about it in the April 22 issue of *O'Dwyer's*. The eight-inch report in *O'Dwyer's* cited key features of the *NYT* story and provided additional information about some of the principals involved and about new developments.

According to *O'Dwyer's*, The Rowland Company, a well-known public relations counseling firm, won the Princeton Dental Resource Center account in 1990. *O'Dwyer's* identified Samuel Ostrow as senior executive VP and president for public affairs in Rowland's New York office. It cited him as saying that his firm also does "some work" for M&M/Mars and that several Rowland staff members were working with the Princeton Dental Resource Center on producing material for various publications, including six two-page newsletters sent once a year in camera-ready format to dentists for reproduction.

"One problem," stated *O'Dwyer's*, is that M&M/Mars is nowhere named or its relationship to the research organization in the newsletter."

O'Dwyer's cited Ostrow as stating that M&M/Mars had never attempted to tell the Princeton Dental Resource Center what to include in its newsletter or its other publications.

As to the future, according to *O'Dwyer's*, Dr. Hans W. Fiuczynski said the controversy about the newsletter will be taken up at a board of directors meeting at the end of the month; M&M/Mars will consider listing its name on the newsletter to prevent any misperceptions; and it was out of deference to those other companies that contribute funds to the Princeton Dental Resource Center that M&M/Mars remained unlisted on the newsletter.

Calvin Trillin, whose nationally syndicated column is distributed to newspapers via King Features Syndicate, found the *NYT* article interesting enough to use as the basis for a column appearing on April 23. His lead paragraph ends this case:

> I can't say I was surprised to read in the *New York Times* that the Princeton Dental Resource Center, whose newsletter to dentists extols the cavity-fighting properties of chocolate, turns out to be a front for the M&M/Mars Company. It made me feel nostalgic: Now that the Communists are gone, I sort of miss front groups.

MAST'S DILEMMA AT BASIC CHEMICALS*

Basic Chemicals International (BCI) was a multinational company with two major divisions: Basic Chemicals U.S. and Basic Chemicals International. Approximately 60 percent of its $600,000,000 in annual sales came from the United States and 40 percent from its international operations.

The 20,000 employees of BCI (about one-third serving with the international unit and two-thirds in the United States) worked in 25 plants and research facilities at 20 locations, 12 of these in the United States. Listed on a major exchange, the company had 75,000 shareholders.

Approximately 60 percent of the products of the company were in the chemical industry category; this included the firm's own consumer products as well as chemical product ingredients the company sold to other chemical manufacturers. The remaining 40 percent of the firm's business was divided among a variety of nonchemical fields, including beverages, drugs, paper, electronics, and textiles.

BCI corporate headquarters occupied 14 floors of a 30-story modern office building at 845 Third Avenue in mid-town New York City. Executive offices were located

---

*All names, places, and dates in this case are disguised.

on the 28th floor, and the nine-member corporate public relations staff had offices on the 10th floor. The published organization chart of the department (Exhibit 10–1) shows the members of the staff.

Hubert Stanley, 44, director of public relations, had been with the company in this position for six years. He was acknowledged to be an excellent writer, particularly of speeches; he had eight years' experience in public relations with another major chemical company and four with a chemical trade association. His media experience was limited to two years in his late twenties as a reporter with a metropolitan newspaper.

Stuart Jonza, 42, manager of editorial services, had joined the company three years ago. He was responsible for publication of the following: monthly management newsletter, monthly employee publication, monthly headquarters office publication, the news flash bulletin board system, college recruiting brochures, and the pension plan report. He had five years' experience as director of employee publications for a multiplant manufacturing concern, six years as news service director of a major food concern, and four years as public information manager of a chemical firm.

George Welch, 41, was manager of press relations. He joined the company last year when Mast gave up his press relations work to devote full time to other corporate public relations staff duties. He had worked eight years as a reporter for a major metropolitan newspaper and two years in a press relations capacity for a national trade association.

Peter Mast, 36, manager of special projects, had been with the company three years (he and Jonza were hired at the same time). He joined the public relations staff with responsibility for both press relations and general corporate staff work. He had served as a reporter for one year with a 60,000-circulation newspaper, as news editor of a general magazine for two years, and as a public relations counselor for four years.

Ramona Copley, 34, manager of investor relations, had joined the company last year. She had several years' experience on a 125,000-circulation newspaper as a financial writer and two years' experience with a press association in a major eastern city.

Peter Brent, 54, manager of plant-community relations, had joined the company five years ago. He was responsible for supervision and guidance of the company's plant public relations managers. He had 14 years' experience as a reporter for various medium-sized daily newspapers, 10 years as editor of a plant newspaper for a heavy industrial firm, and two years as a salesman.

Janice Cohen, 40, manager of government relations, had joined the company four years ago. She had six years' experience as city hall reporter for a metropolitan daily, ten years as a Washington representative for a national trade association, and three years as administrative assistant to a Congressman. She spend most of her time in an office the firm maintained in Washington, but she also worked in one of the offices the department had on the 10th floor.

Leesa Pucci, 28, editor, had joined the company two years ago after four years of Army service (two in public information work) and three years as editor of an employee publication for a large drug company.

Judy Porter, 23, editorial assistant, joined the company this year. She had an undergraduate degree in public relations from Utica College of Syracuse University and a master's degree in public relations from American University. She had worked as an editorial assistant for one year with a chemical trade journal.

Stanley's Management Philosophy

In handling the staff, Stanley gave each manager a wide degree of latitude and a minimal amount of supervision. He operated on the theory that if one hires men and women with sufficient experience and expertise in their areas of competence, there should be no need for close supervision. As he explained to Mast one day during lunch:

"When I hire a person to handle press relations, I expect him to do his job without need of supervision. If he doesn't measure up after a suitable period, then the time has come to consider replacing him with another person, or moving him to another slot, if one is available.

"Besides, I just don't have time for supervision. Dorn (president of the company and the man to whom Stanley reported) keeps me busy enough writing speeches, advising, and suggesting action on policy matters relating to public relations."

Clapping Mast lightly on the back, Stanley added: "Anyway, the people in the department know they can always go to you if they need help or direction."

In actuality, some of the managers did and some did not. Though each manager reported directly to him, Stanley was usually too busy with his own work to spend time on supervision, held few staff meetings, and gave others in the department the understanding that Mast could and should handle matters of daily routine. When inquiries relating to various public relations matters filtered into the department, they were usually relayed first to Mast. He, in turn, relayed them to the appropriate managers.

Mast himself felt that personal relationships in the department were good. There had never been a major dispute, and no one had been dismissed since Stanley took over. But he also felt that supervision of the managers was too loose; there wasn't any real direction given to the people in the department. In effect, Mast felt, each manager worked in a specialized area of public relations activity, and there was little coordination of effort. Starting with just two people six years ago, the department had expanded with expanding business—but at no time had anyone set down a formal set of objectives or a formal plan of action. As Stanley explained when Mast was hired:

"We've just been too damned busy doing the job for which we're paid. Besides, basic objectives really don't change: we all know full well that we're here to gain goodwill for the company and acceptance for its products. We know that we're here to assist in the marketing of company products and head off present and potential trouble for the company and its executives; and, of course, to provide the executives with public relations assistance."

Mast recognized that each person in the department was productively busy, but he felt that the department wasn't functioning as it could have under closer supervision and a concerted plan of action. It was also his belief that some of the managers—particularly Jonza and Welch—failed to demonstrate sufficient creativity and were too content to follow routine ways of handling their work. However, though he was critical in his own mind about the state of the department, Mast wasn't certain what could be done to improve matters and felt that he wasn't in any position to bring about changes.

Mast's hopes for improvement in the workings of the department were raised in January when Stanley moved his office to the 28th floor at the suggestion of the president. The action, explained Stanley at a special staff meeting called to announce the change, was made because the president wanted him to be close at hand rather than far removed on the 10th floor. The move, he said, reflected greater management acceptance of the public relations function.

At the same time, Stanley announced that Mast would become assistant director of public relations and would take over his old corner office on the 10th floor. Stanley advised the staff that the assistant directorship represented a "proxy" when he was not available for routine matters. Stanley asked if there were any questions, and when none were forthcoming he distributed the new department organization chart shown in Exhibit 10–2.

Mast, who had received a significant raise with the announcement of the departmental change, felt the move would be beneficial to the department; he decided, however, to withhold judgment for six months. One afternoon in May, Mast reviewed the departmental setup and concluded that he had three major problems: the department itself, Welch, and Jonza.

THE DEPARTMENT

Mast felt that he was more of an assistant to the director rather than the assistant director. He felt that, while personal relationships between him and the other staffers and between him and Stanley remained good, he was being used mainly as a sounding board. When other managers thought they had problems, they went first to Mast rather than to Stanley. Mast advised action but did not order it because he felt he didn't have the authority.

Mast realized that he could ask Stanley to give him line authority in the department, but, at the same time, he felt that asking for this authority would clearly imply to Stanley that Mast was critical of Stanley's own failure to provide direction. Further, Mast felt that he personally had no proven record of administrative effectiveness and no real supervisory experience—although it was his opinion that he had administrative talent and ability. Finally, he recognized that he was among the youngest of the staff, even though he had about the most experience with the company. For these reasons, he hesitated to press the issue.

WELCH

Mast was definitely dissatisfied with the level of work done by the press relations manager. He also viewed the function differently. Welch, Mast knew, saw himself as a "press officer" who answered press inquiries when they were directed to him. Mast, on the other hand, believed that the press relations manager should be more aggressive in initiating placements and "selling" stories to media representatives.

In the past year, Mast reflected, he had suggested at least three assignments to Welch, but somehow they had never been carried out. Most of Welch's output consisted of routine stories about promotions and financial items, but his record of direct placements of major stories in major outlets was nil. Stanley himself had acknowledged some dissatisfaction with Welch's work. Yet when Mast had suggested that Welch needed closer supervision, the director had replied that those at the manager's level were expected to handle their areas without close supervision. Further, Stanley had said, such close supervision was in itself too time-consuming because it cut into the supervisor's own work. Neither Stanley nor Mast had expressed to Welch their dissatisfaction with his work. Stanley, Mast felt, would agree to any strong recommendation Mast might make regarding Welch.

JONZA

Considering Jonza's performance over the past three years, Mast recalled that Jonza had accepted the job at BCI at the same salary he was getting on his old job because he had strongly wanted to get back to New York City. He spent the first two years with BCI getting management acceptance of a full-blown publications program; Mast knew this had been a wearing experience. Constantly irksome also was the fact that Jonza's work involved major contact with a personnel director who was not particularly cooperative and who tended to undervalue Jonza's counsel and work.

Both Stanley and Mast recognized that Jonza's workload was heavy; to assist him the department had taken on Leesa Pucci two years ago as editor and Judy Porter as editorial assistant this year. Both Stanley and Mast had a very high opinion of Pucci's work, and thought she had a great deal of promise.

Both Stanley and Mast knew that Jonza had some major personal problems; a recent ulcer operation, some undefined but rather obvious family troubles, and a financial drain due to the fact that he had on his hands an unsold house at his previous location in Iowa and a new one in the New York City area.

And both recognized his problems in a general sort of way. Stanley had mentioned to Mast that Jonza could not be counted on for creative initiative because he had lost his drive. Mast felt (and Stanley agreed) that Jonza was a very competent writer; his broad experience in employee communications also represented an unusual resource for the department.

Mast was of the opinion that Jonza needed some help to regain the promise of his earlier years, but he wasn't certain how this could be done. Neither Stanley nor Mast had expressed their doubts about Jonza to Jonza personally, and Mast felt that Stanley would agree to any strong recommendation Mast might make regarding Jonza.

Finally, Stanley called Mast to suggest lunch that week at the University Club, to be followed by a long talk in one of the club's private rooms. "It's been five months since we made the change in the department setup," Stanley said. "I think an all-afternoon session, without interruptions, would be fruitful."

The two set their lunch date for that coming Friday.

Exhibit 10-1

**Department
Organization Chart**

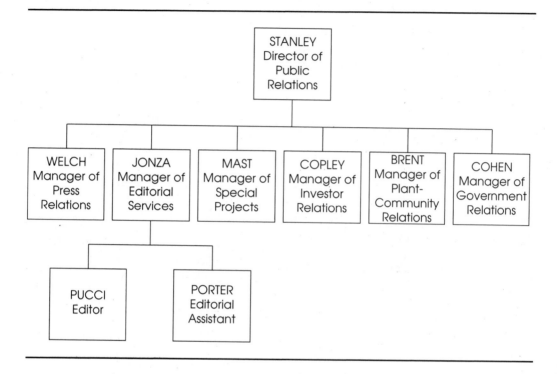

Exhibit 10-2

New Department Organization Chart

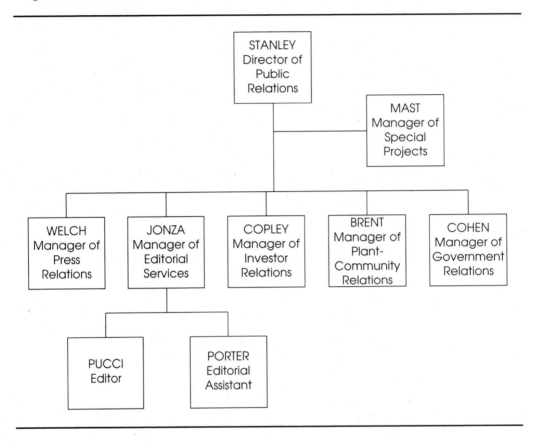

BRENT'S MULTIPLE PROBLEMS AT BASIC CHEMICALS*

You are Peter Brent, manager of plant-community relations for Basic Chemicals International, and as noted in the first BCI case material you work in the public relations department of BCI in New York City. Working for you are a part-time writer and secretary. There are plant-community public relations managers at 10 of the 12 major locations throughout the country where BCI has either a plant or a research facility. These managers report and are directly responsible to the general managers at their plant or research facilities, and they operate under the budget of these facilities.

Your office provides the field public relations managers with advice and counsel and with print and other public relations "hardware" that generally have a company-wide connection. The public relations managers at the field installations are not obligated to use the material you send them nor to take your advice and counsel, but you have built up a sound rapport with them, and generally the material is used and the advice and counsel taken.

Once a year, usually in late June, you sponsor at a suitable location a three-day plant-community relations communications conference to which the field people are invited. Attendance in the past has been excel-

---

*All names, places, and dates in this case are disguised.

lent because the conference programs have generally been of high calibre and the discussions at the conference of real value to the participants. Your budget covers all conference expenses at the conference site, but the participants are expected to cover their travel and routine expenses through their own public relations budgets. This year's conference is scheduled for Arden House, Harriman, N.Y., June 28–30.

Today is Monday, June 15. You have been away from your office since Wednesday, June 10, attending a national public relations seminar at San Jose State University. Your secretary has arranged on your desk various letters, memoranda, etc., (Exhibits 11–1 through 11–8) that have accumulated since you left for the conference, and you have started to leaf through them.

Exhibit 11–1
Memorandum

Thursday, June 11

From: Hubert Stanley

To: Peter Brent

Re: Query from Charles Sturbin

Sturbin, the new man handling public relations at our Syracuse installation, called me this morning. He's gotten a request from the mayor of Syracuse and the Clinton people asking permission to have Governor Clinton address people in our plant there on Wednesday, June 17. As you know, Syracuse is a nominally Republican city, but the mayor is a Democrat. We have no company-wide policy on this sort of thing. I'll be working out a policy as soon as I can get to President Dorn to discuss it with him.

Meanwhile, I'd prefer that you handle this when you get back to your desk Monday. I told him to check with you sometime Monday for guidance. I have no idea what Mike Potts (manager of the Syracuse plant) thinks about this.

By the way, I would appreciate it if our plant PR people would work directly through you rather than call me, especially at this time of the year.

cc: Peter Mast

Exhibit 11–2
Memo from Your Secretary

Friday, June 12

As you requested, I checked the status of our various account numbers today with the comptroller's office. We are generally on target at this time in terms of our budget allocations for the year. In fact—and I am taking into consideration our projected expenses for the coming Arden House conference—we should be about $7,000 to the good on our Community Projects account at the end of the six-month period ending June 30.

Exhibit 11–3
Memorandum

From: Peter Mast   Friday, June 12

To: Peter Brent

Re: Query from Charles Sturbin

As you know, Hubert sent me a copy of the memorandum he sent you yesterday regarding the query from Sturbin. As I will be out of the city Monday, I thought I'd pass along my reflections and observations. They may be of some help.

On the one hand, there's the fact that Governor Clinton is a very hot press personality these days. The national press is covering him like a blanket, so we're sure to be mentioned in connection with any remarks he might make in our Syracuse plant on Wednesday if we give the go-ahead. It never hurts, either, to keep on the good side of the mayor and the Democratic Party.

On the other hand, President Dorn in the past has been a heavy contributor to Republican campaigns and will probably continue to be so. I have always known him to be fair-minded, but I just don't know how he feels about the matter of speeches made at our plants.

Regarding the last item in Hubert's memo, I'm sure that Hubert would not object if your plant PR people checked with me when they can't get to you. The important thing is to make sure they don't bother Hubert.

I'm sure you will use your good judgment on Sturbin's request. By all means let me know what your decision was when I get back.

Exhibit 11-4

Fax

Baxter Drug Division
Basic Chemicals International
Joplin, Missouri

Thursday, June 11

Mr. Peter Brent
Manager, Plant-Community Relations
Basic Chemicals International
845 Third Avenue
New York, NY 10017

Dear Pete:

In talking with me today, one of the top editors of our influential local paper told me he's going to be attending an editors' conference in NYC June 18-20, and he said he would sure love to be able to see "Phantom" on Saturday night, June 20. I told him I'd see what I could do for him. Can you get two tickets for that night? I'm sure it would be much appreciated.

See you at Arden House. Best regards.

Cordially,

Ray Bolger, Manager
Plant-Community Relations

Exhibit 11–5
Fax

Nutron Textiles
Basic Chemicals International
Metro, Illinois

Wednesday, June 10

Mr. Peter Brent
Manager, Plant-Community Relations
Basic Chemicals International
845 Third Avenue
New York, NY 10017

Dear Pete:

The local CBS television station has come up with a very interesting proposition, which I am relaying to you in the hopes that you may see fit to share some of the costs and benefits involved.

They are proposing that we take over sponsorship of a one-and-a-half hour segment of TV time every Saturday evening (11:30 p.m. to 1 a.m.) for 30 weeks, from October through April. The segment would be called the "Nutron Movie of the Week," and for $2,500 weekly we would be entitled to opening and closing "billboards," a maximum of 12 minutes of air time for public relations messages, and a specified but as yet undetermined number of promotional announcements during the week. Normal charges for the above would usually amount to $2,800 a week, but if we sign up for 30 weeks we would get the special rate, the program name, and the use of commercial time for any public relations messages we want to put on the air.

Plant Manager Walter Craig is very interested in the station's proposal because he sees it as a fine public relations vehicle to counteract much of the negative public reaction to problems we have had with pollution, etc. He feels, however, that headquarters public relations should share some of the costs because the program would obviously resound to the credit of BCI as well as to Nutron Textiles. He is willing for us to cover $2,200 of the weekly cost but would like your office to cover the remaining weekly expense.

I hope the answer will be affirmative. I imagine that you are committed in terms of budget to the usual items, but I thought it might be possible for you to find a way to cover this new item. It would represent, I should imagine, a trial run here which might well be wise for the corporation to duplicate elsewhere if it proves successful.

Please let me know your reaction at the earliest.

Cordially,

Kaisten Smith, Manager
Plant-Community Relations

cc: Walter Craig

Exhibit 11–6

Fax

Mason Textile Division
Basic Chemicals International
Greensboro, North Carolina

Wednesday, June 10

Mr. Peter Brent, Manager
Plant-Community Relations
Basic Chemicals International
845 Third Avenue
New York, NY 10017

Dear Pete:

Unless you can figure out a way of shaking me loose, I'm afraid I won't be able to make the Arden House conference.

When I casually broached the upcoming conference on Monday to George Madden, division manager, he blew his stack and said that he had been trying to hold down expenses this year because of our poor earnings picture. He said, and I quote him: "I don't want any of my staff people wasting division money attending fun and games at places like Arden House."

Unless you can do an end run by getting to George through someone at headquarters who carries more weight with him than I do, I don't see me attending the conference. I hope you can work out something, because it looks like a fine program and I'm sure the conference would be very helpful to me.

Cordially,

Karen Ascot, Manager
Public Relations

Exhibit 11-7
Telephone Message

From: Sally Olcott, Walnut Plant, Los Angeles

Time: 10:00 a.m. June 11

Ms. Olcott called to say that she's terribly sorry but she cannot attend the Arden House Conference because of a lack of funds. She said that through an error of the account department she had been advised she still had $1,500 in her conference budget account, but she was told yesterday that she has already overspent the budget. If you can cover her expenses, she'll be glad to attend. She says she finds the conference very helpful and a great way of exchanging ideas with other plant-community managers at BCI.

Exhibit 11–8

Fax

Red Lion Division
Basic Chemicals International
Newark, New Jersey

Friday, June 12

From: David Story III

To: Peter Brent

Re: Upcoming Boycott

I recall when I took over this job as manager of public relations for the Red Lion Beverages Division of BCI, you told me that you would always be available for consultation and that I would have a relatively free hand so long as things seemed to be moving smoothly.

You have been as good as your word, and I should hope that matters have worked out smoothly. I haven't had to bother you with my problems, but a really tough one has arisen and I would certainly appreciate some advice.

First, a brief summary of pertinent details. We're the largest producer, distributor, and seller of soft drinks here in Newark, and sales in the city comprise about 30 percent of our total sales. African-Americans, as you know, are the majority in Newark, and it is estimated that about 60 percent of our sales are to blacks.

About three months ago a group of 12 black leaders representing the Newark Black Alliance met with Raul Walsh, our general manager, to discuss our employment policies. Stating that they represent the total black population of Newark, the leaders very politely told Walsh that they hoped Red Lion would take positive steps to increase the number of qualified blacks in responsible positions in the organization.

That meeting and two others that followed ended cordially enough, but at the last one the visitors requested, and Walsh agreed to, another meeting in three weeks. That meeting took place yesterday, and Walsh told me the details about it today. Rather upset, he told me that the black leaders this time specifically requested that Red Lion take steps in the next three weeks to hire 20 office workers (we have a total office work force of 200 with one black among them) and to upgrade into supervisory positions within six months a number, not specified, of the bottling plant work force. (There are no blacks in supervisory positions in the plant.)

Walsh told me he reminded the black leaders that we operate in a free enterprise economy, but in reply they said that there hadn't been much freedom for blacks in an economy and work situation such as exists at Red Lion. They said, according to Walsh, that unless the situation changed according to their request, they would call a city-wide black boycott of all Red Lion products commencing July 1 and would maintain the boycott until the company changed its employment policies. About 40 percent of our yearly sales occur between July 1 and September 30.

Walsh is well aware of the fact that within the last year the Newark Black Alliance has made similar demands on three other Newark organizations that deal in consumer products. In one case, I understand, the company acceded to the demands within the scheduled time, but in the other two the Alliance called boycotts that lasted two months in one instance and three months in the other.

After informing me today about the meetings he's held with the Alliance, Walsh said the final decision is his, but he would like my advice and counsel. I am meeting with him again at 4 p.m. Wednesday, June 17, and I would certainly welcome any advice you can give me.

Exhibit 11–9
Overnight Mail

CHI 195 BU NMA 22LNPD. Cedar Rapids, Iowa. June 14. Peter Brent, Basic Chemicals Intl, Third Ave, NYC.

Local Sunday paper has a wire service story out of Washington citing informed sources that, if true, can have dire consequences for our Cedar Rapids Plant. Story says it has been learned that William Reilly, administrator of the Environmental Protection Agency, is expected to issue an order Wednesday, June 17, banning almost all uses of DDT. This would be the culmination of almost three years of administrative and legal proceedings, scientific reports, and public hearings. Crux of the expected decision, says the story, will be a 40-page statement in which Reilly will declare that the continued use of DDT is an unacceptable risk to the environment and most likely detrimental to the health of man. Story says that the order will be effective December 31, and that it represents a defeat for the makers and formulators of DDT and for the Department of Agriculture. If the report is true, this could be a disaster for our plant because, as you know, we are one of the major formulators of DDT, and it's our major product at the plant.

I'm sure the local paper will want to be following up the wire story and will be trying to contact us at the plant tomorrow (Monday) for a statement regarding the effects on us of the DDT ban if the EPA order is issued Wednesday. Fortunately, the plant closed down Friday for our annual two-week vacation. This means, of course, that the paper will not be able to reach me at the plant. However, it also means that I can't reach Larry Ruth, plant manager to whom I report, because he has taken off for the upper Michigan region and left no forwarding address or telephone number.

Can you check out whether the wire story has validity and if the order will be made as the story has reported? Second, if there is to be a ban on DDT, does BCI have any plans for our plant? Third, what, if anything, should I say to the media? I can use all the help you can give me, but do not call me at home because I will not be answering the phone. I will call you 4:00 P.M. your time Monday. Hope you have some answers for me.

Nancy Stacy

Reprint for Discussion

Preparation Is the Best Crisis Insurance

William Corbett

Crisis communication has come a long way from the early days of commercial aviation when the key role of airline public relations officials was to go to the scene of a crash and paint over the airline's name before press photographers arrived.

Preparation is the Key to Success

. . . .

It is our job as professional communicators to enable our clients and employers to come out of crisis situations with as little damage as possible and in some cases with no lasting harm at all. Occasionally, a potentially threatening incident can actually prove to be beneficial.

We can never predict what challenge the next phone call will bring. Some practical suggestions to prepare you for those calls:

1. Be prepared to operate from your home or a remote site since crises often occur during off hours. At home and the office, have at your fingertips an annual report, prepared statements covering hot topics, and biographies and photos of senior management and board of directors. You never know when you'll have to produce an obituary on a weekend.

2. Keep copies of the most recent proxy statement, quarterly report, and a list of home and

*Reprinted with permission from "Tips & Tactics" supplement of *pr reporter*, Exeter, N.H., Vol. 29, No. 16, December 2, 1991.

weekend phone numbers of senior management and communications staff members, key media, wire services, Businesswire and PR Newswire. The latter are necessary since your firm might legally be required to inform the public if some event might significantly impact the price of the corporation's stock.

3.   Have an up-to-date fact sheet and economic-impact statement on each facility, along with home phone numbers of local management.

4.   Have a fax machine at home for normal and emergency use. Needless to say, a typewriter or word processor and portable phone are also essential.

5.   Keep updated safety statistics at your fingertips. There will be no time to gather them when everything "hits the fan" and you're besieged by the media, government officials, and your own employees and management.

6.   Make sure top PR executives know how to type, send a fax, set up a conference call, and use a copying machine. You don't know when you'll have to handle after-hours emergencies.

7.   Have 24-hour access to a copying machine in your home community and know the phone number of a reliable round-the-clock messenger service.

8.   Have written procedures in place that ensure there is only one source of information so the press cannot whipsaw you by getting seemingly conflicting information from others in your organization.

9. Keep internal audiences informed promptly and continuously to prevent rumors and inaccurate information from spreading.

10. Ensure that the switchboard, duplicating, mailing, and messenger facilities remain open after hours.

11. Keep a time log of each phone call handled and interview given since inevitably someone will come along later and evaluate your performance.

12. Communicate fully and rapidly. Unfortunately some CEOs like to take the safe way out and go along with their lawyers' advice to "say nothng." While lawyers are always looking ahead to litigation in the courtroom, they overlook the larger court of public opinion, which is much more important.

13. Be as fully informed as possible. Make arrangements with a monitoring service or a large public relations firm to monitor all news wires and to call or fax you immediately each time a story or a new detail breaks. Also notify a radio and TV monitoring service and fax clipping service to alert you of any developments.

14. Appoint a staff person with good media skills to be your organization's spokesperson. I used to believe the senior person in each organization should be the spokesperson. I've since learned how ill-equipped some are for the job. Some CEOs will not spend the time for training. Others—no matter how much training they receive—just can't hack it. With some, their real personalities show through,

arrogance and all, and what is seen is not always pleasant to the discerning viewer.

15.   A request to PR firms on behalf of corporate PR officers: if you are brought in to help during a crisis, don't denigrate the in-house staff. When some of these outside "heavyweights" come in and deal directly with the CEO and totally exclude the in-house staff from the deliberations, they undermine the staff. When the large firm departs, it leaves a trail of problems and hurt feelings because rapport with the press and others has been destroyed.

A crisis provides the opportunity for public relations personnel to prove their worth and impress management with their skills and talent. The key is preparation and getting management involved in developing a crisis communication plan and guidelines long before they are needed. The planning process will help to sensitize management to the communication challenges that arise during a crisis.

Sometimes it's helpful to the in-house staff to invite an outside expert to help guide management through the planning process. There may be things that need to be said that in-house personnel would not be comfortable saying to the people with whom they work. For example, it's easier for an outside expert to tell top management that the communication staff must have direct access to the CEO on an immediate and continuing basis during a crisis. It's also often necessary for an outsider to keep the lawyers with whom the in-house staff deals every day from exercising inordinate control while drafting the crisis communication procedures.

EMPIRE ENTERPRISES SEEKS IDENTIFICATION*

A little more than a year after the events described in "*Basic Chemicals,*" Peter Mast was offered and accepted a position as vice president of media relations at Empire Enterprises, a large conglomerate headquartered in St. Louis, Missouri. At the suggestion of Charles Scully, his superior at Empire, Mast prepared and mailed out to the public relations and advertising trade press and to the heads of public relations at the 62 companies that comprised the Empire family of firms a release announcing his new job and describing his prior experience in public relations.

The corporation Mast joined had started out 80 years ago as a small oil company. It began to branch out in the early 1960s and by 1992 it had become one of the nation's largest corporations. As a result, in 1992 total revenues of Empire Enterprises amounted to $14.5 billion; total employment reached 180,000; and the number of wholly owned firms operating under the Empire banner reached a record 62.

In apprising Mast of these facts a few weeks after Mast joined the firm, Scully, senior vice president of public relations at Empire, expressed a concern he shared with the board of directors at Empire.

---

*All names, places, and dates in this case are disguised.

"Our acquisitions, mergers, and buyouts," Scully said, "have made us one of the largest corporations in the world, but our surveys of public opinion show that most Americans know virtually nothing about us. Obviously we have a public relations problem." Scully directed Mast's attention to a chart he took from a folder on his desk. It was headed "Empire Enterprises Public Relations Staff."

"You'll note that we have a total of 15 professionals on the corporate public relations staff here at headquarters," said Scully, and he then pointed to the bottom half of the chart, "but if you look down here you will see that there are more than 94 other public relations professionals working in the total corporate structure of Empire Enterprises. Every time we've absorbed another company, we've absorbed the staff who work for that company. This past year, for example, when we bought Ocra Foods, we absorbed Ocra's 15-member public relations staff, and when we merged Shore Ship Containers into Empire, their four-member public relations staff joined us.

"Many years ago we made a conscious decision to maintain a lean public relations staff here at corporate headquarters. We're responsible for the public relations activities of the total corporation on a national level and for the advice and counsel we provide top management here in St. Louis. The other 94 professionals are responsible for public relations activities and counseling within their own firms. They operate under the budgets of these firms and report to the management of these firms.

"This arrangement worked well when Empire was not as large as it is today, but we recognize that one of its major defects is an identification failure."

"You mean, non-identification with Empire?" Mast cut in.

"Exactly. There are other faults, such as a wide disparity of quality among the 94 professionals out there, but our board of directors is mainly concerned about the fact that the Ocras and the Shore Ships in our corporate family fail to identify with Empire Enterprises, and this is where you come in."

"Just what do you have in mind?" Mast asked.

"Well, I'm not sure myself," said Scully. "At the last quarterly board meeting one of the board members said we ought to do something to identify all companies and divisions within Empire Enterprises as being members of the Empire family. No formal vote was taken on this idea, but the chairman of the board said he would discuss the matter with me, and he subsequently did last week. He said it was clear from discussion at the meeting that the board is in favor of having all entities within Empire identify publicly with Empire Enterprises—in their advertising, their publications, and their releases to the media. The chairman did not specify how we should bring this about, but he did say that he expects a progress report from me by the next board meeting, which is two months from today."

Mast nodded that he understood, but said nothing.

"I've decided we must start somewhere," Scully continued. "We have only two months leeway, and that doesn't give us enough lead time to do anything substantive about advertising and publications. I've therefore decided that we ought to start with media releases and media conferences, and of course that's your area of responsibility. You can handle this any way you want, but I expect to have a report from you six weeks from now. Okay?"

"That doesn't leave me much time," Mast said, "but of course I'll get right on it."

In the next few days Mast reflected on his options, and he concluded he didn't have many. In the month since he had assumed his new position he had spent most of his time reading through files, getting to know people at corporate headquarters, and in general sizing up the nature of his job and role in the organization. He had visited with the head of public relations at Chicago Products when he was in Chicago on a trip to introduce himself to key media people in that city, but this was the only personal contact he had had with public relations people in the Empire family. Mast knew that he could arrange to take a trip around the country to meet with some of the public relations professionals in the 62 firms that made up Empire Enterprises, but he felt he didn't have nor could spare the time for personal visits. Mast concluded therefore that his only option was to draft and send out a letter to the head public relations person of each of the 62 firms. His letter, which was mailed one week after his meeting with Scully, appears in Exhibit 12–1.

Mast considered sending a copy of the letter to Scully and also noting at the bottom of the letter that a copy was being sent to Scully, but after some deliberation he decided not to do either.

For the next four weeks Mast carefully scanned as many major and national publications as he could get his hands on. These included the *Los Angeles Times; New York Times; Chicago Tribune;* the Dallas, Fort Worth, and Houston newspapers; *Boston Globe; Washington Post; The Wall Street Journal; USA TODAY; U.S. News & World Report; Time;* and *Newsweek.*

A total of 46 stories relating to firms in the Empire family appeared in the publications scanned by Mast. These stories ranged from small (two inches deep) to large (one or several columns). Five stories carried a phrase identifying the firm as being a part of Empire Enterprises, and of these five, three related to one firm.

As he absorbed this information, Mast glanced at his calendar and realized his report to Scully was due in one week.

Exhibit 12-1

Letter to Heads of Public Relations Firms

Empire Enterprises
1114 Mathews Avenue
St. Louis, MO 63101

August 19, 1993

Office of Vice President of Media Relations

To: Executive Head, Public Relations
All Subsidiaries

When I notified you via a press release of my appointment as vice president of media relations, I intended to follow it up as quickly as possible with a personal visit. Recognizing that there are 62 public relations departments among the firms that comprise the Empire Enterprises family, I realized that commitment would take some time to fulfill, but I hoped to achieve it within a reasonable time.

Unfortunately, a matter of serious import to all of us has developed that requires immediate action, and I am therefore forced to use this impersonal communication to deal with it.

Recent public opinion surveys have shown that most Americans have little knowledge of Empire Enterprises, despite the fact that we are one of the world's largest corporations. At the last meeting of our board of directors, concern was expressed that many of the firms within Empire's family fail to identify with the parent corporation. We at corporate public relations were subsequently directed to ensure that all entities within the Empire family identify publicly with Empire in their releases to the media.

As a start in seeking to reach this objective, I am writing to direct that all releases from your office sent to major and especially national media incorporate appropriate phraseology identifying your firm with Empire Enterprises. In most instances this can be achieved by means of a phrase such as "a wholly owned subsidiary of Empire Enterprises" or "a division of Empire Enterprises of St. Louis, Missouri" or "a member of the Empire Enterprises family of firms."

I expect we can see immediate implementation of this directive and, of course, feel free to call me if you have any questions relative to it. I appreciate your cooperation.

Sincerely,

Peter Mast
Vice President of Media Relations

Don't Sweat It Pal, They'll Never Find Out*

Your boss is Hedrick Hardstone, president of Unified Car Parts, and you're the public relations manager. You handle product promotion for the company's trouble light, an inexpensive version of the lights mechanics use when working on cars.

Things have been going well but three months ago a consumer reporter for an Atlanta TV station warned about the light and said electrical leaks sometimes caused shocks.

Unified ordered tests in its own lab that revealed a potential hazard, particularly if the lights were used near moisture. But the tests were called "inconclusive" by the company and you told this to the press. When two small-town newspaper stories appeared about consumer shock situations, the company said these were isolated instances, caused by product misuse.

This morning you got two phone calls that changed the day's agenda. One was from the company's southeast regional manager who had received several complaints about the light. One customer had threatened to demand a recall to save others users.

The other call was from a city-desk reporter at the *Chicago Tribune* who told your secretary he wanted to ask about the product. He said a man had been using one of the lights on a ladder, gotten a shock, and broken his collarbone when he fell.

You meet with Hardstone. "If this thing is showing up in Chicago, we're going to have to get out a response," you say. "Listen," Hardstone shouts at you through the smoke of his cigar. "You're here to make publicity, not to make waves."

You feel a bit naive. After all, Unified has sold thousands of these units over many years, and most products can be hazardous if they're not used according to instructions. But the "inconclusive" tests still gnaw at you.

"What about those tests?" you ask Hardstone. "Don't they make us vulnerable?"

"Don't worry, pal," Hardstone replies. "Those media types are aggressive, but they'll never find the tests— right now they're decomposing in our sewerage system, 20 feet under this building."

You say . . .

CRISIS AT SEARS AUTOMOTIVE CENTERS

The sequence of events and the pace of the action in consumer protection cases are particularly important but often difficult to follow. In presenting this case involving the California Department of Consumer Affairs (DCA) and its charges against Sears automotive repair centers in California, the authors have used a chronological approach to make it easier to understand the events and action as they took place. Media, state, and Sears sources will be clearly identified, including a log kept by Gerald Buldak, national manager of public affairs at Sears corporate headquarters in Chicago.

The first entry in Buldak's crisis log was dated Wednesday, June 10, 1992, but the negotiations mentioned in his entry for that date commenced months earlier. In December 1991, the Bureau of Automotive Repair (BAR), a unit of the state Department of Consumer Affairs, notified Sears that it had conducted an 18-month undercover investigation of Sears automotive centers in California. BAR's allegations included charges that Sears' auto repair centers had been systematically cheating customers and as a result the DCA would seek to suspend or revoke the registration of the 72 Sears auto centers in the state. From December 1991 to June 10, 1992, BAR and Sears representatives met at various intervals to try to negotiate a mutually acceptable solution to the charges raised by BAR.

These sessions ended when the BAR representatives walked out of the last meeting held prior to June 10, 1992. That date starts this chronology of the crisis that followed.

(Wednesday, June 10, 1992)

Sears Log

On learning that BAR had bolted from the negotiation table and may go public, alerted store managers to expect publicity and local interest. Provided them with talking points to accommodate interviews.

Denise Gellene, of the *Los Angeles Times*, calls late in day to ask if we are aware of the California Bureau of Automotive Repair making an announcement of an investigation of a major auto repair retailer. Not knowing what BAR told her, Sears declines to comment.

Sears Alert

In the alert mentioned in Buldak's log above, Gordon Jones notified store managers in California that DCA and BAR "are expected to hold a press conference Wednesday morning [sic] regarding Sears automotive service. Some comments have already been made to news media by state officials. You may use all or part of the following statement to respond to new media inquiries or questions from customers or associates." The statement below then followed.

AUTOMOTIVE SERVICE IN CALIFORNIA

We strongly disagree with the allegations made by the Department of Consumer Affairs and the Bureau of Automotive Repair and will vigorously oppose them in court. We have always cooperated fully with these state agencies.

We believe that the Bureau's undercover investigation was incompetent, very seriously flawed, and simply does not support the allegations.

Sears has offered automotive repair for more than 60 years. We have a hard-earned and outstanding reputation for trust with our customers.

Our policy has always been to put the safety of our customers first when recommending repairs to their vehicles. The service we recommend and the work we perform is in accordance with the highest industry standards.

We have built our reputation on quality automotive products and professional services for our customers. Our technicians have earned more than 14,000 Automotive Service Excellence (ASE) certifications, second only to Ford Motor Co. and General Motors.

(Thursday, June 11, 1992)

BAR Headquarters In a letter to co-author Frank Wylie, Kate McGuire, BAR public information officer at BAR headquarters, Sacramento, explained BAR's communication plan in announcing its charges against Sears. Here are excerpts from her letter:

We did a "layered" media event with the Sears case, and divided the media plan into the five major markets—Los Angeles, San Diego, San Francisco, Sacramento and Fresno—and the smaller markets in the cities where undercover runs were conducted.

Because this story would be of great interest to so many consumers, we wanted to communicate with as many folks as possible. Since the Bureau of Automotive Repair (BAR) has 40 field offices statewide, and all the office supervisors have been media trained (they know how to approach local media and how to pitch a story and handle interviews), we knew we could get good grassroots coverage if:

a. we provided the field offices with the tools which included media lists, directions telling them how and when to contact the media, B-rolls (of our undercover shop where the undercover vehicles used in the investigation were prepared) for local TV stations, and media kits. My office supplied these tools to the offices in the towns and cities where undercover runs were conducted.

b. we localized the stories. We did this by providing a list of the locations of each undercover run, address of each store (so local reporters could go there and get pix and/or interviews), the amount of and the date when the investigators were sold the unnecessary parts and service.

A decision was made to conduct four press conferences in four of the five major media markets all in one day in order to give reporters an opportunity to talk and directly question Department and BAR officials. We put together two teams of folks and began the day in Los Angeles. After that press conference, we separated the teams, with the Director of the Department of

Consumer Affairs and his team members heading off to San Francisco, and the Chief and Deputy Chief (who is Hispanic and handled Spanish press in both San Diego and Los Angeles) of BAR went to conduct the press conference in San Diego. From there the two teams rendezvoused in Sacramento for the final press conference of the day.

Meanwhile our field office supervisors were handling the smaller markets all over the state and providing reporters with excellent local coverage since they all had someone to interview, a press kit, B-roll, etc.

The press release was also put on Business Wire to be picked up in the areas where there was no field office. That release listed me as the contact person. My staff and I stayed here in Sacramento . . . to respond to those calls that came flooding in from all over the country that day and for several days thereafter. We spent the day taking calls and faxing press releases and supporting fact sheets to hundreds of smaller and larger out of state papers and TV stations.

Furthermore, the two teams were armed with cellular phones (ah, technology) and as they landed at their destinations I would call them with the names and phone numbers of reporters who had requested to speak directly with the Director or the Chief. Every reporter who needed one got a call back, and some got several. In addition, we also had our public relations consulting firm begin booking follow-up appearances on public affairs radio and television shows, both local and network.

According to our Chronology sheet, Sears was informed of the findings of our investigation at a meeting in December of 1991 in Oakland where Department and BAR officials met with their National Service Manager, National Sales Manager, Senior Counsel, and Auto Training Manager.

P.S. We calculated that we reached about 67 million people with print and more than 160 million people in "audience impressions" with the broadcast media.

The DCA/BAR press release cited in McGuire's letter, ran to six double-spaced pages. The press materials from BAR also included a map of the locations visited by the undercover agents, a sample Sears brake ad, three pages documenting where investigators went and what they allegedly were overcharged in each location, a sheet recording alleged oversell (90 percent in the initial investigation and 70 percent in the checks after they had notified Sears), and three pages of questions and answers on the investigation and charges.

Following are the first five pages of the DCA/BAR press release (the sixth page was a generic account of BAR):

FOR IMMEDIATE RELEASE
CONTACT: KATE McGUIRE (BAR)
(916) 366-5060
LOUIS BONSIGNORE (DCA)
(916) 322-2463

SEARS AUTO REPAIR REGISTRATIONS IN JEOPARDY STATEWIDE

SACRAMENTO—State Department of Consumer Affairs (DCA) Director Jim Conran announced today that the Department's Bureau of Automotive Repair (BAR) is seeking to revoke or suspend the registration of all 72 of Sears' auto repair shops in California for violations of provisions of the State's Auto Repair Act.

In accusations issued and currently being served on Sears, one of the largest retail chains in the country, BAR is charging the auto repair shops with false or misleading statements, fraud, willful departure from accepted trade standards, failure to clearly state parts and labor on an invoice and false advertising.

The charges are the result of a year-long undercover investigation conducted by BAR, which conducted 38 initial undercover runs on the shops during which investigators were sold unnecessary service and parts 90 percent of the time.

After notifying Sears officials of the findings of the initial investigation, BAR's undercover operators did runs on an additional 10 shops in January of this year. During those runs, while the amount of items oversold declined, some overselling continued.

"This is a flagrant breach of the trust and confidence the people of California have placed in Sears for generations," Conran said. "Sears has used trust as a marketing tool, and we don't believe they've lived up to that trust."

"We are here today to send this message to the entire automotive repair industry: if you are ripping off the consumers of the State of California, we are after you," Conran continued. "We have zero tolerance for abuse of the public trust."

"The automobile is one of the things that unites us as Californians," he added. "Whether urban, suburban or rural, rich, poor or middle class we depend on our cars daily. The repair and maintenance of those cars is vital to our quality of life. The violation of the faith that was placed in Sears cannot be allowed to continue and for past violations of the law a penalty must be paid."

According to Jim Schoning, Chief of the Bureau of Automotive Repair, BAR launched its investigation in December 1990 after detecting a pattern in consumer complaints received against Sears. Between December 1990 and December 1991, BAR conducted 38 undercover runs at 27 Sears shops throughout California, and in January 1992 did the 10 follow-up runs at various locations.

In 34 of these undercover runs, Sears employees recommended and performed unnecessary service and/or repairs. In some cases, undercover operators were overcharged as much as $550 for needless repairs.

Schoning said that in some cases, Sears employees even resorted to scare tactics to sell repairs. "One of our undercover operators was told that the front calipers on his car were so badly frozen that the car would fishtail if the brakes were applied quickly," said Schoning. "The calipers on that vehicle were in fine working order."

Sears attracted customers through print advertising offering a $48 (or in some cases, $58) brake job. When BAR undercover operators brought vehicles requiring a simple brake job, they were often told that calipers, shock absorbers, coil springs, idler arms and/or master cylinders needed to be repaired or replaced.

Although the brake pads on some of the undercover vehicles were in need of replacement, the coil springs, shock absorbers, master cylinders, calipers and idler arms were in good working condition, usually with less than 20 miles of use.

For the Sears investigation, BAR used undercover vehicles in need of a minor brake repair. Prior to taking the vehicle to Sears for repair, BAR disassembled the brakes and suspension, and inspected, marked and photographed the parts to ensure accuracy. The automobiles were then moved by transporter to a location near the shop, where they were dropped off to be driven by an undercover operator to the targeted Sears shop.

Upon arrival at Sears, the undercover operator typically requested a brake inspection. In 34 of 38 runs conducted, undercover operators were told additional, and more expensive, repairs were needed. The undercover operator then authorized the repair, paid the amount due and the vehicle was transported back to BAR's undercover facility for examination.

Company Encouraged Repairs

According to Schoning, BAR's investigation revealed that Sears instructed employees to sell a certain number of repairs and/or services during every eight-hour work shift.

According to BAR investigators, employees were asked to sell a specified number of alignments, springs and brake jobs every eight hours.

In addition, employees were pressured to sell a specified number of shock absorbers or struts for every hour worked. According to BAR, current and former Sears employees said that if they did not meet these goals, they often received a cutback in their work hours or were transferred to another department within Sears.

In addition to selling customers unnecessary repairs and service, BAR officials said the undercover vehicles were often returned to the undercover operator in worse—and sometimes unsafe—condition, with loose brake parts or improperly installed coil springs.

Problems at Sears Not Unique

Schoning warned that consumers should be aware that problems of overselling continue to exist in the automotive repair industry: "The persons with the ultimate responsibility in the market place are consumers, who must learn to protect themselves, and the many honest men and women in the industry, whose reputations and livelihood are victims of this sort of conduct."

Conran also offered advice to consumers who may be victims of auto repair fraud. "You may not be able to trust some of these shops, but you can trust yourselves, if you're informed," he said.

"Offers that appear too good to be true are often just that," he said. "Consumers should be aware that they can—and should—seek a second opinion if they have doubts about the advice they are receiving."

Sears Log

Los Angeles Times story breaks resulting in a flood of media inquiries.

Sears issues press release denying allegations of fraud, but says we will continue to work with California authorities to resolve the matter.

Sears uses Dirk Schenkkan as spokesman for *Los Angeles Times, New York Times, Chicago Tribune, Wall Street Journal,* Associated Press and other major media. Sears refutes specific charges, challenges methodology and acknowledges that honest mistakes occurred. Says "Satisfaction Guaranteed" will resolve customer concerns.

Sears issues e-mail to staff updating them on situation, giving store and auto center managers talking points in working with media, encouraging managers to hold storewide staff meetings immediately, introducing the topic at Pure Selling Environment (PSE) meetings that weekend, encouraging staff to reassure inquiring customers.

As regards the Sears Log items cited above, here

are some amplifying details fleshing out the necessarily brief mentions in Buldak's log:

1.   The *Los Angeles Times* story on Thursday, June 11, started on page 1 and ran over on an inside page for a total of 50 column inches. It was written by Denise Gellene, who had called Buldak the evening before, and its lead stated that the state DCA will seek revocation of Sears' license to perform auto repairs. DCA director Jim Conran was quoted as charging Sears with "the systematic looting of the public." Gellene reported that she had reached Sears spokesman Gordon Jones at Sears headquarters in Chicago, and that he said the company would have no comment until after the charges were filed. Most of the rest of the long story cited details concerning findings of the undercover investigation.

2.   The press release mentioned in Buldak's log was six paragraphs long. Datelined Chicago, the release stated that "We strongly disagree with the allegations made by the Department of Consumer Affairs and the Bureau of Automotive Repair. We have always cooperated fully with these state agencies and look forward to continuing our dialogue with them. We believe that the Bureau's undercover investigation was very seriously flawed and simply does not support the allegations." The rest of the release stressed Sears' reputation for trust, integrity, and quality of products and professional services.

3.   Dirk Schenkkan, cited in the log as the spokesman used by Sears in relating to major national media on Thursday, June 11, was the company's external counsel in San Francisco. In responding to questions about why Sears used a

lawyer in this instance, Buldak pointed out that Schenkkan had lived with the case for more than six months and was the local person who best knew the answers. Buldak said that Sears had used lawyers in the past as spokesmen and would use them in the future. He also pointed out that Sears handled about 150 media calls out of Chicago on June 11.

Media Coverage (Friday, June 12, 1992)

The DCA's investigation and charges against Sears received extensive coverage in the nation's press as well as on radio and television newscasts on Friday. The stories in such major papers as the *Chicago Tribune, New York Times,* and *The Wall Street Journal* ran from 16 to 22 column inches. Their lead paragraphs centered on the DCA's investigation, charges, and decision to seek suspension or revocation of the licenses of Sears automotive centers to repair cars in California. The stories then cited either Conran for the DCA, the first-day Sears statement, or comments made by Schenkkan in San Francisco or by Perry Chlan, a spokesman at Sears' headquarters in Chicago. The bulk of the stories dealt with details of the investigation with examples of alleged violations of the Auto Repair Act.

The quote from Conran that most of the print media used was his charge that there was "a systematic looting (of) the public." Most of the stories cited Sears' statement that called the investigation incompetent and seriously flawed, and which vowed to contest the charges in court. Several of the major papers, in citing the response by Sears, carried comments by Schenkkan alleging political motivation behind the investigation. One major paper quoted him as declaring, "If you wanted to embark on a massive publicity campaign to demonstrate how aggressive you are and how much need there is for your services in your state, what better target than a big, respected business that would guarantee massive press coverage?"

The following Associated Press story, which was carried throughout the country in such disparate (in terms of circulation, size, and location) papers as the *Philadelphia Daily News* and the *Santa Cruz Sentinel*, could be considered typical of those that ran on Friday, June 12. The story, as it appeared in the *Sentinel,* is reprinted with permission of the paper.

Sears Auto Shops Accused of Bilking Customers

The Associated Press

LOS ANGELES—The state Thursday sought to revoke Sears' license to repair cars because undercover investigators were overcharged an average of $223 per visit during a probe that lasted more than a year, authorities said.

California officials alleged that the 106-year-old Sears, Roebuck & Co. used its reputation as a reliable American institution to fleece customers.

"There's a saying, 'You can count on Sears.' I'm here to tell you in auto repair you cannot," said Jim Conran, director of the California Department of Consumer Affairs. He charged that there was "a systematic looting (of) the public," and that customers outside California may have been affected.

Sears blasted the investigation as incompetent and seriously flawed. The company vowed to vigorously contest the charges in court.

"We've offered auto repairs for more than 60 years and we have a hard-earned and outstanding reputation for trust with our customers," said Perry Chlan, a spokesman at Sears' headquarters in Chicago.

California officials alleged that employees were forced to meet sales quotas through a restructuring of wage and commission structures.

"Employees were instructed to sell a certain number of repairs and services every eight-hour shift, such as alignments, springs and brake jobs," said Jim Schoning, chief of the Bureau of Automotive Repair.

"Current and former employees have told the bureau that if they didn't meet these goals they often received a cutback in their working hours, or they were transferred to another department," he said.

Authorities said the investigation began in December 1990 after a rapid near-doubling of consumer complaints.

The state moved to revoke or suspend the auto repair registration of all 72 Sears auto shops in California through an administrative law challenge.

Such action does not involve any fines or criminal penalties. If the registration is not entirely revoked or suspended, there can be intermediate measures such as forbidding certain types of repairs, such as brake jobs.

But Conran said that his department would also work with state or local prosecutors who might seek to investigate the auto repair operations.

The Bureau of Automotive Repair sent undercover investigators 48 times to 33 Sears repair shops statewide. Agents used cars with systems that had been carefully assembled, documented and sometimes left with a minor problem.

Sears Log

Media inquires continue . . . Sears issues news release reminding customers of "Satisfaction Guaranteed" hallmark and urging customers to visit local auto centers if they have questions about the service they have received. Sears reminds customers of 1-800 number to locate nearest auto center . . . Sears position continues; however, we are stressing more our cooperation with California officials . . . Sears continues to update staff through e-mail . . . National print ad prepared and approved . . . Sears learns that New Jersey will announce the results of its investigation Monday.

Some amplifying details about the Sears Log items follow. The one-page "Satisfaction Guaranteed" release was FOR IMMEDIATE RELEASE, June 12, 1992, and it ran as follows:

CHICAGO—Reaffirming its century-long "Satisfaction Guaranteed" promise to consumers, Sears, Roebuck and Co. today encouraged its automotive customers to call their local Sears Auto Center if they are concerned about the service they received because of recent allegations made in California.

"For 105 years Sears has promised Americans "Satisfaction Guaranteed" when it comes to quality products and services," said Forrest R. "Woody " Haselton, president, retail. "While we disagree with the allegations made about us in California, we will correct any mistakes that may have been made and will work in the coming months to resolve these issues. We immediately want to reassure our customers that this commitment to satisfaction continues unabated."

Sears reminded customers that they can call the company's automated customer service number—1-800-669-AUTO—which was introduced in March to obtain the location and telephone number of their local auto center.

"Our service technicians at those locations are prepared to answer any questions, resolve any differences and satisfy all customers," Haselton said.

The national print ad referred to in the June 12 log resulted from a decision by Sears to shift its response from a legal one to one dealing more directly with the concerns of customers.

Charles Ruder, Sears vice president for public affairs, was cited in a June 17 *New York Times* story as stating that the company wanted to stress that "the key is trust and integrity and that if mistakes were made we will rectify them. In a business where trust is important, we wanted to make sure we got that across."

Sears Chairman Edward A. Brennan cancelled an out-of-town meeting to work on the ad with the team planning its execution and placement in national media. The ad was scheduled to run on Sunday. It was in the form of an open letter from Brennan to Sears customers. (See Exhibit 13–1.)

Sears Log (Saturday and Sunday, June 13 and 14, 1992)

Media inquiries continue on Saturday and Sears hosts press conferences and open houses in its auto centers in four key markets—Los Angeles, San Francisco, San Diego and Chicago—to show how we work with customers in providing quality service . . . No media calls on Sunday when Mr. Brennan's full-page ad breaks nationally.

Sears Log (Monday and Tuesday, June 15 and 16, 1992)

Media calls continue . . . New Jersey announces results of investigations . . . Sears questions methodology of tests but says it will work with state officials to resolve issues.

. . . .

Media

The Associated Press transmitted a story Monday from Newark, citing New Jersey state officials as charging that Sears auto repair shops in the state recommended unnecessary repairs each time undercover investigators visited the chain during a four-month investigation. Consumer Affairs Director Emma Byrne was cited as stating that in 12 visits to six Sears shops mechanics gave written estimates for a new battery or alternator—or both—when the car needed only to have a wire reconnected. Byrne, the AP reported, said that Sears was not specifically targeted in the investigation, which also centered on independent repair shops.

"The finding," said the AP story, "mirrored complaints filed by the California Department of Consumer Affairs, which on Thursday moved to revoke the licenses of all Sears repair shops in California." After noting that California officials claimed that Sears employees were pressured to meet sales quotas, the AP said that investigators had no information about a quota system operating in New Jersey.

According to the AP, Sears spokesman Perry Chlan said the company could not respond to the charges until it received more details on the New Jersey probe. Chlan was quoted as saying: "The charges made are of extreme concern to us. We want to see what happened in each case."

A Reuters story, transmitted Tuesday, had this lead sentence: "Hit by new charges after an undercover investigation in New Jersey, Sears, Roebuck & Co. said Tuesday it is moving quickly to respond to allegations that its auto repair stores are recommending unnecessary work to customers."

Reuters followed this with several paragraphs about the probe. In two later paragraphs, Reuters amplified the lead as follows: "A Sears spokesman said the company asked for additional information from New Jersey officials to 'address the situation.'

"He added: 'The charges made are of extreme concern to us. We are beginning an internal review as to what happened in each case and will work closely with New Jersey officials to resolve the situation as quickly as possible.'"

Sears Log (Wednesday–Friday, June 17–19, 1992)

Media calls continue . . . Mr. Brennan writes all attorneys general . . . SVN shown in stores throughout weekend. [See Exhibit 13–2.]

Media

On Wednesday, June 17, the *New York Times* carried on the first page of its Business section an article by Richard W. Stevenson critiquing Sears' handling to date of the auto repair crisis. Crisis management experts cited in the article expressed the belief that the company erred in the initial stages of the crisis by trying to duck and in using lawyers as primary spokesmen.

Stevenson cited Charles Ruder, the public affairs chief at Sears, as saying that the company's response was proper under the circumstances, as was the decision to shift from the legal approach to one emphasizing trust and the concerns of customers. Ruder was also cited as stating that Sears found it appropriate to have Brennan involved in developing the full-page ad but did not think it wise for him to hold a press conference or appear on television to respond to the state's charges against the company because "we did not think it was necessary to take it to a higher level of escalation."

Sears Log (Saturday–Wednesday, June 20–24, 1992)

No media calls Saturday and Sunday . . . On Monday Mr. Brennan holds press conference to announce changes in compensation programs for automotive service advisors and to announce industry-wide initiatives. Mr. Brennan conducts telephone interview with *Los Angeles Times* . . . Mr. Brennan sends letter to New Jersey officials; new national advertising approved; industry meeting held (all on Tuesday) . . . Media calls continue.

The press conference mentioned in the log was held at noon in Chicago in the Sears Tower. In his remarks before answering questions from press representatives, CEO Brennan said Sears management had gone through some "very painful soul searching" and made a thorough review of the allegations. He said the company came to the conclusion that "our auto center incentive compensation programs and goal setting process for service advisors created an environment where mistakes did occur. . . We have talked to enough people over the last 12 days to believe that the policies for compensation and goal setting created by management for our service advisors in the auto centers were mistakes. And, when I refer to management, the buck stops with me." Brennan then detailed the steps and actions the company had decided to take. (The Sears press release appears in Exhibit 13–3.)

In a message sent to all store general managers, district managers, district automotive managers, and auto center managers, Gerald Buldak notified them about the scheduled press conference; said the release will be coming through by e-mail; summarized key points of the release; and urged them to cooperate with local media to get the story across using talking points he set forth. "Regarding California," he stated, "we continue to have major disagreements with the results of its investigation. We continue to believe that the preventive maintenance measures we recommend were appropriate and are consistent with industry standards. We will continue to work with California officials to resolve this matter."

Media coverage of the Sears press conference announcements can be summarized by the following leads:

> Associated Press: "Sears, Roebuck and Co., stricken by charges of car repair fraud, admitted on Monday that it erred and killed a commission program for auto repairs that 'created an environment where mistakes could occur.'"

> USA TODAY: "Sears Roebuck says it will quit paying commissions to auto-repair workers—removing an incentive to sell parts and services customers don't want."

> New York Times: "In the wake of charges that Sears, Roebuck & Company defrauded customers in California and New Jersey, the retailer said today that it would eliminate its commission-based pay structure for its employees who propose auto repairs."

The *NYT* story carried a reaction from Jim Conran, director of California's DCA, who was quoted as saying that the Sears announcement meant that "they apparently have recognized that the process they set up for merchandizing products did not reconcile with what they perceived to be their policy." Conran called the announcement "a step in the right direction, but it does not mean they have resolved their problem here in California."

Sears Log (Thursday–Thursday, June 25–July 9, 1992)

Thursday: Media calls continue . . . National print, broadcast and radio ads break, appear through Saturday . . . Mr. Brennan conducts interview with *San Diego Union-Tribune* . . . Former San Bruno, Calif., auto employee sues Sears for wrongful discharge, saying he refused to pro-vide customers with service they didn't need . . . Friday: Media calls continue . . . Class action suit filed in Chicago . . . Saturday/Sunday: No media calls . . . Monday: Few media calls . . . New class action suit filed . . . Tuesday: Few media calls . . . Wednesday: Associated Press runs story on auto union shops, resulting in new stories in cities affected . . . Thursday: stores pull Brennan ad sign in most shops. Hartigan role announced.

The print ad cited in Buldak's June 25 log and shown in Exhibit 13–4 was another full-page ad in the form of an open letter to Sears customers signed by CEO Ed Brennan. It ran in major newspapers throughout the country. Broadcast media carried a 60-second television spot and a two-minute radio spot. Both broadcast spots featured Brennan talking directly to the audience about the actions taken by the company.

Discussions between Sears and state representatives in New Jersey and California in late spring and in the summer culminated with resolution of the automotive repair dispute in the two states.

The announcement in New Jersey was made on Tuesday, July 21, 1992, by New Jersey Attorney General Robert Del Tufo and Consumer Affairs Division Director Emma Byrne. The lead of the Associated Press story on the settlement stated that Sears "agreed today to pay $200,000 to settle accusations arising from a consumer fraud inquiry into its auto-repair centers in New Jersey." The story said that Sears will cease paying commissions to car repair employees and will eliminate goals for selling specific products.

According to the AP, the company agreed to settle immediately any complaints by consumers already filed with the Consumer Affairs Division and will also pay $3,000 to the state for not posting consumer rights notices in the auto centers visited. The state, said the AP, "settled with the company before formal charges were filed." Exhibit 13–5 shows the release Sears distributed from its Chicago headquarters on July 21.

On September 2, 1992, the State of California and Sears agreed on terms resolving the dispute concerning Sears's automotive repair centers. The state and Sears put out their own press releases on the settlement; they appear in Exhibits 13–6 and 13–7 as the end to this long public relations case study.

To illustrate how different media handled the settlement, here are the leads to the story which ran in the *New York Times* and the story sent out by the Associated Press. The *NYT* lead: "Sears, Roebuck & Company has agreed to pay $8 million to settle civil charges that its auto repair shops systematically overcharged customers for routine repairs in California." The AP lead: "Sears, Roebuck and Co. said yesterday it has agreed to settle charges across the nation that it cheated customers by doing shoddy or unnecessary work at its auto repair shops."

Exhibit 13-1

An Open Letter to Sears Customers:

On June 10th, the California Bureau of Automotive Repair made charges concerning the practices of Sears Auto Centers in California.

With over 2 million automotive customers serviced last year in California alone, mistakes may have occurred. However, Sears wants you to know that we would never intentionally violate the trust customers have shown in our company for 105 years.

You rely on us to recommend preventive maintenance measures to help insure your safety, and to avoid more costly future repairs. This includes recommending replacement of worn parts, when appropriate, before they fail. This accepted industry practice is being challenged by the Bureau.

Our repair policy is to:

1. Consult with you before the repair.
2. Prepare a written estimate.
3. Perform only repairs you authorize.
4. Guarantee all work performed.

Sears has been providing Customer Satisfaction in auto repairs for over 60 years. In addition to our own extensive training program, our technicians have over 14,000 Automotive Service Excellence (ASE) certifications.

Sears hallmark has always been Satisfaction Guaranteed or Your Money Back. If you have any doubt or question about service performed on your car, we urge you to call or stop by your local Sears Auto Center.

I pledge we will do our utmost to resolve any concern you may have.

Ed Brennan

Ed Brennan
Chairman and Chief Executive Officer
Sears, Roebuck and Co.

Exhibit 13-2
**Letter to State
Attorneys General**

SEARS, ROEBUCK AND CO.
SEARS TOWER
CHICAGO, ILLINOIS 60684
JUNE 19, 1992

EDWARD A. BRENNAN
Chairman of the Board

Dear (Attorney General name):

As I am sure you are aware, California and New Jersey officials have recently raised questions about our company's auto repair practices. Although we believe that these allegations are unfair and not supported by the facts, we are extremely concerned about them and about their impact on Sears reputation for integrity and trust with consumers in (State).

Sears has always shared with your office a profound interest in protecting the consumer. In a very real way, our respective missions are much the same: assuring that consumers are dealt with fairly and with integrity. Without consumer good will and trust, companies like Sears simply cannot exist and flourish over time.

I am sending you materials relating to Sears auto repair policies, procedures and Sears Code of Ethical Conduct which each of our employees is expected to live by.

I urge you to review Sears auto repair standards and practices. While I believe you will find that they are among the highest in the industry, if there appear to be any material differences between our standards and practices, and those of (State), we would like to discuss them with you. We want to work with you or the person you may designate to assure that consumers in (State) receive only the best and most honest auto repair service. I have asked Mr. Al Dombrowski, Vice President—Automotive, to head this effort for Sears. You will be receiving our materials in the next few days. If you have any questions, please call Mr. Dombrowski at 312-875-9108.

You have my personal assurance that our company and its employees are committed to the highest ethical and business standards.

Exhibit 13-3
Sears Press Release, June 22

News from
SEARS, ROEBUCK AND CO.

<u>CONTACT</u>
Gerald E. Buldak
(312) 875-8371

<u>FOR IMMEDIATE RELEASE</u>
June 22, 1992

SEARS ANNOUNCES AUTOMOTIVE CHANGES, INDUSTRY INITIATIVES

CHICAGO—Sears, Roebuck and Co. today announced that it is eliminating its incentive compensation program for automotive service advisors and taking a series of related actions in response to recent questions about its auto repair practices in California and New Jersey.

"We are taking these actions to preserve the most precious asset we have, namely the more than century-old bond of trust between Sears and the American consumer," said Edward A. Brennan, Sears chairman and chief executive officer.

Brennan outlined the following actions:

• Sears will immediately eliminate its incentive compensation program for automotive service advisors and replace it with a new non-commission program designed to achieve and recognize higher customer satisfaction levels. The role of the service advisor is to inspect vehicles, identify problems and explain and recommend appropriate measures to the customer, who then determines whether repairs will be made.

• Sears will immediately discontinue product-specific sales goals for automotive service advisors to remove any programs which could affect public perception and undermine customer confidence.

• Sears has asked every state to compare the company's auto repair standards and practices with those of the state to determine whether differences exist. In a letter to every state attorney general last Friday, Brennan said Sears would send its automotive repair policies and procedures and code of ethical conduct to every state.

- Sears will aggressively pursue and help fund and organize an industry-consumer-government effort to review current auto repair practices and recommend uniform industry standards.

- Sears will retain an independent organization to conduct ongoing unannounced "shopping audits" of its automotive services to ensure company policies and standards are met. This will be in addition to existing internal monitoring of services, which will be reviewed and expanded.

"Sears Auto Centers provide the American consumer with quality, cost-efficient and honest services and we continue to deny strongly allegations of fraud and systemic problems," Brennan said. "We believe the governmental investigations in California and New Jersey were flawed and their results misleading.

"Much of the current debate centers around what is appropriate preventive maintenance for vehicles," Brennan said. "Sears traditionally has taken a prudent, diagnostic approach in recommending preventive maintenance to its customers, not only to ensure their safety, but the safety and longevity of their vehicles. We will continue this approach. Our research indicates our customers expect it from us. If our service advisors see something wrong in a vehicle—or something that could go wrong—we bring it to the attention of our customers to decide whether the service should be performed. However, this approach has been viewed erroneously by some as recommending unnecessary repairs as a means to increase sales.

"We have the utmost confidence in our 34,000 automotive associates nationwide who provided superior service on more than 20 million vehicles last year. In the automotive repair business, mistakes can and will occur. At the same time, our compensation and goal-setting programs for automotive service advisors created an environment where, in some instances, mistakes have been made. They may have been the result of rigid attention to goals, or they could have been the result of aggressive selling. However, we strongly believe that these instances were isolated and there has been no pattern of this conduct," Brennan said.

Sears continued to urge customers who have concerns about auto service to visit their local Sears auto center. To locate the nearest center, customers may call 1-800-669-AUTO toll-free.

"Charges made against Sears in recent days have seriously challenged our integrity and the trust the American consumer has placed in us for the past 105 years," said Brennan. "We believe the forceful actions and changes we are announcing today as an honest and responsible industry leader will help preserve that trust."

Exhibit 13–4

An Open Letter to Sears Customers:

You may have heard recent allegations that some Sears Auto Centers in California and New Jersey have sold customers parts and services they didn't need. We take such charges very seriously, because they strike at the core of our company— our reputation for trust and integrity.

We are confident that our Auto Center customer satisfaction rate is among the highest in the industry. But after an extensive review, we have concluded that our incentive compensation and goal-setting program inadvertently created an environment in which mistakes have occurred. We are moving quickly and aggressively to eliminate that environment.

To guard against such things happening in the future, we're taking significant action:

- We have eliminated incentive compensation and goal-setting systems for automotive service advisors—the folks who diagnose problems and recommend repairs to you. We have replaced these practices with a new non-commission program designed to achieve even higher levels of customer satisfaction. Rewards will now be based on customer satisfaction.
- We're augmenting our own quality control efforts by retaining an independent organization to conduct ongoing, unannounced "shopping audits" of our automotive services to ensure that company policies are being met.
- We have written to all state attorneys general, inviting them to compare our auto repair standards and practices with those of their states in order to determine whether differences exist.
- And we are helping to organize and fund a joint industry-consumer-government effort to review current auto repair practices and recommend uniform industry standards.

We're taking these actions so you'll continue to come to Sears with complete confidence. However, one thing we will never change is our commitment to customer safety. Our policy of preventive maintenance—recommending replacement of worn parts *before* they fail—has been criticized by the California Bureau of Automotive Repair as constituting unneeded repairs. We don't see it that way. We recommend preventive maintenance because that's what our customers want, and because it makes for safer cars on the road. In fact, 75 percent of the consumers we talked to in a nationwide survey last weekend told us that auto repair centers should recommend replacement parts for preventive maintenance. As always, no work will *ever* be performed without your approval.

We understand that when your car needs service, you look for, above all, someone you can trust. And when trust is at stake, we can't merely *react*, we must *overreact*.

We at Sears are totally committed to maintaining your confidence. You have my word on it.

Ed Brennan
Chairman and Chief Executive Officer
Sears, Roebuck and Co.

Exhibit 13–5
Sears Press Release, July 21

News from
SEARS, ROEBUCK AND CO.

CONTACT
Gerald E. Buldak
(312) 875-8371

FOR IMMEDIATE RELEASE
July 21, 1992

CHICAGO—Sears, Roebuck and Co. said today its agreement with the New Jersey Department of Consumer Affairs further expands its commitment to seek uniform auto repair standards and is in the best interests of not only New Jersey motorists, but all U.S. drivers.

New Jersey Attorney General Robert Del Tufo and Consumer Affairs Division Director Emma Byrne announced Tuesday resolution of the state's inquiry of six Sears auto centers and settlement of any claims it might have had as a result of the investigation in January through April of this year.

Sears Chairman and Chief Executive Officer Edward A. Brennan said, "Through several weeks of discussions with New Jersey officials, our prime concern was the safety and welfare of our customers and their vehicles and our agreement today addresses these objectives."

Brennan said the agreement also recognizes the initiatives Sears announced June 22 to preserve customer confidence and trust. Those programs, which have been or are being implemented, include: elimination of commissions for Sears auto service advisors; elimination of product-specific sales goals and incentives; and introduction of independent "shopping audits" of Sears auto centers.

The agreement also expands Sears support of activities to seek uniform auto repair standards by underwriting the initial cost of $200,000 to the National Association of Attorneys General for an Automotive Repair Industry Reform Fund. On June 22 Sears announced it would aggressively pursue and help fund an industry-government-consumer effort with similar goals.

Sears will also pay a $3,000 penalty for not posting appropriate consumer rights signs in the six auto centers the state visited.

Exhibit 13–6
California Press
Release

GOVERNOR PETE WILSON

FOR IMMEDIATE RELEASE

.CONTACT: KEVIN ECKERY
916/653-4090

GOVERNOR ANNOUNCES $8 MILLION SETTLEMENT WITH SEARS AUTO CENTERS; RECORD AMOUNT INCLUDES COMPENSATION TO INDIVIDUAL CONSUMERS

SACRAMENTO—Governor Pete Wilson announced today an $8 million out-of-court settlement with Sears, Roebuck & Co., concerning charges that Sears sold unnecessary auto repairs and service to its California customers. The settlement, which also provides restitution to individual consumers, is the largest in the history of the Department of Consumer Affairs (DCA).

"This settlement is tough, but fair. It sends a clear message that business practices that harm consumers will not be tolerated by this Administration," said Acting Secretary of State & Consumer Services Andrew Poat on behalf of Governor Wilson.

The announcement was made at a noon press conference with Attorney General Dan Lungren, Contra Costa County District Attorney Gary Yancey and Director of Consumer Affairs Jim Conran.

Under the agreement, Sears will establish a $4.5 million restitution fund. $3 million of the restitution fund, in the form of $50 coupons, will be used to reimburse consumers for questionable repairs and $1.5 million will be used to provide tools and equipment at vocational training programs for auto technicians within the state's Community College system.

Additionally, for those customers who can demonstrate that receipt of the $50 coupon does not adequately address their loss, Sears will honor its policy of "satisfaction guaranteed."

The remaining $3.5 million will be used to reimburse the Department of Consumer Affairs' Bureau of Automotive Repair, the state Department of Justice and the Contra Costa County District Attorney for costs associated with the Sears investigation, and monitoring the auto repair industry.

While all 72 Sears Auto Repair Centers in California will remain open for business, the agreement temporarily invalidates their registrations for 30 days. This provision will not take effect, however, if Sears complies with this settlement for a period of three years.

After DCA announced the filing of accusations in June, Sears Chairman Edward Brennan announced that Sears was voluntarily halting a commission-based compensation plan they believe may have led to some abuses in their auto centers.

"I believe this is an agreement that takes into consideration the best interests of the consumers of this state while sending a very strong message that we take our consumer protection role seriously," said Jim Conran, Director of the Department of Consumer Affairs. "I am gratified that Sears voluntarily changed its compensation policies, and that it has taken important steps to restore the century old trust it has traditionally had with its customers."

The agreement concludes three months of intense discussions between the Department of Consumer Affairs and Sears to resolve charges that the firm had engaged in numerous violations of the California Auto Repair Act.

In accusations filed in June, Sears was charged with making false or misleading statements to undercover investigators, willful departure from accepted trade standards, failure to clearly state parts and labor charges on invoices, and false advertising.

The Bureau of Automotive Repair (BAR), part of DCA, began its investigation in December 1990 after receiving a number of consumer complaints involving Sears. Working on its own and with the Contra Costa County District Attorney's office, BAR conducted 48 undercover runs against 33 Sears shops over a 12 month period. In the formal accusations directed against Sears, BAR investigators charged that they were sold unnecessary repairs 90 percent of the time.

In addition to the financial terms of the settlement, Sears is prohibited from recommending repair or replacement of a given item unless it is established by manufacturer's specifications, accepted trade standards, or another reasonable basis exists for the recommendation.

"We sincerely hope that this agreement will begin to heal the wounds that the consumers of this State and Sears, a major employer and contributor to California's economy, have suffered over the last 18 months," Poat said.

The Settlement

Sears establishes $4.5 million Restitution Fund:
- $3 million to Sears automotive customers;
- promises additional funds as necessary to fulfill "satisfaction guaranteed" pledge;

- $1.5 million for the purchase of automotive repair tools for California Community Colleges auto repair facilities.

Sears pays $3.5 million in costs:

- funds paid to Contra Costa County District Attorney's office, Department of Consumer Affairs' Bureau of Automotive Repair and the state Attorney General's Office for investigative and settlement costs;
- aids in monitoring the auto repair industry.

Registrations at 72 Sears Auto Centers invalidated for 30 days.

- Stores will remain open for business.
- Invalidations stayed for three years pending completion of all terms and conditions of settlement.

Exhibit 13–7
Sears Press Release, September 2

News from
SEARS, ROEBUCK AND CO.

CONTACT
GERALD E. BULDAK
(312) 875-8371

FOR IMMEDIATE RELEASE
September 2, 1992

SEARS SETTLES AUTOMOTIVE ISSUES

CHICAGO—Sears, Roebuck and Co. today announced resolution of issues concerning Sears Auto Centers with the State of California, resolution of all 19 automotive class action suits, and launched new operating, educational and customer initiatives to benefit California and U.S. motorists.

In the settlements, Sears denied any liability or intentional wrongdoing, but said it reached the agreements to avoid the burden, expense and uncertainty of prolonged litigation.

Sears also announced that attorneys general of 41 states, led by New Jersey Atty. Gen. Robert Del Tufo, agreed to join with Sears in an effort to develop a comprehensive program to standardize auto repair practices. Del Tufo, said, "Those of us who have reviewed this new package of Sears initiatives feel it is an important opportunity to foster national change in the auto repair industry and that it extends equitable financial settlement terms and other consumer protection to consumers in each of our states."

A group of former attorneys general, led by Neil F. Hartigan of Illinois, has been working with various states on auto repair issues on behalf of Sears. The Hartigan group includes W. J. Michael Cody of Tennessee; Anthony J. Celebrezze, Jr. of Ohio; Brian McKay of Nevada; Tom Miller of Iowa; and LeRoy S. Zimmerman of Pennsylvania.

Sears also announced that it would offer a national merchandise coupon redemption program for certain auto customers to supplement its long-standing "Satisfaction Guaranteed" policy, to serve as a good faith effort with customers in all states, and to resolve national class action suits and State of California issues.

Additionally, Sears said that it would not charge customers for cost of repairs beyond the estimate it gives customers.

California Gov. Pete Wilson and Sears Senior Vice President and Chief Administrative Officer Charles F. Moran outlined the terms of the settlement with the state:

- Sears will reimburse California $3.5 million to cover investigative costs, attorneys' fees, general automotive repair monitoring costs and related items.

- Sears will establish a fund, of at least $1.5 million, to finance auto repair training programs at California community colleges.

- Sears will offer all California auto customers—and extend to all U.S. auto customers—who purchased and had Sears install selected products during the period from Aug. 1, 1990 to Jan. 31, 1992, a $50 coupon for each such item or pair of items. These products include a master brake cylinder or idler arm, or a pair of shock absorbers, brake calipers or coil springs. The coupons can be used for the purchase of any merchandise or service in any U.S. Sears retail store, during the year staring Nov. 1, 1992. Sears will advertise details of the coupon program beginning Nov. 1, 1992, and has established a customer phone number (1-800-659-7057) to answer additional questions. If coupon redemptions total less than $3 million in California, Sears will contribute the difference to the college automotive training fund. Sears said about 933,000 transactions nationwide are affected by the coupon redemption agreements. The company said the financial impact of the agreements will not be material and estimated the net after-tax effect on Sears will be less than $15 million.

- In addition to the coupon program, Sears will continue to honor its long-standing policy of "Satisfaction Guaranteed or Your Money Back" for all its customers.

- All 72 Sears auto centers in California will remain open for business and continue to provide the same products and services.

- Sears will continue to provide a preventive maintenance auto repair program to its customers, but will be more specific when informing customers why Sears is recommending such repairs. For example, Sears will specify whether the manufacturer, auto industry standards, or Sears, based on its 60 years of experience in auto repair, is making the recommendation.

Sears also said that as a result of its work with the states' attorneys general it will expand the automotive responsibilities of Richard Quinn, Sears vice president for customer-focused quality. New areas include strengthening annual customer surveys and tracking mechanisms, developing consumer education materials, coordinating independent audits, and forming a technical advisory panel to assure quality of products and services.

Moran said, "We are pleased to reach a final resolution which we believe is in the best interests of our customers, associates and shareholders. Today's announcement and the previous actions we've taken show that Sears wanted 'to go the extra mile' to assure our customers that they can be more confident than ever in visiting our auto centers. While we regret any mistakes and inconveniences to customers that occurred, they were not intentional. We are confident that the overwhelming majority of the more than 27 million vehicles we serviced in 1991 and 1992 were done properly and safely, but more important, we believe these settlements should help restore the trust our customers have placed in us over the last 105 years."

Reprint for Discussion

The Matter of Survival

Ronald Rhody

I'm not quite sure how I got myself in this position, and even less sure how I'm going to get myself out of it. Who, in their right mind, would undertake to advise an audience like this on survival—personal survival I've come to understand—in situations of mergers, acquisitions, downsizings, or takeovers? Unfortunately, I don't have any answers.

I do have some suggestions that may help improve the odds a little, though, and that's where I want to focus my remarks . . . on improving the odds.

Be damn good at what you do. That's Odds Improvement Suggestion #1.

Just being good, though, isn't enough. The key players are not only good, they are perceived as being good. They are seen as the experts, the people whose knowledge of the subject matter is complete, whose judgment is sound, and whose ability to execute is total. In short, the key players are the ones who know what to do, know how to do it, and who deliver the results.

It seems to me that what corporate management needs, craves, and values most these days is performance excellence and hands-on management. What the CEO wants and needs most is people who know what to do, know how to do it, and who can do it expertly themselves—people who can handle the tough media situation personally; can spin the memorable phrase for policy speech, or annual report, or employees message, if necessary, themselves; who can set the communications strategy and manage the

*Talk by Ronald E. Rhody, senior vice president, Bank of America, at the Public Relations Management Seminar, Palm Springs, California, June 26, 1990. Bank of America Corporation. Reprinted with permission.

execution of the various actions adroitly by virtue of their own personal experience and capabilities.

Which raises another basic question having to do with both survival and success. And that is, how you see your role in the organization's mission. How you see yourself determines how you act and what you do. Which in turn determines how you are perceived and valued.

The choice, it seems to me, is either to be a "professional manager," or a "managing professional." That is, to be an employee . . . or a professional.

[Thus] Odds Improvement Suggestion #2. Be a professional.

Employees have a certain emotional attachment to the institution, an attitude of belonging that gives warmth and succor and is motivating and satisfying. Employees are a "part of" something. A portion of their identity and ego is wrapped up in that something. They see themselves as, say, "an Alcoan," rather than as a professional employed by Alcoa. They look to a career track as a "manager" that will move them through a variety of jobs to (ultimately and hopefully) either job security or senior management, or both.

Professionals have a different perspective. They owe, and pledge, loyalty to the employer, and carry passion for the employer's causes (if they are right and just, of course). But in the final analysis, professionals see themselves as hired to bring expert professional skills and talents to bear on the problems and opportunities at hand. For the most part they do not aspire to be general managers, or sales executives, or heads of line operations. Their minds just don't work that way. They do, however, see themselves as crucially important players and full members of the management team.

The case can be made that professionals functioning as professionals in this context are more valuable to corporate management than professionals functioning as employees.

Keeping the CEO warm and secure is Odds Improvement Suggestion #3. I'm using the phrase "CEO" as a metaphor for senior profit-center management in general, but only in part. If anyone is to be kept happy, it's the CEO.

. . . .

A Complex Matter

Keeping the CEO happy is a complex thing—not a function of performance or ability alone. Performance and ability are givens. Without them, no one survives. But they are not enough. There must also be the very highest level of trust and respect between the CEO and the CPRO [Chief Public Relations Officer]. Trust is earned, not granted. Respect is won, not conferred. And both grow from the working understanding the two hold.

Let me give you an idea of the sort of working understanding many of the key players have with their CEOs.

First, they are professionally assertive. Politely and calmly, they assert that they are the experts in matters of public relations and communications and they exercise their authority as such. They allow the lawyers and the financial people and the profit-center managers expertise in the things that lawyers and financial people and profit-center managers do, but not in matters of public relations. They believe the job they do is too important to be left to amateurs, that it is a job for professionals; and they assert their professionalism.

In doing this, they take responsibility. They take responsibility for understanding the CEO's goals and actions and for fashioning the communications strategies and tools to help him reach those goals. They take responsibility for the success or failure of their ideas and initiatives. They take the responsibility for seeing the institution clearly, unimpaired by tunnel vision or internal politics, and for transmitting what they see and think candidly to the CEO, without regard for whether the CEO will like what they have to say or not. And they take responsibility to pay as much attention to costs and efficiencies in their operations as the profit-center managers do in theirs.

In the CPRO's areas of competence, they do not wait to be asked. They take the initiative. They assume personal charge of the really crucial situations and they make the decisions that are theirs to make. Their confidentiality can be relied on completely. The boss can expect their unvarnished candor, their full commitment, and their earned loyalty. He can be secure in the knowledge that they have no axes to grind or agendas to advance, except when, and as, the best interests of the CEO and corporation are at issue.

Which brings me to Odds Improvement Suggestion #4: Know what game you're playing.

No one is paying us to practice public relations. We're being paid to help our clients reach their operating and profit goals. Applying the tools of public relations and communications happens to be how we do it.

The distinction is important . . .

Cornell Maier, former CEO of Kaiser Aluminum, one of the finest executives I've known and a prior boss, had a very simple rule:

"Anything that doesn't contribute to making or selling the product is a luxury. I like luxury as well as the next guy, but I can't afford it." . . .

Which brings me to Odds Improvement Suggestion #5: (Don't be a luxury.)

The profit-center manager's attention is focused on the bottom line. Key players make sure their attention is focused there, too.

Back to Maier's rule. We work for fairly complicated institutions competing in a highly contentious world. However large or small they may be, none are, or can be, "simple" anymore. There are too many pressures from communities, and shareholders, and competitors; too many demands from employees, government, and customers to allow management to focus simply on making and selling the product. If the pressures and demands of all these groups aren't met, our companies won't be permitted to make and sell their product. So those actions which contribute to "making and selling" the product now extend to a wide range of other necessities.

Therefore, you make a direct contribution to the bottom line if your efforts motivate employees and educate and inform shareholders, helping create a proper and appropriate understanding of your performance and value(If your activities draw attention to your products and create interest in them through publicity (the kind of interest and attention that advertising can't generate, but which wonderfully extends advertising's impact), or help keep the community on your side, you make a necessary contribution to the bottom line. If your work can help avoid restrictive legislation or build public support for your actions, defending where necessary, persuading where needed, you count. If your efforts help move people to do something, not do something, or let you do something (that something being to take the action steps which advance your organization's goals), you make a direct contribution to the bottom line.)

These things, my friends, are not luxuries. They are necessities.

If the profit-center managers, the people who control the budgets, don't understand this, it's our fault—not theirs.

Said another way, survival and success requires that we be as effective selling our function to the people who pay the bills as we are in selling our clients to their constituents.

Very few executives have any real grasp or understanding of the scope of what we do, unless they've been in a real crisis situation or under heavy fire from shareholders or their communities. More to the point, very few have any real appreciation of how important what we do is to their success. That's not only a pity—it is a major hazard to survival. If we don't tell them and show them what we do and how they benefit from it . . . regularly, repetitively, persuasively, and compellingly, they ain't gonna know. No one will tell our story for us unless we tell it ourselves.

Success and survival, then, is first of all a matter of performance. After that, it is a matter of effectively marketing that performance back to the client.

Which is a fair enough bridge into the final point I want to make. This involves what is a much more likely case for most than merger, acquisition, or takeover. In fact, it is the likeliest case: budget pressure and downsizing.

Avoid Being Dead Meat

· ·

Long before the bad news man comes around with word of a 10% across-the-board cut or other sobering suggestions, you will either have justified a need for what you do within your organization and established its value, or not. If the first time you try to make your case is when the call for cutbacks and downsizing comes . . . you're dead meat.

To avoid that, the function must be viewed through a profit-center manager's eyes and managed to profit-center manager standards. Look at it this way: If you were the profit-center manager, and paying the freight for this or that public relations activity, would you buy it? Would you see the value that would justify your costs?

If the case can't be made convincingly in your own mind, then it can't be made to the profit-center manager—and it probably falls in the "luxury" category.

Luxuries, remember, are those things we have concluded none of us can afford.

What then can the institution afford? In coming up with that answer, the CPRO winds up in a unique situation—at the same time enviable and chancy to the extreme.

Let me explain.

For the Chief Counsel, the Human Resources head, the Management Systems and Accounting people—their costs are dictated almost entirely by the demands of their clients: for legal help, for recruiting and training, for better reports, sharper information systems, etc.

Very few people inside corporations "demand" public relations in quite the same way—except, as I say, in real crisis situations.

Compared to almost all other corporate expenses, of course, the public relations budgets are, as the attorneys would say, "de minimis." But that isn't the point. The point is that most of what we do is the result of our own initiative . . . of our own assessment of what needs to be done. The "demands" which drive our budgets are, by and large, the result of our own conclusion about the action steps necessary to advance our client's goals and our success in convincing the client to fund the effort. Which, as I said, is both enviable and chancy to the extreme.

There's nothing wrong with this. In fact, there is almost everything right about it. The most cost-effective and successful public relations and communications programs are always those in which the opportunity is seen and the initiative seized. They are also almost always the consequence of professionals doing what they are paid to do . . . taking the initiative on opportunities and problems rather than waiting around to inquire what management wants done (when most frequently management doesn't know and is relying on the professionals to propose).

So, within reason, our budget levels are driven by what we believe needs to be done to advance both the corporation's interests and the specific goals of the profit-center managers, and what we can persuade the CEO and the profit-center managers to support on this basis.

This fact about the way we operate gives us a considerable responsibility. Consequently, we had better understand what really affects the bottom line (in both a short- and long-term sense) and concentrate our efforts there. And we had better demonstrate hard-nosed business sense in the process. . . .

Nothing is so "survival ensuring" as running the sort of operation the profit-center managers see as bottom-line oriented and which helps them make their goals.

Let me close with this observation. Success and survival in the Nineties will depend almost as much on what the people who pay the bills "know" and understand as on what we know. In the successful operations, the CEO and the profit-center managers will know that the public relations and communications function is a hard-edged management tool which produces valuable results that cannot be obtained in any other way. They will understand the objective is to affect behavior . . . to get their constituents to buy in to what they are trying to achieve . . . to hold opinions and take actions which advance their goals. They will know and understand these things because the professionals with whom they work make sure they do.

And they will buy in.

If one can create buy-in, can success be far behind?

Well, what have I said? . . .

Among the suggestions were these:

Be very good at what you do.

Be a managing professional, not a professional manager, and most importantly, be the expert.

Understand the game you're playing. It's not PR. It's results.

Don't, at the risk of immediate extinction, be a luxury.

Don't expect to be loved and understood automatically. If you want clients to know what you're doing and how they benefit from it, you've got to produce results and market them.

Face up to the hard decisions, make them realistically, and get on with getting the job done.

TARGET MARKETING IN PHILADELPHIA (A)

In December 1989, the R. J. Reynolds Tobacco Company announced that on February 5, 1990, it would commence a six-month test market of Uptown, a new menthol cigarette whose advertising would be targeted primarily at black smokers. Estimates then were that more than two-thirds of all black smokers nationally preferred a menthol cigarette.

At the time, the top menthol cigarette brands were Lorillard's Newport, Reynolds' Salem, and Brown and Williamson's Kool. Newport had the least menthol of the three brands and Salem the most. With research showing that blacks preferred a lighter menthol, Reynolds decided to introduce Uptown, with a less pronounced menthol taste, and to package it in black and gold rather than in green, the traditional color for menthol cigarettes. Market research also showed that many blacks opened cigarette packs from the bottom, and so Uptown cigarettes were packed with the filters facing down, reverse of the usual arrangement.

To test the cigarette, Reynolds selected Philadelphia, whose population was about 40 percent black. Estimated cost was in the range of $2–10 million. Most of the print advertising was scheduled to appear in two Philadelphia black newspapers and in such national black magazines as *Ebony* and *Jet*.

The Anti-Test Coalition

On Thursday, January 11, 30 representatives of black, Hispanic, health, civic, and religious organizations met in Philadelphia to express their opposition to the planned test of Uptown. Included among the 30 local groups were representatives of the Black United Methodist Preachers, the Conference of Black Clergy of Philadelphia and Vicinity, the American Cancer Society, the American Lung Association, and the city health department. Their discussions culminated in an announcement the next day (Friday, January 12) that they would fight the efforts of R. J. Reynolds to test-market the new menthol cigarette in Philadelphia.

In its edition of Saturday, January 13, the *Philadelphia Inquirer* ran a long story about the planned test and the protest movement under the headline: "GROUPS TO FIGHT CIGARETTE; WANT TO BLOCK TEST-MARKETING."

Following the lead, which reported the announced protest, the story quoted Pastor Jesse Brown of the Christ Evangelical Lutheran Church and president of the Committee to Prevent Cancer Among Blacks, as declaring: "They're taking their own brand of death and trying to market it to the black community. . . . We will galvanize the black community and educate folks that they should not accept this cigarette."

Robert Robinson, president of the National Black Leadership Initiative on Cancer in Philadelphia and associate member of the American Oncologic Hospital, Fox Chase, was quoted as declaring: "I'm very opposed to the idea of a cigarette being developed and targeted to the African-American community.

"The African-American community is already suffering the highest rate of cancer in the country. They develop more cancer and die from cancer more than anyone else, especially from smoking-related cancers—cancer of the lung, cancer of the esophagus."

Pointing out that Robinson holds a doctorate in public health, the story quoted him further as stating that "This is about life and the quality of life. Cigarettes cause disease and death. It is irresponsible and immoral for R. J. Reynolds to target this community."

The *Inquirer* story cited Maura Payne, a Reynolds spokeswoman, as responding as follows to the criticisms of the company's plans to test-market Uptown in Philadelphia:

"We are marketing a legal product and have a right to compete on legal footing with other manufacturers of cigarettes. There seems to be a bit of bigotry here. . . . People are arguing that black customers don't have a right to buy a product for which they have expressed a desire. We believe black smokers have a right to choose between Newport, Salem, Kool, and Uptown."

Payne was further cited as stating that it is not uncommon for a company to target a segment of the population. "We're just trying to take smokers away from our competition. It's purely business."

The *Inquirer* story followed up on Payne's freedom of choice comment by referring to a column about a tobacco company advertising in black publications that ran in the *Michigan Chronicle,* a Detroit newspaper. In that column, according to the *Inquirer* story, Benjamin L. Hooks, executive director of the National Association for the Advancement of Colored People (NAACP), was quoted as stating, "Blacks (don't) need some guardian angel to protect their best interests. Blacks, like the rest of the population, can make the choice of whether to smoke or not."

New York Times Article

In a long article reporting the Uptown controversy and running on the first page of its Business section, the *New York Times* dealt mainly with the marketing and business aspects of the situation. Written by Anthony Ramirez and with a Winston-Salem, N.C., dateline, the article in the Friday, January 12, issue first summarized the basics of the conflict between the cigarette company and its critics. It quoted Patti LePera, vice president of marketing and communications for the Philadelphia branch of the American Cancer Society, as declaring: "We want to halt it [the test] before February 5. We want R. J. Reynolds to know we don't want it here."

Mary L. Clarke, president of the Charlotte-Mecklenburg, N.C., branch of the NAACP, was quoted as declaring: "With the poor health among black folks today, we do not need anything else to cause even more health problems. R. J. Reynolds' targeting of blacks is unethical."

Ramirez noted in his article that "black publications find themselves in the middle." He quoted the president of the *Philadelphia Tribune* (circulation 108,000), which plans to carry Uptown advertising, as declaring: "We don't have the right to make a choice for our readers. What we're doing is not illegal or immoral."

Jeff Burns, vice president of Johnson Publishing, parent company of *Ebony* and *Jet* magazines, which are scheduled to carry Uptown advertising, was quoted as stating: "R. J. Reynolds has been an advertiser for a long time. This is just another product."

Barbara A. Britton, national advertising manager for *Essence*, commented as follows: "It's unfair to single out minority publications on this issue. Given the health issue in America, this is a question that should be posed to the white media as well."

According to Ramirez, David Iauco, senior vice president of marketing at Reynolds, was not surprised by the controversy. "Everything we do is going to be assaulted and picked at by the anti-smokers," he stated. "But taking away business from our competitors is the only thing that Uptown is about."

In concluding his long article, Ramirez stated: "Despite the heavy marketing to blacks, Reynolds does not say that Uptown is a cigarette designed for blacks. Rather, the company says it is a cigarette for the entire market but which is likely to attract a disproportionate number of black smokers."

TARGET MARKETING IN PHILADELPHIA (B)

On Wednesday, January 17, Dr. Louis W. Sullivan, Secretary of Health and Human Services and one of the highest black officials in the Bush Administration, sent a letter to James W. Johnston, chief executive of R. J. Reynolds, urging him to cancel plans to aim the Uptown advertising at blacks.

"Cigarettes are the only legal product on the market that are deadly when used exactly as intended," Sullivan wrote to the Reynolds chief executive (reported in the *New York Times*, January 19, 1990). "Claiming an estimated 390,000 deaths each year in the United States, smoking is by far the country's leading cause of preventable death."

According to the *Washington Post* of January 19, Sullivan also wrote in his letter: "Higher smoking rates among blacks, especially black males, are a major reason why blacks experience higher rates of lung cancer, other cancers, heart disease and stroke compared to whites. I strongly urge you to cancel your plans to market a brand of cigarettes that is specifically targeted to black smokers."

The day after sending his letter to Johnston, Sullivan was scheduled to address medical students and faculty at the dedication of a building at the medical school of the University of Pennsylvania in Philadelphia. In this talk on Thursday, January 18, Sullivan angrily attacked Reynolds's test-market plan in very explicit language.

"This brand," Sullivan said about Uptown, "is cynically and deliberately targeted toward black Americans. At a time when our people desperately need the message of health promotion, Uptown's message is more disease, more suffering for a group already bearing more than its share of smoking-related illness and mortality.

"At a time when we must cultivate greater responsibility among our citizens, Uptown's slick and sinister advertising proposes instead a greater degree of personal irresponsibility."

Calling on Reynolds to reverse its plans, Sullivan said his remarks were the start of a campaign against Reynolds and other cigarette companies.

"We must resist unworthy efforts of the tobacco merchants to earn profits at the expense of the health and well-being of our poor and minority citizens," said the health secretary. "This trade-off between profits and good health must stop. And it will stop if, around the country, our citizens rise up and say, 'Enough—no more!' "

Talk Makes Front Pages

Dr. Sullivan's blunt criticism of Reynolds's Uptown plans received front-page coverage in the *New York Times, Washington Post*, and other daily newspapers of Friday, January 19. The *NYT* lead ran as follows: "The nation's top health official, Dr. Louis W. Sullivan, expressed outrage today at the R.J. Reynolds Tobacco Company for 'deliberately and cynically' test-marketing a cigarette aimed primarily at blacks, and he assailed the company for 'promoting a culture of cancer.' "

The *Post* lead in its story on January 19 read: "The nation's chief health official yesterday denounced the R.J. Reynolds Tobacco Co., calling for the company to withdraw its plan to market a brand of cigarette called Uptown and promoted specifically for blacks."

In their stories, both papers referred to Betsy Annese as a spokeswoman for Reynolds. The *NYT*, identifying her as vice president of communications for the company, quoted her as saying, "The company will respond directly to Dr. Sullivan" and stated that she declined any further comment about his criticism. The paper also reported her as saying that the company will go ahead with plans to market Uptown as a cigarette that "appeals most strongly to black smokers."

The *Post* stated in its story that "a spokeswoman for the company said it had decided not to comment on the speech, adding that Reynolds will respond to Sullivan in two weeks." The *Post*, identifying the spokeswoman as Annese, quoted her as follows: "We believe that black smokers have the right to buy products that fit their preference. The introduction of a new brand will not affect the decision to smoke."

According to the *NYT* story, "officials at the Department of Health and Human Services said it may be the first time a Secretary has ever openly attacked a specific company and brand." As had the *Washington Post*, the *NYT* reported Sullivan's denouncement of Reynolds's "slick and sinister advertising" and said that he called on the company to reverse its plans for Uptown.

The *NYT* story, headline, and head-and-shoulder picture of Sullivan ran to 26½ column inches. The *Post* story and headline ran to 20½ column inches.

TARGET MARKETING IN PHILADELPHIA (C)

On Saturday, January 20, the *New York Times* (*NYT*), *Washington Post,* and *Philadelphia Inquirer* carried front-page stories reporting that the R.J. Reynolds company had decided late Friday night to scrap its plans to test-market Uptown in Philadelphia. The announcement was made from company headquarters in Winston-Salem, North Carolina.

The *NYT* headline and lead read as follows:

Reynolds, After Protests, Cancels Cigarette Aimed at Black Smokers

Under fire for developing a cigarette aimed primarily at blacks, the R.J. Reynolds Tobacco Company abruptly decided yesterday to cancel the cigarette.

The company said a planned market test that was to begin in three weeks would no longer be reliable because of what it called "the unfair and biased attention the brand had received."

The *Post* headline and lead read as follows:

Reynolds Cancels Plan to Market New Cigarette

The R.J. Reynolds Tobacco Co., stung by a public attack from the nation's top health official, yes-

terday canceled plans to market a brand of cigarettes aimed at blacks.

The company acted one day after Health and
Human Services Secretary Louis W. Sullivan delivered a startling speech in which he accused
Reynolds of "promoting a culture of cancer"
with its new Uptown brand, which company officials had said they would market heavily among
blacks.

The *Inquirer* headline and lead read as follows:

Plan for Test of Cigarette Here Halted
R.J. Reynolds Tobacco Co., stung by a growing
public relations debacle, said last night that it
had scrapped plans to test-market in Philadelphia a new cigarette aimed primarily at black
smokers.

The company declined to say whether the
new Uptown brand would be introduced elsewhere, and indicated that its future was uncertain.

"We don't know what future plans we'll
make," a spokeswoman said.

All three papers carried the following prepared
statement by Peter Hoult, Reynolds's executive vice
president for marketing:
"We regret that a small coalition of anti-smoking
zealots apparently believe that black smokers are somewhat different from others who choose to smoke and
must not be allowed to exercise the same freedom of
choice available to all other smokers. This represents a
loss of choice for black smokers and a further erosion of
the free enterprise system."

The *NYT* also quoted Hoult as declaring in his statement that "our intentions in test-marketing Uptown in Philadelphia have been misconstrued and misrepresented by the anti-smoking lobby. Our sole purpose, plainly and simply, was to test-market a cigarette among smokers who currently buy competitive products." The *Inquirer* did not quote Hoult directly on the company's intentions, but said that "in its statement, Reynolds blamed anti-smoking forces for the cancellation of the marketing test, and said the controversy had wrecked any chance that it would get useful test results."

David B. Fishel, Reynolds's senior vice president of public relations, was quoted in the *NYT* story as stating in a telephone interview, "There's a feeling here that we were cheated on this one. Maybe in retrospect we would have been better off not saying we were marketing to blacks. But those were the smokers we were going after, so why shouldn't we be honest about it?"

According to the *Inquirer*, Reynolds "declined to respond publicly to Sullivan's remarks, saying he would communicate directly with the secretary himself."

When informed about the company's decision to cancel its test-marketing plan, HHS Secretary Sullivan, according to the stories in the *Inquirer* and the *Post*, said the news is a victory for the citizens of Philadelphia, for minority citizens, and for all Americans.

The *Times* and the *Inquirer*, in their Sunday, January 21, editions, carried editorials about Uptown, Sullivan's remarks, and Reynolds's decision to cancel its test-marketing of Uptown in Philadelphia. The *NYT* said that Sullivan spoke a "tragic truth" when he spoke of a group "already bearing more than its share of smoking-related illness and mortality." Said the *NYT* in its editorial conclusion: "One need not endorse Dr. Sullivan's charge that Uptown's advertising was 'slick and sinister' to share his anger and applaud his exemplary use of his office. During his term as Surgeon General, Dr. C. Everett Koop mounted a powerful and successful campaign to reduce the smoking rate among all Americans. May Dr. Sullivan be equally effective among black Americans."

In its editorial on Sunday, headlined "Uptown's Outatown," the *Philadelphia Inquirer* said that by late Friday R.J. Reynolds "knew the PR war was lost. It canceled the test-marketing in Philadelphia, saying the new brand was getting 'unfair and biased attention.' You bet it was getting attention, though it was fair and on-target."

Referring to Reynolds as the "pushers from Tobacco Road," the editorial said the company received "the perfect comeuppance" from the community. After citing the company statement that the incident was "a further erosion of the free enterprise system," the editorial replied: "We'd call it a victory for the people of Philadelphia. A triumph for a community that was about to be taken for a ride. A milestone for anti-smoking organizing. So good riddance, Uptown. We hope you learned a lesson from your welcome in these parts. Philadelphia certainly did."

In a long round-up story of the week's test-marketing events, the *Inquirer* on Sunday stated that the Philadelphia protesters advised Reynolds to examine its marketing approach. The story reported that David Fishel of Reynolds said that the protest condition "created such an environment through media manipulation we did not feel we could get an honest test."

After noting that Reynolds's research showed that black smokers preferred less menthol and more taste than its Salem brand provides, the story cited Fishel as follows:

"Our one and only motive was to say to black smokers smoking Newport or Kool, here's another alternative. The way anti-smoking people in Philadelphia were telling it, this was some dark, awful plot to cause people to smoke who already don't smoke. It's a silly comment from people who don't know anything about advertising."

Reprint For Discussion

Playing the Role of Organizational Ethicist*
John Paluszek

Here are five things we can do to play an effective role as "ethicists" within our organizations.

1. Let's really perform the early warning function. That is, let's be sure that we're positioned to see the kind of changes in values that develop constantly in a self-correcting society. Because changing values eventually change laws. Psychographic as well as demographic research is important here.

For example, the values and lifestyles research system. Primary as well as secondary research too.

Remember, at first the Vietnam War was opposed mainly by scruffy, alternative-lifestyle advocates. But eventually the opposition became mainstream. Exactly when did that happen? Who was smart enough—informed enough—to warn American companies and the American government on that critical evolution of ethical position?

2. We also owe it to our employers and clients to be familiar with the experts on applied ethics and their readiness to help on the sticky questions of the day. Sure, everyone knew that Harvard University got a $30 million grant in this area, but

*Remarks made by John Paluszek, President, Ketchum Public Affairs, at the 1991 Public Affairs Conference, The Conference Board, Washington, D.C., May 15, 1991. Reprinted with permission of Mr. Paluszek.

what about the lesser known but very capable institutions?

Here are a few: the Carnegie Council on Ethics and International Affairs, the Center for Applied Ethics, the Manhattan College Business Ethics Division and the Institute for Ethics and Leadership.

3. Let's keep our advice simple and practical. If we can't think through all of the moral dimensions of a problem, how about just asking, "How will this look on page one of the local daily paper?" That's practical, my friends, and CEOs can relate to it.

4. Fourth, let's be sure we're familiar with, and live by, the ethical codes of our societies—such as the Public Affairs Council, the American Association of Political Consultants and the Public Relations Society of America. And where necessary, let's strengthen those codes.

And, of course, we all have to be fully conversant with the Ethics Reform Act of 1989 which, beginning this year, placed heavier career restrictions on federal workers.

5. Fifth, and finally, let's take a good look at how we might encourage the media changes that I reported on earlier (reform of media coverage of election campaigns so that the realities of substance rather than the staged photo opportunities make the news).

Let me conclude this apologia re ethics with one overreaching piece of advice. Whenever I'm in doubt on an ethical issue, I reflect on it.

The late Donald McCammond, a distinguished public relations professional and a former chairman of the PRSA Ethics Board, drew a very effective bottom line. He said, "Remember, you have to live with yourself."

2 NONPROFIT ORGANIZATIONS

HANDLING A TOWN/GOWN DISPUTE* (A)

Crescent State University (CSU) is a state institution in the eastern United States, located in the city of Jackson, population 51,000. CSU appears to have good, friendly relationships with both Jackson and the nearby major city. Walking across campus one afternoon, the new public affairs director, Diana Morrissey, spied a familiar face and warmly greeted the number-two campus facility man, David Delacompagni. "What's going on today, anything special?"

Delacompagni squinted in the afternoon sun, thought a bit, and then said, "A couple of things, maybe."

"Anything that would be of interest to me and the public affairs office?"

Delacompagni hesitated. He knew Morrissey had joined the university just a month ago. She worked for the CSU president and had an office in the president's suite on the eighth floor. Years on the job had taught him that you have to be careful with the brass and anyone connected to them. But then he thought, she's only been here a few weeks. She needs me more than I need her, but if she works out, she could be helpful to me. I don't have anything that's really news, so we'll talk about it.

"Well," he said, "We're going to take out those

---

*All names, places, and dates in this case are disguised.

palms and put in some silk trees. It will make the place look better, but people will complain. They always think each palm is the last one on earth."

Morrissey listened carefully, spoke slowly. "I suppose that whatever you do, someone will be upset. Who do you think it will be?"

Delacompagni thought: at least she listens. "I can't tell you who will gripe, but they will as soon as the crane shows up to lift the palms," he said. "Then the student paper will send someone to take a picture and make a big deal about nothing. I don't know why that is, but they always do it."

"There's one reason," said Morrissey. "It's easier to write a story about someone doing wrong than someone who's doing right. It's what's called 'lazy journalism.' "

Delacompagni said, "I never figured it that way, but it sure makes sense. Those kids will do it the easiest way every time. They may not know much, but they're sure proud that they're students and work on that paper."

Morrissey paused a moment. She found she learned a lot by letting silence move the other person to speak. Also, she found that by wandering around campus and talking with students, faculty, and staff, she had learned quite a bit. The day before she was interviewed for the job, she'd been on campus in slacks and a casual top. She walked all over, listened to anyone who would talk, and asked questions. When the job interview had taken place, the president and academic VP were surprised at how much she seemed to know about the university. She'd gotten the job. There were 312 applicants.

Delacompagni paused, looked around, spat, and then said, "And then the town people are trying to give us some trouble, too. But our university lawyer says it won't amount to much. The town wants to close Locust Avenue at the east side of the campus, but the lawyer says they can't. I called him."

Morrissey was all ears. She'd sat in university-wide

administrative and faculty meetings all morning where every issue, no matter how trivial, was discussed in great detail, and no one had mentioned this. She wondered why. Did they all know? Was it an old story that only she didn't know about? Was there something she didn't understand?

"Dave, when is the city planning on closing the street?"

"I don't know, but I do know that they will be voting on it tonight at the city council meeting," he replied.

"Has someone got a plan on what they're going to do at the city council meeting tonight, Dave?"

"I can't say as I know. No one told me anything about a plan, but the university's lawyer says they can't close it anyway."

"Who have you talked to about this?" Morrissey asked.

"I heard about it from a guy at City Hall. Then I called the lawyer, because he's the guy we deal with on stuff like that."

"Did you, or anyone, tell the president?"

"My boss might have. He's the one who talks to the president. That guy has a temper, and I give him lots of room."

"Well, Dave, I've got to get back to the office. Nice talking with you. See you around."

As she walked into a nearby campus building, Morrissey made some quick calculations. She had about four hours if the meeting started at a typical time. She predicted that it represented more of a problem than it seemed. The campus had 25,000 students, a couple thousand faculty and staff, and only three entrances. The south entrance came off the freeway, and was always a bottleneck. The north entrance wasn't used much, although it was the shortest route for Morrissey to commute to work. It was the quickest way home and seemed to have the least traffic. The east entrance, Locust Avenue, was the main exodus road in the afternoon and evening. People wanted out in a hurry, and the freeway was stop and go from at least 4:30 to 6 p.m.

Locust Avenue was once the main east-west thoroughfare through these suburban residential, commercial, and industrial towns. Then the freeway came. Locust now was a residential street in the area immediately adjacent to the campus and commercial about a mile away.

Morrissey decided it was important for her to make a quick auto tour of the Locust Avenue area at the university, but she first called her office and asked her secretary to find out how many university employees and students lived in the Rosedale section of Jackson, the section in which CSU was located. She felt it was important to know who could speak as a resident of the area and argue the university's case capably. She therefore asked her secretary to get a list of all employees who lived in Rosedale, by address and phone number, and have it ready when she returned to the office.

Morrissey walked to the parking garage, got her car, and drove out the east entrance of the campus on Locust Avenue. From there to the next main road was exactly a mile of residential street. There were no stop signs and a speed limit of 30 mph. It was a nice area, with moderate houses well kept. The residents she saw seemed either quite old, probably retirees, or members of young families. She did a U turn and drove slowly back. Going this way there was one stop sign, about halfway down. A maze of little streets led off Locust. There were few through streets, and many of them wound with the contours of the land. Morrissey meandered through some of these side streets. The streets were all narrow, and many of them were cul-de-sacs. The best houses, lawns, and gardens were on Locust.

It was easy to see why the neighbors might object. The traffic moved briskly, sometimes fast. Tough scene for an area with young kids and elderly people. She could also understand what had happened: upset at people racing down their street, the locals had probably complained to council members, and now it was coming up for a vote.

As Morrissey headed back to the office, her thoughts were going almost as fast as her car. She knew that eminent domain often gives cities the power to close a street, and that city councils care a lot more about the residents than the university. Clearly, voters usually get attention when they complain. The main point, she thought, is to keep this from becoming a town-gown controversy. She would have to play it as low-key as possible. However, she believed that in many cities it takes two readings and two votes before anything can become law, but she didn't know if that was the procedure in Jackson. Nor did she know whether or not an Environmental Impact Report (EIR) was required or had been done in a situation such as the Locust Avenue closing.

Morrissey recalled in a vague way that she had read about a city that had to vote twice and then put up notices that a road would be permanently closed in 30 days. Then, as she recalled, the authorities put up steel barriers and "dead end" street signs. But is that what was planned here? She had many questions relating to governmental procedures, the council itself, and the university's actions to date, if any.

Returning to the office, Morrissey put in a call to the Jackson City Clerk. "Miss Murphy," she began. "Is it true that tonight the council will be considering a motion to close Locust Avenue at the university?"

"Why yes, that's so," she replied.

"Will it be a big issue? Are there a lot of people lined up to comment on both sides?"

"Who can tell?" she said. "I'm sure the neighborhood people will be here, but I'm not sure about others."

"What time do you think it will be on the agenda?"

"We start at 7:00, but we have a lot of announcements, proclamations, and awards. It could be 8:00 to

8:30. I know they'll get it on as quickly as possible, because there will be a lot of people here for that issue, and they'll get restless if they have to wait a long time."

"Thank you very much, Miss Murphy," said Morrissey. She scanned the partial list brought in by her secretary. On this list of six Rosedale residents she recognized the name of one dean and two professors she had met. They'd impressed her as being quite articulate, the dean especially.

Morrissey drifted down the hall to the president's secretary. "Mary, have you heard anything about Jackson wanting to close down Locust Avenue?" she asked.

"No, I haven't heard a thing. That's crazy."

"Do you think the president knows about it?"

"I doubt it. He would have said something. He's in. Want to see him?"

"Yes, I would. It's a bit of a crisis."

As Morrissey walked into the president's office, she wished she had more information. However, she reasoned that she was new. Morrissey also felt that the problem was important enough to start dealing with it now. She didn't know how this president reacted to things like this, but she quickly sketched out what she had learned and done.

"I don't care what anyone says, they can't do that," said the president. "What are you going to do to stop them?"

HANDLING A TOWN/GOWN DISPUTE* (B)

Diana Morrissey, the new public affairs director at Crescent State University, had hoped to spend enough time with the president to arrive at a plan of action, but unfortunately he cut the meeting short because of an important out-of-town engagement. However, Morrissey was able to get answers to some questions, and his final words, "I'll leave it to you," left her with both a challenge and the opportunity to handle Locust Avenue as she saw fit.

Morrissey knew she had little time before the evening council meeting, and therefore she could not develop a complete plan of action based on solid research. It was her opinion that she, as DPA, should not surface at council meetings as a representative of the CSU on the Locust Avenue issue. It was chiefly for this reason that she had sought the names and phone numbers of university staffers and faculty who lived in the Rosedale section of Jackson.

She phoned the six Rosedale residents who were affiliated with the university, explained the situation, and asked if they would be willing to attend the council meeting that evening and speak against the planned closing. Two of the six—Professor Thomas Royal of the

---

*All names, places, and dates in this case are disguised.

English department and Elaine Lofton, a clerical employee of the Human Resources office—refused to speak at the meeting. Professor Royal said he was hired to teach, not to deal with university business in the evening. Ms. Lofton said she considered the request from Morrissey to be an imposition on her personal freedom of expression and as an officer of the clerical union at the university she would file a grievance.

The other four said they would be glad to attend the meeting and express their opposition to the planned street closing. All four asked Morrissey if they should identify themselves as university staffers.

"I think it would be advisable if you did not mention your university affiliation," Morrissey told them. "Simply identify yourself by your residency." The four agreed to do so.

Morrissey tried to reach Kevin Stoga, the university's director of campus facilities, but was unable to do so before the evening meeting. She was surprised to find him at the meeting but was not able to talk to him before the session got underway because the meeting room was packed.

The audience proved to be strident and upset about speed, safety, and heavy traffic. Most of those who spoke favored the immediate closing of Locust Avenue. The university dean, saying he spoke as a resident of Locust Avenue, addressed the need for an Environmental Impact Report (EIR) dealing with the subject of smog, gasoline consumption, where the traffic would go if Locust Avenue were closed, and how many cars would be on each street then as opposed to now. The university professor who had been called earlier by Morrissey suggested what she termed a simple solution: put stop signs at every intersection to eliminate the speeding cars. The two other university people who had been phoned by Morrissey also spoke against the closing of Locust Avenue. None of the four mentioned affiliation with the university.

One who did mention his university affiliation was Stoga. He read out and asked to have put in the record an official letter of protest about the closing in his capacity as the director of campus facilities for Crescent State University.

Following the public comments, the council voted 5 to 0 to close Locust Avenue.

The Second Meeting

At the second meeting, held two weeks later, a parade of residents once again spoke in favor of closing Locust Avenue. They stressed that they were voters and that this was a vital issue for their part of the community. As one stated, "If this road is not closed now, the issue will go on until it is—and we'll remember how each of you votes."

Speaking against the closing, the dean filed a formal protest on an informal EIR that had been started but not completed, citing its shortcomings and then making a formal request for a completed EIR, which he estimated would cost the city about $30,000. The council president agreed that it would be improper to close the road without a completed EIR. The council again voted 5 to 0 to close Locust Avenue and by the same vote to have the EIR completed.

In the week prior to the meeting at which the EIR was to be presented, the university, through Diana Morrissey, contacted a prominent resident and asked him to look at the situation and talk before the council. Bob McLurry, the man contacted, was a prominent area businessman, owner of the state's largest minority-owned auto dealership, former head of the city's Chamber of Commerce, and a major source of sales tax income for Rosedale. McLurry agreed, drove to Locust Avenue with Morrissey, watched the traffic for an hour, and concluded that Locust Avenue should not be closed.

McLurry testified before the council to this effect at the meeting scheduled to receive the completed EIR. He told the council that the matter was more fuss than substance, that he had observed the traffic, and that there wasn't any problem that a few stop signs couldn't cure.

Following presentation of the completed EIR, residents living on the streets off Locust said they wanted Locust Avenue to remain open and didn't want all Locust traffic diverted to their streets.

Taking the floor, the dean suggested that the city manager and his staff be given two weeks to review the EIR and make a recommendation to the council for further consideration or action to be taken at that time. The council voted 5 to 0 to refer the matter to the city manager.

Now that the EIR had been presented to the council, Morrissey decided to disseminate its findings. Her office made copies of EIR data and provided them door-to-door to those living on the streets that would be adversely affected by shunted traffic if Locust Avenue were closed. A simple fact sheet quoted the EIR. The projected traffic for each street was highlighted in yellow so that residents wouldn't miss it. The sheet also listed the names and phone numbers of the council members and the city staff who were involved. The sheets were either handed to the residents of all the streets affected or placed on their doorknobs. Those who lived on Locust Avenue, or within four houses of Locust, did not get information sheets. The EIR was the only source cited for the information in and distribution of the sheets.

Following the last council meeting, the city staff evolved a plan. There would be a series of stop signs for traffic going either way on Locust, and additional stop signs on campus as well. After some weeks, the matter was placed on the agenda again. Before the council's vote on the city staff's recommendation, there was a lot of public discussion, some of it heated. The Locust residents objected; the residents of the other streets, which would have gotten more traffic, approved. After listening to all testimony, the council voted 5 to 0 to approve the city staff's recommendation.

In the next few days the new stop signs were put in place. Locust Avenue remained open.

· ·

Some Afterthoughts

Dianna Morrissey had taken a public relations cases course years ago when she was in college, but she didn't remember too many details about the cases. She did remember, however, a major lesson she had learned from the course: following a public relations crisis or problem situation, it's a good idea to spend some time reviewing and assessing how well you handle yourself, others, and the situation. In so doing, you may avoid making the same mistakes twice, and you may well improve your chances of being successful in your field. (See Exhibit 18–1.)

Exhibit 18-1
Diana's
Self-Assessment

Questions	Diana's Answers
1. Did I achieve my major objective?	Yes, Locust Avenue was not closed.
2. Did I achieve my objective of avoiding a university/community conflict?	Not sure to what degree.
3. Did I, by my actions, exacerbate the situation?	In some ways, probably to some degree. Otherwise, no.
4. Did I handle myself in a professional, ethical manner?	Yes, in most instances, no in others.
5. If the same situation were to arise again, what would I do differently, and why?	I'm too close to the situation but will seek counsel from others who have read this case.

The National Arrhythmia Association*

You, Maria Hostos, are the Ohio public relations director for a health service agency, the National Arrhythmia Association (NAA). You have been in the field a number of years, and you have very good relations with the volunteers but a less close relationship with the media.

A professor-writer, Alphonso Stevens of Pettigrew University in Arizona, has a syndicated column. He has written a number of articles on nonprofit agencies, criticizing them for their high overhead expenses, excessive salaries, and alleged misleading of the public as to how their donated funds will be used. Stevens bases his columns on his analysis of annual reports and other public documents that the health service agencies must file with their state. He seems to be a thorough, accurate researcher. Stevens has concentrated mostly on other types of agencies, but recently he did a long, critical piece on the Washington state NAA. He criticized them for having a fleet of cars, extensive real estate holdings (buildings in which they have their offices), and a large reserve account.

Your state's NAA chapter owns one building, has three executives making over $100,000 a year, a rather liberal system for handling expenses (including payments for limousines and lavish dinners), and a car and a private club membership for the executive director. Your reserve account is roughly three times the size of the Washington chapter's reserve account.

The phone buzzes, and your secretary advises you that Professor Stevens of Pettigrew University is on the phone and would like to talk with you about the Ohio chapter of NAA. Your executive director is out of town.

How, in brief terms, would you initially address this mini case? You need not go into detail. Perhaps just describe the first three or four moves you'd make and state why.

---

*All names, places, and dates in this case are disguised.

A TALE OF TWO EYE BANKS* (A)

Background

When this case was written, there were 100 nonprofit eye banks in the United States. Most of them (90 percent) were members of the Eye Bank Association of America (EBAA) and were sponsored and supported by state and local Lions Clubs.

Each eye bank is an independent, nonprofit agency incorporated in the state where it operates and usually serving an entire state or part of a state. The main service they provide is to collect human eyes within six to eight hours after death from persons who have authorized this use while living and to distribute the eyes to ocular surgeons when a cornea is needed for grafting or transplantation. All donated eyes not suitable for corneal transplantation are used for research and education.

The corneal transplant is by far the most frequently performed human transplant procedure. In recent years, there were more corneal transplants than all other organ transplants combined. More than 90 percent of corneal transplant operations are successful. The healthy corneal tissue collected by eye banks and used

---

*This case is an amalgam of events and situations involving eye banks and personnel at various times and locations. All names, places, and dates in this case are disguised.

in these operations is made available to ocular surgeons on a no-cost, first-come-first-served basis to patients.

. . . .

University and Zenith

When this case was written, two eye banks—University Eye Bank and Zenith Eye Bank—were in operation in a mid-Atlantic state. University Eye Bank, the newer and larger of the two, was located in a wing of University Hospital and Medical Center in Metropolis, the capital city of the state (population 540,000). Established 12 years ago, University Eye Bank had a five-person staff: Lynn Heywood, executive director; John Bascomb, assistant administrator; Laurie Scott, M.D., medical director; Nina Ortiz, technician; and Cynthia Stone, secretary. Its facility—reception area, offices, laboratory, etc.—was considered to be one of the finest among the nation's eye banks. Last year, 90 percent of all eye and corneal donations obtained in the state were handled by the University Eye Bank.

The remaining 10 percent of eye and corneal donations obtained in the state were handled by the Zenith Eye Bank. Established 20 years ago in the city of Zenith (population 71,000), which was 200 miles east of Metropolis, the Zenith Eye Bank had a three-person staff: Larry Boone, executive director; Olmstead Pantel, M.D., medical director; and Stuart Little, technician. Its facility barely met the standards set by the Eye Bank Association of America (EBAA), but the bank had the strong support of the Lions Club of Zenith and had been praised in editorials at various times by the Zenith *Observer*, an afternoon daily (circulation 35,000). Dr. Pantel, 72, not only had founded the eye bank, but also had been its medical director since its inception. He is a member of the bank's seven-member board of directors and of the Lions Club of Zenith.

At various times in the past two years, Executive Director Lynn Heywood of University Eye Bank had discussions with members of her board of directors concerning the decline in the number of small eye banks nationally and the figures showing decreasing procurement on the part of the Zenith Eye Bank. Heywood and her medical director were especially concerned about Zenith's problem of meeting EBAA quality control standards and about Zenith's inability in recent years to obtain sufficient eye donations to meet the demand for corneal transplants in Zenith. Heywood was all too well aware, however, that recognizing a problem and being able to resolve it were two different matters.

For a variety of reasons Heywood did not believe it would be feasible or wise for her or her board to attempt to do anything about the problems of the Zenith Eye Bank. Because of these reasons Heywood had not made any recommendations to her board regarding the Zenith bank.

However, as a result of developments that occurred in recent months, Heywood began to change her mind about recommendations concerning the Zenith bank. There were three such developments:

> 1. The state legislature passed and the governor signed a required request law, to take effect January 1. This law made it mandatory that next-of-kin be advised of the opportunity to donate the tissue, bone, and organs of the deceased for surgical transplant and research.

> 2. Dr. Pantel announced he is retiring from active practice and expects to resign as medical director of the Zenith Eye Bank at the end of the year. Both the Zenith *Observer* and the Metropolis *Dispatch* carried news stories about the announcement, but neither made mention of Dr. Pantel's intentions regarding his membership on the Zenith Eye Bank board.

> 3. At its annual meeting, held three weeks ago, the Zenith Eye Bank board elected Drs. Tad

Binder and Jonas Kover, board-certified ophthalmologists, to serve three-year terms on the board. The two outgoing board members they replaced were members of the Zenith Lions Club and the only club representatives on the board (other than Dr. Pantel).

Reviewing these developments early in April, Heywood concluded that the time might well have arrived to attempt to bring about a consolidation or meshing of the University and Zenith eye banks. Recognizing the delicate nature of such an endeavor and realizing it had public relations ramifications, she talked about these with John Bascomb, the bank's assistant administrator, whose responsibilities included public relations and public affairs.

"I'm sure you realize we have to proceed very carefully if we do decide to move on this," Heywood said. "That's why I'd like you to bring me up to date on the media situation."

"As you know," replied Bascomb, "we have three network-affiliated TV stations, eight AM and eight FM radio stations, and one daily newspaper in Metropolis. We've been getting only minimal news coverage from TV and radio and occasional appearances on talk shows.

"The morning *Dispatch* and its Sunday edition is by far the most important media outlet in Metropolis and in the entire state, for that matter. It has a daily circulation of six hundred twenty-five thousand and a Sunday circulation of eight hundred fifty thousand. In some cities its circulation is larger than that of the dailies published in those cities.

"That doesn't hold true in Zenith, though, where the *Dispatch* circulates twenty-two thousand daily compared to the *Observer*'s thirty-five thousand. I think the *Observer* holds its own because it's more aggressive in its coverage of local Zenith news and in its self-promotion of the city and the area.

"Unfortunately for our eye bank operation here in Metropolis, ever since the *Dispatch* absorbed the afternoon newspaper here a year ago and made this a one-newspaper city, coverage of our activities has plummeted. We no longer have the option of 'playing off' one paper against the other, but more crucial is the fact that all health and medical news has to go through Diane Sands, and you know what that means."

Heywood nodded in agreement. As she knew, Sands had been brought in as health and medical editor shortly after the *Dispatch* bought out the afternoon paper. Married to an internist who joined a medical group when the family moved to Metropolis, Sands was a veteran newspaper woman who had covered health and medical news and features for the Associated Press, three major women's magazines, and one of the Chicago dailies. Proof that her work was appreciated by *Dispatch* management is the fact that the paper's space coverage of health and medical news and features had quadrupled since she joined the staff. In concluding his briefing, Bascomb said he had been trying for the past six months to find a feature story angle that might interest Sands, but she kept rejecting his suggestions.

"I think she may go for a story, with art, about Susie Loughlin," said Bascomb. "The fact that she was once legally blind and as a result of a corneal transplant is now in charge of our satellite office in Durham (100 miles south of Metropolis) interested Sands when I spoke to her last week. I've sent background info with art and will be calling her about them."

An incoming long-distance phone call interrupted the discussion, and so Bascomb returned to his office. The call was from Dr. Binder in Zenith, who said he and Dr. Kover expected to be in Metropolis on April 9 and would like to talk to Heywood about an eye bank matter that should be of interest to her. It was agreed that the three would meet in Heywood's office at 11 a.m. on April 9.

After some preliminary chit-chat when the two doctors came in on the 9th, Dr. Binder explained why he and Dr. Kover had sought the meeting.

"I'm sure," he said, "you are aware that for the past year the need for eyes in Zenith for corneal transplants has been greater than the supply of eyes available through the Zenith Eye Bank. I imagine you also know about Dr. Pantel's decision to retire at the end of this year. Dr. Kover and I feel that the time is ripe for some sort of merger or consolidation of our two eye banks. Both of us are confident that if given the right kind of terms and if the approach is carefully made, a majority of the Zenith Eye Bank board would approve of such a merger. It won't be easily accomplished, but we're here to tell you of our interest, learn where you stand on the matter, and what you suggest be done as the next step."

"Let me add a point or two," said Dr. Kover. "Both of us are doctors, not administrators and not public relations experts. However, we know that how this matter is handled is crucial to the success of the undertaking. Our question is: should it be attempted, can it succeed, and how should it be brought about?"

The doctors sat back in their chairs. Heywood knew it was her time to respond.

A TALE OF TWO EYE BANKS* (B)

In the week following her meeting with the two Zenith doctors, Heywood met individually with the chairman and members of her board and with Bascomb. In talking to each person, Heywood reported what the two doctors had said and her responses. She cautioned each person about the need to respect the confidential nature of the meeting and asked for the person's opinion.

Bascomb and a majority, but not all, of the board members said they were in favor of having Heywood pursue the consolidation/merger matter further and arranging an unpublicized meeting in Zenith.

Heywood did not talk to Dr. Scott about the meeting nor about the board members' reactions for the following reasons:

1. Heywood felt that this was not a medical matter and therefore was one that she, as executive director, and the board should handle.

2. Heywood knew that Dr. Scott and Dr. Pantel referred patients to each other from time to time as circumstances warranted, and she was con-

---

*This case is an amalgam of events and situations involving eye banks and personnel at various times and locations. All names, places, and dates in this case are disguised.

cerned about premature disclosure of the upcoming discussions.

3. Heywood recognized that she and Dr. Scott did not make a harmonious team. In part, she reflected, this might be due to an age difference (Heywood was 32 and Dr. Scott was 46), or it might be due to an educational/professional difference. Dr. Scott was a college and medical school graduate and board-certified specialist. Heywood, former head nurse at a university-affiliated hospital, was a college graduate and had a master's degree in public health administration.

4. The two women had had differences in the past when decisions had to be made that were not purely medical and not purely administrative. Resolving these differences resulted in very uncomfortable confrontations about ultimate authority.

In this particular instance, Heywood concluded, it would be best not to risk another such confrontation if the two disagreed about steps to be taken. Therefore, she did not talk to Dr. Scott nor seek her opinion.

In talking to Bascomb, Heywood was reminded by her associate that the Zenith Eye Bank was the core of Dr. Pantel's professional and personal life. Mindful of this point, when Heywood phoned Dr. Binder to arrange a meeting in Zenith she asked if Dr. Pantel would be present.

"I don't think we should bring in the medical directors at this point," said Dr. Binder. "We'll have two members of our board—Dr. Kover and me—and our board president, Herman Muskatt."

"I see," said Heywood. "I think it's a mistake to exclude Dr. Pantel, but that's your prerogative. Our group will include me, Lewis Pinella, our board president, and another board member. As you may know, we're not officially tied to the Metropolis Lions Club, though they've been helpful in many ways, so we won't have a club rep in our group. I am surprised, though, that you don't want to have a Lions Club representative in your group."

"We don't think it would be wise at this time," Dr. Binder said. Heywood did not pursue the matter further.

The two then settled on a date and place: Saturday morning, April 20, at Dr. Binder's country club. Dr. Binder had at first suggested the meeting be held at his office, but when Heywood stressed the need to be discreet, the doctor then suggested a private dining room at his club. Heywood said that would be fine.

Before leaving at 4 p.m. on Friday, April 19, with the other members of the Metropolis group, Heywood had a brief meeting with Bascomb. She again cautioned him about the need to keep the meeting under wraps and told him who would be representing each eye bank at the meeting. She did not tell him exactly where the meeting would be held, but she did say it was the next morning and that she and the others from Metropolis would be staying overnight somewhere on the road.

About a half hour after Heywood and the others left for Zenith, an incoming phone call from Diane Sands of the Metropolis *Dispatch* was taken by Cynthia Stone, the eye bank secretary. When Sands asked to speak to Heywood the secretary said she had gone out of town.

"It's important that I reach her," said Sands. "Do you know where she's gone?"

"No," said Stone, who knew that Heywood had gone to Zenith. "However, if it's important you may want to speak to Mr. Bascomb. I believe he's still here."

"This is Diane Sands, John," the editor said when Bascomb got on the line. "I've been hearing some rumors about a takeover by Metropolis of the Zenith Eye

Bank, so I'm checking them out and preparing a story for tomorrow's *Dispatch.* Heywood seems to have gone out of town. Do you know where she's gone? I'd like to talk to her."

"I'm sorry, Diane, but Lynn doesn't tell me everything," said Bascomb. "I can't say I know where she's gone."

"I see," said Sands. "Does that mean you don't know where she's gone, or you're prohibited from saying where she's gone?"

"Hey, give me a break," said Bascomb. "The weekend is here."

"Well, before you take off for the weekend, perhaps you can be of some help about the rumors I've heard about a takeover."

"I wish you wouldn't use that word," Bascomb interrupted.

"Oh, you mean it isn't a takeover?" Sands responded quickly.

"I didn't say that," said Bascomb.

"I'm aware of that, but you're mighty touchy about the word," Sands said. "In any case, I was mildly interested when I first heard about it, so I started to make inquiries, checked my files, that sort of thing. Among other things I found a backgrounder from the EBAA that indicates that nationally, and I quote, 'the number of small eye banks is slowly declining' and 'the trend is moving toward more eye banks becoming larger,' end quote.

"So what seems to be happening here is symptomatic of a national trend, and that's a good enough peg for me to do a major story for the Life Styles and Health section we run every Saturday. That's what I'm preparing for tomorrow's paper.

"What I have so far is some historical material about both eye banks, statistics relative to procurement of eyes, and the numbers on transplants. A source told me that a representative from the Zenith Eye Bank came to Metropolis on an official visit to sound out your board president about taking over the Zenith operation. My source told me that your board by a unanimous vote authorized Lynn Heywood to pursue the matter, and therefore a meeting has been scheduled between representatives of the two eye banks.

"So, I'm calling to confirm all this and to flesh out more details for the story that will run in tomorrow's *Dispatch.* By the way, I've been giving serious thought about running that Susie Loughlin feature, probably some time next week. Nothing firm, mind you, but a lot depends on this takeover story and the kind of cooperation I get on it from you people here and those in Zenith."

When Sands paused, Bascomb knew she expected a response. The two subsequently conversed for several more minutes. Before hanging up, Sands asked for and received Bascomb's unlisted home telephone number.

"I may want to get back to you later tonight from the office as I write the story," Sands said. "Have a pleasant weekend."

"Yeah, you too," Bascomb replied.

A TALE OF TWO EYE BANKS* (C)

After staring at the wall for 20 minutes, Bascomb called Dr. Binder's office and was informed by the answering machine that Dr. Binder was out of town until Monday, but in an emergency the caller should contact Dr. Pantel. Bascomb then called Dr. Kover, and his answering machine provided the same message. Bascomb went home to dinner and at 7 p.m. phoned Sands at the *Dispatch*.

"About that story you're writing, I can't confirm it but I would like to correct some of the details you now have," Bascomb said. "However, I want your assurance that you won't use my name or identify me in any way."

"Of course," said Sands. "I can understand your position."

"Good. Now, first of all, Lynn was approached by two representatives from the Zenith board, but it was an unofficial approach. Nothing was said about a takeover. A majority of our board, but not the whole board, authorized Lynn to pursue the matter. A meeting between representatives of the two boards has been set, but I do not know where it is being held."

"When is it being held?" Sands asked.

---

*This case is an amalgam of events and situations involving eye banks and personnel at various times and locations. All names, places, and dates in this case are disguised.

"I can't comment on that," Bascomb replied.

"Who were the two representatives from Zenith who first approached Heywood?"

"I can't comment on that," Bascomb said.

"If all this isn't to be classified as a takeover, then what is it?" Sands asked.

"Look," Bascomb said, "I've said more than I should, and that's all I know. I hope you appreciate my position."

"Don't worry, John," replied Sands. "I do understand your position and will be careful. I appreciate your help."

Bascomb slept fitfully that night and was at the front door early Saturday morning when the *Dispatch* was delivered at 6:45. His eye quickly saw the story. It ran under the fold on the front page and continued on the first page of the Life Styles and Health section.

"The Metropolis and Zenith Eye Banks, whose laudatory work has brought the 'gift of sight' to thousands, may well be in need of a transplant themselves," read the lead. The story continued:

"Recent attempts to bring about a takeover of the Zenith Eye Bank by the Metropolis Eye Bank have been clouded by efforts to maintain secrecy.

"According to authoritative sources, two representatives from the Zenith bank visited Metropolis in recent weeks and sought to ascertain if the Metropolis bank would be interested in a possible linkage of the two banks.

"The answer from a majority of the Metropolis board, according to a staffer at that eye bank, was a clear yes. Subsequently, Lynn Heywood, executive director, was empowered to arrange a meeting between representatives of the two banks.

"That meeting continues to be a mystery. Asked when the meeting is scheduled to be held, the Metropolis staffer said, 'I can't comment on that.'

"Asked who the representatives from Zenith are,

the same staffer said, 'I can't comment on that either.'

"Efforts to secure information about the secret meeting turned up few substantive leads. Heywood and Dr. Laurie Scott, medical director of the Metropolis bank, were reported to be out of town. Dr. Pantel, founder and medical director of the Zenith Eye Bank, did not return phone calls made last night to his home and office.

"Officials of the two banks recognize the need to do something about the continued inability of the Zenith Eye Bank to procure enough eyes to meet the transplant needs of that city. They are also aware that the local situation mirrors a national problem in eye banking."

The rest of the story cited national statistics relating to eye bank procurement and transplants and similar statistics relating to the two local banks. The story ran to 14 column inches and was topped by a 36-point headline: SECRECY SURROUNDS EYE BANK TALKS. The story carried a Diane Sands by-line.

"That's what comes from answering questions," Bascomb said to his wife.

"What are you going to do about it?" she asked.

"That's a better question, to which I have no answer at the moment," Bascomb said.

Reprint for Discussion

Possibilities*

John L. Paluszek

I think we need to remind ourselves—and , of course, others—that today's public relations is based on a staggeringly simple idea.

That idea is this: People count. Their opinions count. Their feelings count. Their intelligence counts. Their culture and values count. Their working and buying decisions count. And, quite literally, their votes count—immensely.

As a result, public relations today is a lot broader, deeper, and more impactful—beneficially impactful—than many people realize.

Beneficial impact?

I know public relations people and perhaps you do, who have helped save lives, by teaching Americans the importance of using auto safety belts.

I know public relations people, and perhaps you do, who by their work have eased the pain of a factory closing through a communications program spurring economic development of the factory community.

And I know public relations professionals, and perhaps you do, who by their work have significantly increased the chances for world peace. How is it that democracy has spread like a raging firestorm around the world during the past few years? Partly because for almost 50 years the folks at the U.S. Information Agency have been telling the story of a democracy through the Voice of America, and Fulbright Scholarships, and media relations programs such as Worldnet and many other programs.

*From a talk delivered by John L. Paluszek, president, Ketchum Public Relations, at the *PR News* Gold Key Awards Banquet, New York, N.Y., June 3, 1992. Reprinted with permission of Mr. Paluszek.

In other words, public relations people are building bridges, working for consensus, and de-polarizing.

We've evolved. Harold Burson has capsulized that evolution something like this:

1   They used to tell us: "Here's the message. Go deliver it."

2   Then it became: "How should we say this?"

3   Now it's: "What should we do?"

We now improve reputations—mainly by helping to improve policy and performance relative to current expectations. But also through two-way communications, listening as well as projecting.

That, folks, is not "your father's old PR."

Management—not only of corporations and trade associations, but also of universities, hospitals, nonprofit organizations, government and yes, media organizations, too—seeks our advice on the right thing, and the best thing, to do.

That advice is increasingly related to listening better. Listening to what groups of people—"publics"—expect. What they expect *today*, not yesterday, or last year, or ten years ago. And what they may expect tomorrow.

Who invented the community advisory committee? Or the outreach-to-critics dialogue? Or the scientific advisory board?

These and many other de-polarizing, consensus-building activities came from the fertile brows of public relations people.

You could look it up, as Casey Stengel used to say.

Do we have too much influence? Only if you believe that Americans are naive. We believe that today Americans—and publics the world over—have an innate common sense and instinct for truth. So we practice with that in mind.

At the other extreme, some say we're superficial. But our involvement in virtually every major contemporary issue, and public relations growth, especially during the past ten years, would make you wonder about that.

Growth? Our work is so highly valued that the 50 top counselling firms tripled their fee income from 1984 to 1990 to $1.2 billion a year.

Do we have miscreants? About as many as other professions.

Are we advocates? Unquestionably. Advocates (but not adversaries) who respect the truth and operate in the public interest within an ethical code.

The Albatross

But we've saddled ourselves with an albatross.

The first is the notion that we have to convince top management of the value of what we do.

Nonsense.

Do you think Keith McKennon of Dow-Corning needs to be convinced? Do you think the 100 Gold Key Award winners would have achieved their responsibility and recognition without top management buy-in to public relations? Did you see the *PR News* survey last month that documented top-management appreciation of public relations?

The truth is that more and more smart top executives understand the essence of what we do. They know how important it is to build and maintain quality relationships with the groups of people who can help them, or prevent them, from accomplishing their objectives. They know that:

> Managed public relations develops quality relationships with the groups of people—the "publics"—who are important to an organization.

. . .

And now one last thought: What a great time to be in public relations! Here in America, we have a rare opportunity—no, a rare *imperative*—to build a new national agenda. As a nation, as a society, we are truly at a critical juncture—a crossroads.

Can we maintain "American Exceptionalism"? Will

we be comfortable as "the first among equals" in a new economic order? The possibilities abound.

But they'll require consensus building on an unprecedented scale—much work for public relations professionals.

And what about the global agenda?

The world came apart in the late Eighties. But the good news is that this generation of leaders has an opportunity to put it back together—the right way.

The world is arguably entering a new era of global discovery dwarfing that which began in 1492—an era of potential progress not on geography but on demography, not of exploitation but of cooperation. The possibilities are enormous.

Consider:

Five hundred years ago, the Great Explorer landed in the New World opening up all kinds of possibilities for mankind. He wrote in his journal:

"It is certain . . . that when there are such lands there should be profitable things without number; but I tarried not in any [one] harbor because I sought to see the most countries that I could."

Last month, another historic world figure, Mikhail Gorbachev, visited America and, at Fulton, Missouri (with a certain historical symmetry), outlined the possibilities of a new epoch. He said:

"Humanity is at a turning point. This is not just some ordinary stage of development, like many others in world history. . . . Today, before our eyes, and with our participation, [changes] enter their decisive, watershed phase—when all spheres of human activity—production, economics, finance, the market [the market!] politics, science, culture and the like—become integrated on a worldwide scale. . . .

"The attention, and the resources, of the world community can be focused on solving problems in non-military areas: demography, ecology, food production, energy. . . .

"This major international effort will be needed to render irreversible the shift in favor of a democratic world—and democratic for the whole of humanity, not just half of it."

Note the link between free markets and democracy.

It's Gorbachev finally buying into Friedrich von Hayek's idea that markets—groups of people—are "epistemic devices." That's just von Hayek's fancy way of saying that there's infinitely more knowledge and wisdom spread among the thousands, or millions, of people in a market than there could possibly be in any economic or political centralized-planning entity.

Add to all that the rapid developments in the European Community, U.S.–Japanese relations, the Pacific Rim and the North American trade pact, and you have a cornucopia of possibilities—and opportunities for public relations. (You may have noticed that in the last five years much public relations counselling growth has occurred overseas.)

Finally—finally—I'll close by reminding you of the school of Italian Renaissance painting called the "Sfumato School," because it has much relevance to public relations today and tomorrow.

For the few who don't *immediately* recall the "Sfumato School," it was a style of painting with unique characteristics. Sfumato artists created paintings which were focused at their center but somewhat unclear at the edges—to give the beholder's imagination something to work on. The Mona Lisa is by far the best example.

I suggest that public relations today is something like that. We do have a clear center—the commitment to developing quality relationships—but there is much for us to do, to evolve, to crystallize, at the edges of our profession.

To me that's exciting.

In fact, there's so much left undone—so much development and application of our profession ahead of us—that I'm envious of many of you here tonight. I'm envious of those with many years ahead in their careers.

You see, there are so many possibilities for public relations that, frankly, I wish that I were starting all over again.

RAPE AT BROOKE COLLEGE* (A)

Brooke College, a small, private, liberal arts college for women, was established in 1892 in the downtown section of the capital city of a northeastern state. In 1946 the college moved to a new campus on 300 wooded acres in Swanwick (pop. 10,000), 16 miles west of the capital, and in 1982 it changed its charter and enrolled its first male students. The change was initially met with protests from loyal alumnae, a sizable number of whom sent their daughters to Brooke, but in time the opposition died down. By 1992, when this case was written, 40 percent of the students were men.

The change to a coeducational institution helped enrollment. Whereas the college had been steadily dropping in enrollment prior to the change, after 1982 each year brought an increase in enrollment. Fall term figures for 1992 showed a total enrollment of 2,000 students. A total of 620 Brooke students came from the state in which the college was located, and 910 came from eight adjoining states. The remaining students came from 32 other states and from 26 foreign countries. A total of 70 percent of the student body had graduated from public schools, the remaining 30 percent from private schools. One quarter of the students had a parent who had graduated from Brooke.

---

*All names, places, and dates in this case are disguised.

The college offered degree programs of study in 15 fields and in four interdisciplinary areas. Most of the programs were in the traditional liberal arts and sciences, but the college also offered programs in education, computer science, public health, public relations, and the performing, visual, and creative arts.

The campus, which was heavily wooded on its outer fringes, contained three large classroom/science buildings; a library of 400,000 volumes; a college center housing the main administrative offices, bookstore, snack bar, and lounge; an 840-seat hall for the performing arts; the athletic center, which included a swimming pool, squash courts, basketball court, and hockey rink; riding stable; and 18 resident houses organized into six main clusters. The professional resident staff consisted of a resident life director, six resident assistants, and 30 floor advisors.

Just before closing time at 1:30 a.m. on Wednesday; September 20, a 19-year-old Brooke College sophomore named Heather Domstedder staggered into The Cedars, a bar-and-grill one-quarter mile from the Valley Road entrance to the college. Her clothes were torn and disheveled, her face was bruised, and it was clear to the bar owner that she was in a state of shock. He called the city police and she told the responding police officer she had been assaulted and raped. She refused to file charges, and no arrest was made in connection with the attack.

President Maxwell Pondexter was given the above information when he received a phone call at home at 8:00 a.m. from the college's director of security. The director informed the president that his contact at the police department told him that the victim told the police that her assailant attacked her from behind, pulled her hard by the hair, punched her, threw her to the ground, and then forced himself on her. According to the director, Domstedder had undergone an examination at Swanwick Hospital which had confirmed the rape. After being treated for bruises and shock, said the security director, Domstedder was given a ride back to the college. She refused to go to the infirmary, but instead went directly to her room.

One of the actions that President Pondexter considered taking when he got to his office was to call the regional editor of the *Gazette*, the daily newspaper published in the capital city. The *Gazette* had a circulation of 120,000, was read throughout the state, and reached 6,000 readers in Swanwick. The president did not know the regional editor personally, but the president knew that he was the editor responsible for coverage of Swanwick news in the *Gazette*.

The president thought it would help if he told the editor the steps the college had taken to prevent such incidents as the attack on Domstedder. (See Exhibit 22–1 for a letter outlining these steps.) After some thought, however, the president decided that it would probably be wiser not to call. Later that morning he and the school nurse visited with Heather Domstedder in her room; while there, the three of them talked to Domstedder's parents on the phone.

Thursday's *Gazette* carried the following story on page 1 of its second, or regional, section:

Swanwick Police Investigate Rape

Swanwick police are investigating the assault and rape of a 19-year-old Brooke College sophomore, which took place early Wednesday morning 200 yards from the college entrance on Valley Road. According to Sergeant Mort Lux, no charges have been filed and no arrests have been made in connection with the report made to the police by the victim, who underwent an examination at Swanwick Hospital after the incident.

After reading this story the president considered calling Elaine Fox, the editor of the Brooke College *Call*, the college weekly that was distributed on campus every Wednesday. This early in the semester, the president had not had a chance to have Fox in for the informal chat he had each year with the new editor. The paper had published only one issue, and as that issue had not contained any editorials, the president had no way of knowing how Fox viewed issues crucial to college students. He thought of asking Fox to stop by, asking her to be discreet in handling the story, and explaining to her the steps the college had taken to prevent such incidents, but in the end he decided not to do so. The issue of September 28 carried the following 24-point headline and story on its front page:

Brooke Sophomore Attacked and Raped

Police in Swanwick are investigating the brutal and vicious attack and rape of a 19-year-old Brooke College sophomore, which took place in the early morning hours last Wednesday.

In the attack, which occurred 200 yards from the college entrance on Valley Road, the Brookie was first beaten and assaulted.

"Her assailant," said a police department source, "attacked her from behind, pulled her hard by the hair, punched her, and then threw her to the ground and forced himself on her."

City police took the victim to Swanwick Hospital, and there she was examined and treated. Confirming that the Brookie has been raped, the hospital said she was treated for bruises and shock and later transported back to her dorm.

According to *Call* files, there were two cases of reported rape of Brooke College students last year, and two were reported the previous year, as were several cases of exhibitionism.

President Pondexter felt that Fox had not handled the story in a discreet manner, but he decided not to say anything to her nor to write a letter to the editor expressing his feelings about the way the paper had treated the incident. On October 10, the president sent the letter in Exhibit 22–1 to all Brooke College parents who had a daughter at the school.

Exhibit 22–1

Letter from President Pondexter

Office of the President
Brooke College

October 10, 1992

Dear Brooke Parents:

As many of you have perhaps heard by now, on Wednesday, September 20, at 1:30 a.m. a Brooke student was raped just off the campus grounds near the Valley Road gate.

I am writing you to ask your help in convincing your daughter that she should take all precautions necessary to assure her own safety. While we do not wish our students to be fearful of leaving their dormitories, we do want them to realize that they must exercise caution. As you know, the campus is large and heavily wooded, and it is impossible for us to provide security coverage for all of it at all times. Our security people regularly patrol the roads and walkways through the campus, but they cannot keep all the property under surveillance constantly.

Our students have been repeatedly told:

1. Not to walk or jog alone at night.
2. To be careful in the woods during the day and stay out of them at night.
3. To travel in groups of three or more at night.
4. To keep their dormitory rooms locked and not prop open exit doors.

As a matter of fact, the very week of the rape, a notice was sent to all students reporting an afternoon incidence of exhibitionism and warning them to take the above precautions.

However, some students assume that "it can't happen to me." We hope it will not. As has always been the case, our security officers and residential living staff are trying to help assure that it does not by patrolling, counseling, and speaking to students privately and in groups. But we need your help and the cooperation of the students as well.

Sincerely,

Maxwell P. Pondexter
President

RAPE AT BROOKE COLLEGE* (B)

Several months after the incident and letter described in this case, President Pondexter decided to add a director of public relations to the college staff, a decision he had been considering for some time. You are one of three finalist applicants who have been invited to the college for personal interviews. Your present job as editorial assistant of an alumni publication at a large university pays $27,500, and you have learned via your interviews that the Brooke position pays $35,000. The successful applicant will be responsible for a staff of two full-time employees and two interns. Your last interview of the day is with President Pondexter. It has been going well; you've been chatting for almost an hour now, and you think you've been making a good impression.

"I would like your opinion about a situation that took place a few months ago," President Pondexter says. He then provides you with information set forth in Part (A) of this case. "I've always felt that the best way to test professional public relations judgment is to measure it against an actual case, so I decided to ask all three of you applicants for your reactions. I'd be glad to answer any questions you may have, but I am primarily interested in knowing your professional opinion about the way I handled the situation." *Should have addressed it immediately.*

*All names, places, and dates in this case are disguised.

My Staff Is Exempt

You are the new public relations director of State University. Your president, I.M. Wright, has been advocating expanded educational opportunities for the state's Alsatian minority.

He recently created a department of Alsatian affairs and appointed a prominent Alsatian, Harry Paws, as its director.

You have arranged a reception at the president's residence to introduce Mr. Paws to public officials and the press corps.

This is your first visit to the president's residence. You are shocked to discover that the household staff consists only of Alsatians. Before the guests arrive, you suggest to President Wright that it might be wise to fill future openings with some non-Alsatians.

President Wright responds: "Don't worry about it. It's not a big issue."

In the next day's paper, a prominent columnist who attended the reception questions President Wright's sincerity. He also speculates Mr. Paws may be a hypocrite who is pleased to heel at the president's side.

President Wright phones and says: "I want you to draft a letter from me to set this do-gooder columnist straight. Build me up as a champion of the Alsatians."

You reply . . . *It appears your case may not carry as much weight had you not had a staff of all Alsatians.*

One of six hypothetical cases in an article entitled "What's Right?" The authors, Richard Truitt and Davis Young, noted that all of the ethical questions in the six cases would be discussed at the November annual national conference of the Public Relations Society of America. Truitt is managing partner, Truitt & Arnold, New York City, and Young is president, Edward Howard & Co., Cleveland.

METRO TRANSIT REVIEW COMMISSION* (A)

Nearing the end of his second consecutive two-year term as mayor of the midwestern city of Metro, Republican Mayor Karl Dorfman foresaw that the privately owned Metro Transit Company would likely become a campaign issue in the coming fall election.

Metro (pop. 120,000) was served by a bus company that had been operating at a loss for the past five years, despite increases in fares and a cost-cutting campaign. Two years ago the head of the company offered to sell it but had no takers. His latest year-end report, which received extensive media coverage, stated that the company would be forced to go out of business unless there was a turnabout in revenues or the city provided a subsidy. Neither the turnabout nor the subsidy had become a reality. Anticipating there could be campaign problems related to the transit company, the mayor decided to set up a Transit Review Commission.

Late in May, therefore, the mayor asked for and received from the Republican-dominated Common Council approval of his commission proposal. He then established a seven-member Transit Review Commission with four Republicans and three Democrats. Only one member, Tad Goodwin, head of the City Planning

---

*All names, places, and dates in this case are disguised.

Department, held a position with city government, and all were well-known citizens of Metro.

Republicans on the commission were Goodwin; John Treiber of the law firm of Treiber and Woolcut; Alan Seals, owner, Seals Toyota; and Thadeus Roosevelt, executive director, the United Way of Metro. The Democrats were Annette Jiminez, president, Jiminez Publishing; Jay Bloom, public relations director, Local 1, the Teamster's Union; and Lorraine Godlewski, director, Metro Head Start program.

The commission was charged with the task of conducting an exhaustive review of the transit situation and recommending proposals for dealing effectively with the transit problem. The mayor set a mid-December date for submission to him (and subsequently to the Common Council) of the commissioner's report and recommendation.

At its first meeting early in June, the commission elected Goodwin, 30, chairperson of the commission. The only son of Stanley Goodwin, president of Goodwin Insurance Company and one of the city's leading businessmen, Tad Goodwin had been appointed head of the City Planning Department three years ago by the mayor. A Northeastern Law School graduate, Goodwin had never practiced law. He joined the legal department of Goodwin Insurance Company after graduation and worked there for several years before taking his present position with the city. Both he and his father were registered Republicans. Stanley Goodwin, 63, was a lifelong friend of the publisher of the *Courier*, an afternoon daily. Both served on the governing board of the city's most prestigious club and lunched there every weekday.

After his election to the chairperson's position and with the concurrence of the commission members, Tad Goodwin contracted with Paula Martin Associates to handle public relations for the commission on an hourly basis, with out-of-pocket expenses at cost. The firm, formed three years ago by Martin, 28, had a number of accounts on an annual retainer basis, including its major account, the Goodwin Insurance Company. Martin also occasionally handled assignments billed either on an hourly or straight fee basis. Paula Martin, who had graduated seven years earlier from a midwestern university with a degree in public relations, worked for four years after graduation with a large Chicago public relations counseling firm as a trainee, assistant account executive, and account supervisor before opening her firm in Metro. The firm consisted of Martin, a secretary/assistant, and free-lancers hired as needed.

The Transit Review Commission also signed a $10,000 contract with Professor Joan Blanchfield, a transportation specialist on the faculty of Metro College. Dr. Blanchfield was to conduct research on private and city-run transit bodies and to submit to the commission by late November recommendations for handling the Metro transit problem. As her research assistant, Professor Blanchfield engaged Thomas McGinty, a graduate student who had worked his way through undergraduate school as a summer graphics and page-makeup replacement on the *Courier*. (Media in Metro included the *Courier*, with a circulation of 84,000; the morning *Bulletin*, circulation 54,000; two television stations; and five AM and five FM radio stations. The two papers and the electronic media were separately owned and highly competitive.

Schedule of Submissions Established

Under the terms of her agreement with the commission, Dr. Blanchfield agreed to submit to the commission chairperson a first draft of her report by October 10, to meet subsequently with the commission to discuss various aspects of the proposal, and to submit a final report by November 25. The parties to the agreement fully understood that Dr. Blanchfield's report was to serve the commission only as a working paper from which the commission would prepare the final document to be submitted to the mayor and the Common Council by December 15.

Paula Martin Associates carried out a nominal number of assignments for the commission during the summer. These consisted chiefly of press releases to the local media and guest appearances by Goodwin on Metro radio and television talk shows. Goodwin felt that matters were proceeding according to plan, and at a meeting with Martin on October 1 he told her that he expected Professor Blanchfield's first draft in the very near future. He also told Martin that he was pleased to have it come in at that time, because this would give the commissioners time to digest the report and discuss its contents.

In responding, Martin suggested that receipt of the first draft would serve as an excellent means of getting out to the public the first solid news of the commission's work. She reminded Goodwin that nothing had been reported about the commission since he was named chairperson. She recommended that a press conference be held to announce receipt of Professor Blanchfield's first draft and to have the professor available to answer media questions. She also said that it could be explained clearly that the draft was only a working paper for the commission's further deliberations. To her surprise, Goodwin said he disagreed with her suggestions.

"I'm sure I need not remind you that we are in the middle of an election campaign; therefore, this is not the proper time to air Dr. Blanchfield's first draft," said Goodwin. "I hope you can keep the media off our backs until we agree to release the report at a time of our own choosing. Is that clear?"

Because she felt it would not be wise to get into an argument with Goodwin at the time, Martin simply nodded. She thought that Goodwin was wrong, but she decided she could make her point more clearly when the professor's first draft was delivered. She therefore suggested that the two of them discuss the matter in more detail some other time, perhaps when the report was actually delivered. Goodwin made no response but changed the discussion to talk about football.

Having worked diligently throughout the closing weeks of summer, Professor Blanchfield and her assistant completed the first draft and submitted it to Goodwin the evening of October 10, five days before a scheduled October 15 meeting of the commissioners. Goodwin spent the next evening reading the 65-page report. At 4:00 p.m. on October 12, Goodwin received a telephone call from Howard Platt, public affairs reporter for the *Courier*. Platt advised Goodwin that he had learned of Professor Blanchfield's report and intended to write a story about its major provisions. Goodwin told Platt that his call came just as he was on the way to an appointment (which was not true), and he promised to call back within an hour.

"That's fine," said Platt, "so long as I get a chance to go over the essentials of Professor Blanchfield's report with you."

"Oh?" replied Goodwin. "And what if you don't?"

"Well, then I'll simply report the facts and information I have on hand: the first draft has been delivered to you, but you refuse to reveal its contents. My lead, in such circumstances, would probably go like this: 'The chairperson of the Metro Transit Review Commission, Tad Goodwin, has declined to make public a $10,000, 60-page consultant's report that recommends that the city buy and operate the Metro transit system and eliminate certain unprofitable routes. Among these, it has been learned, are Route C, serving Metro City Hospital; Route F, serving North Metro; and Route G, serving lower-income South Metro.' "

"I'm late for that appointment, Mr. Platt," Goodwin replied coldly, reflecting at the same time that Platt's facts were correct with two exceptions: the report was

65 pages long and Blanchfield did not recommend elimination of Route G. "I'll call you in an hour."

Goodwin then hung up. He called Martin's office and was informed that she was out of the city and not expected to return until late the next afternoon.

METRO TRANSIT REVIEW COMMISSION* (B)

Keeping his word to Howard Platt, Tad Goodwin called the *Courier* reporter at 5:00 p.m. on October 12. He told Platt that his original decision stood.

"Professor Blanchfield's proposal is merely a rough draft," he said. "The commission hasn't even had a chance to read it, much less review its contents. When the proper time comes, we'll give you information about the proposal, not now."

"Suit yourself, but I think you're making a mistake, Mr. Goodwin," said Platt.

"That may well be, but I don't intend to make the report public at this time," Goodwin replied. "It's not complete and, as I said, it's just a rough draft. We expect to get more information and clarification on some of the sections."

Asked when this would occur, Goodwin told Platt he could not say. He said it would depend on a meeting with the researchers, and he didn't know at this time when that meeting would take place. Although Platt did not ask him when the full commission was scheduled to meet, Goodwin volunteered the information that it would be meeting in three days. Platt thanked him and suggested that he read the next day's *Courier*. His story,

---

*All names, places, and dates in this case are disguised.

carried on page 1 of the second, or local, section of the paper on October 13, ran as follows:

Transit Review Group Won't Release Study

The Metro Transit Review Commission yesterday refused to make public a $10,000, 60-page consultant's report that suggests sweeping changes in the city's transit system.

The report was submitted to Mr. Tad Goodwin, commission chairperson, three days ago and is scheduled to be discussed at a meeting of the full commission on October 15.

Mr. Goodwin said the report would not be made public at this time "because it is incomplete and because we expect to have some of the sections clarified."

Asked when the report would be made public, Mr. Goodwin said "it depends on meetings with the researchers. I can't say when these will be held. They are definitely not scheduled at this time."

Reliable sources indicate that a major recommendation in the report is to have the city buy and operate the transit system and to eliminate certain routes which have proven unprofitable. Among the latter, it has been learned, are Route C, serving Metro City Hospital; Route F, serving North Metro; and Route G, serving lower-income South Metro.

The consultants are Professor Joan Blanchfield of Metro College and Thomas McGuane, a graduate assistant. (See editorial, page 6.)

The lead editorial in the same edition of the *Courier* ran as follows:

The People Have Right to Know

We cannot make sense of the decision of Mr. Tad Goodwin, chairperson of the Transit Review Commission, to decline to make public the report of its consultant's research study.

The commission should be aware that it wants and needs public backing, and for this reason it should not hold back news about proposals for change. If Mr. Goodwin is worried that controversy will impede final acceptance of the commission's report, he fails to understand the value that can come of full and frank discussion. And if he feels that public debate at this time will be diverting, then he does not truly recognize the public's interest and right to know.

So let's hope that Mr. Goodwin's decision to withhold news is a temporary one. If it isn't, then let's hear what the consultant, Professor Joan Blanchfield, has to say. We would also be interested in hearing what the mayor has to say about the decision of the chairperson he appointed. The commission's chairperson is doing Metro residents a disservice by withholding information of so valuable a nature.

Paula Martin, who had to leave Metro the day before to keep an appointment in another city, read the above-cited *Courier* story and editorial when she returned to her office at 5:50 p.m. on October 13. Awaiting her were several notes left by her secretary.

One note read: "Tad Goodwin called at 4:00 p.m. He

would like you to call him as soon as you return. He said it's *very* urgent."

A second note read: "Mr. Goodwin called again at 5:00 p.m. He wanted to know if you had returned and if you had received a call from his father. He said he would be in his office until 6:00 and can be reached after 7:30 at his father's house. He sounded *very* upset."

A third note read: "Joe Lightfoot (city editor of the *Bulletin*) called at 4:50. He did not leave a message but would appreciate a call from you.

The final note read: "Mr. Stanley Goodwin called at 5:10. When I told him you were out of the city but due back, he said he would appreciate it if you would call him as soon as you returned. He said he would be in his office until 6:00 and can be reached at home after 7:30."

The secretary left a note of her own: "I went home at 5:30. Good luck."

Once the Commission was formed, information could have been given to the public as to the purpose it was formed. Dates could have been released, making the public feel they are being kept abreast of what's going on.

Reprint for Discussion

Summary Report of the Independent Commission on the Los Angeles Police Department*

Warren Christopher

On March 3, 1991, Rodney King, an African-American, was brutally beaten by several Los Angeles police officers after a long and unnerving automobile chase. The event became a matter of national interest and concern after a private citizen who took a videotape of the 81-second beating made it available to a Los Angeles television station. In a matter of hours the tape was shown nationally, over and over again, focusing attention on the subject, now quite real, of excessive force.

As a result, an Independent Commission on the Los Angeles Police Department was established. Mayor Tom Bradley appointed the chairman, Warren Christopher, and six other members. Chief of Police Daryl F. Gates appointed the vice chairman, Justice John A. Arguelles, and two other members. Under the leadership of Christopher, a national public servant of unimpeachable integrity and the chairman of the largest Los Angeles law firm, the commission set to work investigating the Los Angeles Police Department. Exhibit 1 is the commission's cover letter; following is the Summary of Report of the Independent Commission on the Los Angeles Police Department.

Summary of Report

The videotaped beating of Rodney G. King by three uniformed officers of the Los Angeles Police Department, in the presence of a sergeant and with a large group of other officers standing by, galvanized public demand for evaluation and reform of police procedures involving the use of force. In the wake of the incident and the resulting wide-

*Reprinted with permission of Warren Christopher, chairman of the Independent Commission on the Los Angeles Police Department.

spread outcry, the Independent Commission on the Los Angeles Police Department was created. The Commission sought to examine all aspects of the law enforcement structure in Los Angeles that might cause or contribute to the problem of excessive force. The Report is unanimous.

The King beating raised fundamental questions about the LAPD, including:

- the apparent failure to control or discipline officers with repeated complaints of excessive force

- concerns about the LAPD's "culture" and officers' attitudes toward racial and other minorities

- the difficulties the public encounters in attempting to make complaints against LAPD officers

- the role of the LAPD leadership and civilian oversight authorities in addressing or contributing to these problems

These and related questions and concerns form the basis for the Commission's work.

Los Angeles and Its Police Force

The LAPD is headed by Police Chief Daryl Gates with an executive staff currently consisting of two assistant chiefs, five deputy chiefs, and 17 commanders. The City Charter provides that the Department is ultimately under the control and oversight of the five-member civilian Board of Police Commissioners. The Office of Operations, headed by Assistant Chief Robert Vernon, accounts for approximately 84% of the Department's personnel, including most patrol officers and detectives. The Office of Operations has 18 separate geographic areas within the City, divided among four bureaus (Central, South, West, and Valley). There are currently about 8,450 sworn police officers, augmented by more than 2,000 civilian LAPD employees.

While the overall rate of violent crime in the United States increased three and one-half times between 1960 and 1989, the rate in Los Angeles during the same period was more than twice the national average. According to 1986 data recently published by the Police Foundation, the Los Angeles police were the busiest among the officers in the nation's largest six cities. As crime rates soar, police officers must contend with more and more potential and actual violence each day. One moment officers must confront a life-threatening situation; the next they must deal with citizen problems requiring understanding and kindness. The difficulties of policing in Los Angeles are compounded by its vast geographic area and the ethnic diversity of its population. The 1990 census data reflect how enormous that diversity is: Latinos constitute 40% of the total population; Whites 37%; African-Americans 13%; and Asian/Pacific Islanders and others 10%. Of the police departments of the six largest United States cities, the LAPD has the fewest officers per resident and the fewest officers per square mile. Yet the LAPD boasts more arrests per officer than other forces. Moreover, by all accounts, the LAPD is generally efficient, sophisticated, and free of corruption.

The Problem of Excessive Force

LAPD officers exercising physical force must comply with the Department's Use of Force Policy and Guidelines, as well as California law. Both the LAPD Policy and the Penal Code require that force be reasonable; the Policy also requires that force be necessary. An officer may resort to force only where he or she faces a credible threat, and then may use only the minimum amount necessary to control the suspect.

The Commission has found that there is a significant number of LAPD officers who repetitively misuse force and persistently ignore the written policies and guidelines of the Department regarding force. The evidence obtained by the Commission shows that this group has received inadequate supervisory and management attention.

Former Assistant Chief Jesse Brewer testified that this lack of management attention and accountability is the "essence of the excessive force problem. . . . We know who the bad guys are. Reputations become well known, especially to the sergeants and then of course to lieutenants and the captains in the areas. . . . But I don't see anyone bring these people up. . . ." Assistant Chief David Dotson testified that "we have failed miserably" to hold supervisors accountable for excessive force by officers under their command. Interviews with a large number of present and former LAPD officers yield similar conclusions. Senior and rank-and-file officers generally stated that a significant number of officers tended to use force excessively, that these problem officers were well known in their divisions, that the Department's effort to control or discipline those officers were inadequate, and that their supervisors were not held accountable for excessive use of force by officers in their command.

The Commission's extensive computerized analysis of the data provided by the Department (personnel complaints, use of force reports, and reports of officer-involved shootings) shows that a significant group of problem officers poses a much higher risk of excessive force than other officers:

- Of approximately 1,800 officers against whom an allegation of excessive force or improper tactics was made from 1986 to 1990, more than 1,400 had only one or two allegations. But 183 officers had four or more allegations, 44 had six or more, 16 had eight or more, and one had 16 such allegations.

- Of nearly 6,000 officers identified as involved in use of force reports from January 1987 to March 1991, more than 4,000 had fewer than five reports each. But 63 officers had 20 or more reports each. The top 5% of the officers (ranked by number of reports) accounted for more than 20% of all reports. . . .

Blending the data disclosed even more troubling patterns. For example, in the years covered, one officer had 13 allegations of excessive force and improper tactics, 5 other complaint allegations, 28 use of force reports, and 1 shooting. Another had 6 excessive force/improper tactics allegations, 19 other complaint allegations, 10 use of force reports, and 3 shootings. A third officer had 7 excessive force/improper tactic allegations, 7 other complaint allegations, 27 use of force reports, and 1 shooting.

A review of personnel files of the 44 officers identified from the LAPD database who had six or more allegations of excessive force or improper tactics for the period 1986 through 1990 disclosed that the picture conveyed was often incomplete and at odds with contemporaneous comments appearing in complaint files. As a general matter, the performance evaluation reports for those problem officers were very positive, documenting every complimentary comment received and expressing optimism about the officer's progress in the Department. The performance evaluations generally did not give an accurate picture of the officers' disciplinary history, failing to record "sustained" complaints or to discuss their significance, and failing to assess the officer's judgment and contacts with the public in light of disturbing patterns of complaints.

The existence of a significant number of officers with an unacceptable and improper attitude regarding the use of force is supported by the Commission's extensive review of computer messages sent to and from patrol cars throughout the City over the units' Mobile Digital Terminals ("MDTs"). The Commission's staff examined 182 days of MDT transmissions selected from the period from November 1989 to March 1991. Although the vast majority of messages reviewed consisted of routine police communications, there were hundreds of improper messages, including scores in which officers talked about beating suspects: "Capture him, beat him and treat him like dirt. . . ." Officers also used the communications system to express their eagerness to be involved in shooting incidents. The transmissions also make clear that some officers enjoy the excitement of a pursuit and view it as an opportunity for violence against a fleeing suspect.

The patrol car transmissions can be monitored by a field supervisor and are stored in a database where they could be (but were not) audited. That many officers would feel free to type messages about force under such circumstances suggests a serious problem with respect to excessive force. That supervisors made no effort to monitor or control those messages evidences a significant breakdown in the Department's management responsibility.

The Commission also reviewed the LAPD's investigation and discipline of the officers involved in all 83 civil lawsuits alleging excessive or improper force by LAPD officers for the period 1986 through 1990 that resulted in a settlement or judgment of more than $15,000. A majority of cases involved clear and often egregious officer misconduct resulting in serious injury or death to the victim. The LAPD's investigation of these 83 cases was deficient in many aspects, and discipline against the officers involved was frequently light and often nonexistent.

While the precise size and identity of the problem group of officers cannot be specified without significant further investigation, its existence must be recognized and addressed. The LAPD has a number of tools to promote and enforce its policy that only reasonable and necessary force be used by officers. There are rewards and incentives such as promotions and pay upgrades. The discipline system exists to impose sanctions for misconduct. Officers can be reassigned. Supervisors can monitor and counsel officers under their command. Officers can be trained at the Police Academy and, more importantly, in the field, in the proper use of force.

The Commission believes that the Department has

not made sufficient efforts to use those tools effectively to address the significant number of officers who appear to be using force excessively and improperly. The leadership of the LAPD must send a much clearer and more effective message that excessive force will not be tolerated and that officers and their supervisors will be evaluated to an important extent by how well they abide by and advance the department's policy regarding use of force.

Racism and Bias

The problem of excessive force is aggravated by racism and bias within the LAPD. The nexus is sharply illustrated by the results of a survey recently taken by the LAPD of the attitudes of its sworn officers. The survey of 960 officers found that approximately one-quarter (24.5%) of 650 officers responding agreed that "racial bias (prejudice) on the part of officers toward minority citizens currently exists and contributes to a negative interaction between police and community." More than one-quarter (27.6%) agreed that "an officer's prejudice towards the suspect's race may lead to the use of excessive force."

The Commission's review of MDT transmissions revealed an appreciable number of disturbing and recurrent racial remarks. Some of the remarks describe minorities through animal anologies ("sounds like monkey slapping time"). Often made in the context of discussing pursuits or beating suspects, the offensive remarks cover the spectrum of racial and ethnic minorities in the City ("I would love to drive down Slauson with a flame thrower . . . we would have a barbecue"; "I almost got me a Mexican last night but he dropped the dam gun too quick, lots of wit"). The officers typing the MDT messages apparently had little concern that they would be disciplined for making such remarks. Supervisors failed to monitor the messages or to impose discipline for improper remarks and were themselves frequently the source of offensive comments when in the field.

These attitudes of prejudice and intolerance are translated into unacceptable behavior in the field. Testimony from a variety of witnesses depict the LAPD as an organization with practices and procedures that are conducive to discriminatory treatment and officer misconduct directed to members of minority groups. Witnesses repeatedly told of LAPD officers verbally harassing minorities, detaining African-American and Latino men who fit certain generalized descriptions of suspects, employing unnecessarily invasive or humiliating tactics in minority neighborhoods and using excessive force. While the Commission does not purport to adjudicate the validity of any one of these numerous complaints, the intensity and frequency of them reveal a serious problem.

Bias within the LAPD is not confined to officers' treatment of the public, but is also reflected in conduct directed to fellow officers who are members of racial or ethnic minority groups. The MDT messages and other evidence suggest that minority officers are still too frequently subjected to racist slurs and comments and to discriminatory treatment within the Department. While the relative number of officers who openly make racially derogatory comments or treat minority officers in a demeaning manner is small, their attitudes and behavior have a large impact because of the failure of supervisors to enforce vigorously and consistently the Department's policies against racism. That failure conveys to minority and non-minority officers alike the message that such conduct is in practice condoned by the Department.

The LAPD has made substantial progress in hiring minorities and women since the 1981 consent decree settling discrimination lawsuits against the Department. That effort should continue, including efforts to recruit Asians and other minorities who are not covered by the consent decree. The Department's statistics show, however, that the vast majority of minority officers are concentrated in the entry level police officer ranks in the Department. More than 80% of African-American, Latino and Asian officers hold the rank of Police Officer I–III. Many minority officers cite white dominance of managerial positions within the LAPD as one reason for the Department's continued tolerance of racially motivated language and behavior.

Bias within the LAPD is not limited to racist and ethnic prejudices but includes strongly felt bias based on gender and sexual orientation. Current LAPD policy prohibits all discrimination, including that based on sexual orientation. A tension remains, however, between the LAPD's official policy and actual practice. The Commission believes that the LAPD must act to implement fully its formal policy of nondiscrimination in the recruitment and promotion of gay and lesbian officers.

A 1987 LAPD study concluded that female officers were subjected to a double standard and subtle harassment and were not accepted as part of the working culture. As revealed in interviews of many of the officers charged with training new recruits, the problem has not abated in the last four years. Although female LAPD officers are in fact performing effectively, they are having a difficult time being accepted on a full and equal basis.

The Commission heard substantial evidence that female officers utilize a style of policing that minimizes the use of excessive force. Data examined by the Commission indicate that LAPD female officers are involved in use of excessive force at rates substantially below those of male officers. Those statistics, as confirmed by both academic studies and anecdotal evidence, also indicate that women officers perform at least as well as their male counterparts when measured by traditional standards.

The Commission believes that the Chief of Police must seek tangible ways, for example, through the use of the discipline system, to establish the principle that racism and bias based on ethnicity, gender, or sexual orientation will not be tolerated within the Department. Racism and bias cannot be eliminated without active leadership from the top. Minority and female officers must be given full and equal opportunity to assume leadership positions in the LAPD. They must be assigned on a fully nondiscriminatory basis to the more desirable, "coveted" positions and promoted on the same nondiscriminatory basis to supervisor and managerial positions.

Structural Issues

Although the City Charter assigns the Police Commission ultimate control over Department policies, its authority over the Department and the Chief of Police is illusory. Structural and operational constraints greatly weaken the Police Commission's power to hold the Chief accountable and therefore its ability to perform its management responsibilities, including effective oversight. Real power and authority reside in the Chief.

The Chief of Police is the general manager and chief administrative officer of the Police Department. The Police Commission selects the Chief from among top competitors in a civil service examination administered by the Personnel Department. Candidates from outside the Department are disadvantaged by City Charter provisions and seniority rules.

The Chief's civil service status largely protects him or her from disciplinary action or discharge by giving him a "substantial property right" in his job and declaring that he cannot be suspended or removed except for "good and sufficient cause" based upon an act or omission occurring within the prior year. In addition, recently enacted Charter Amendment 5 empowers the City Council to review and override the actions of the City's commissions, including the Police Commission.

The Police Commission's staff is headed by the Commanding Officer, Commission Operations, a sworn LAPD officer chosen by the Police Commissioners, who normally serves in that post for two to three years. Because the Police Commission depends heavily on the Commanding Officer to review information received from the Department and to identify issues, it must also rely on his willingness to criticize his superior officers. However, he lacks the requisite independence because his future transfer and promotion are at the discretion of the Chief of Police, and he is part of the Chief's command structure as well as being answerable to the Police Commission.

The Police Commission receives summaries, prepared

by the Department, of disciplinary actions against sworn officers, but cannot itself impose discipline. The summaries are brief and often late, making it impossible for the Police Commission to monitor systematically the discipline imposed by the Chief in use of force and other cases.

The Commission believes that the department should continue to be under the general oversight and control of a five-member, part-time citizen Police Commission. Commissioners' compensation should be increased substantially. They should serve a maximum of five years with staggered terms. The Police Commission's independent staff should be increased by adding civilian employees, including management auditors, computer systems data analysts, and investigators with law enforcement experience. It is vital that the Police Commission's staff be placed under the control of an independent civilian Chief of Staff, a general manager level employee.

The Chief of Police must be more responsive to the Police Commission and the City's elected leadership, but also must be protected against improper political influences. To achieve this balance, the Chief should serve a five-year term, renewable at the discretion of the Police Commission for one additional five-year term. The selection, tenure, discipline, and removal of the Chief should be exempted from existing civil service provisions. The Chief should be appointed by the Mayor, with advice from the Police Commission and the consent of the City Council after an open competition. The Police Commission should have the authority to terminate the Chief prior to the expiration of the first or second five-year term, but the final decision to terminate should require the concurrence of the Mayor and be subject to a reversal by vote of two-thirds of the City Council.

Implementation

Full implementation of this Report will require action by the Mayor, the City Council, the Police Commission, the Police Department, and ultimately the voters. To monitor the progress of reform, the City Council should require reports on implementation at six month intervals from the Mayor, the Council's own Human Resources and Labor Relations Committee, the Police Commission, and the Police Department. The Commission should reconvene in six months to assess the implementation of its recommendations and to report to the public.

Chief Gates has served the LAPD and the City 42 years, the past 13 years as Chief of Police. He has achieved a noteworthy record of public service in a stressful and demanding profession. For the reasons set forth in support of the recommendation that the Chief of Police be limited to two five-year terms, the Commission believes that commencement of a transition in that office is now appropriate. The Commission also believes that the interests of harmony and healing would be served if the Police Commission is now reconstituted with members not identified with the recent controversy involving the Chief.

More than any other factor, the attitude and actions of the leaders of the Police Department and other City agencies will determine whether the recommendations of this Report are adopted. To make genuine progress on issues relating to excessive force, racism and bias, leadership must avoid sending mixed signals. We urge those leaders to give priority to stopping the use of excessive force and curbing racism and bias and thereby to bring the LAPD to a new level of excellence and esteem throughout Los Angeles.

Exhibit 1
Cover Letter

INDEPENDENT COMMISSION
ON THE LOS ANGELES POLICE DEPARTMENT

Warren Christopher
CHAIR

John A. Arguelles
VICE CHAIR

MEMBERS
Roy A. Anderson
Willie R. Barnes
Prof. Leo F. Estrada
Mickey Kantor
Richard M. Mosk
Andrea Sheridan Ordin
John Brooks Slaughter
Robert E. Tranquada, M.D.

Gilbert T. Ray
EXECUTIVE DIRECTOR

Prof. Bryce Nelson
DIRECTOR FOR PRESS
INFORMATION

John W. Spiegel
GENERAL COUNSEL

DEPUTY GENERAL COUNSEL
Percy Anderson
Catherine A. Conway
Richard E. Drooyan
Gary A. Feess
Raymond C. Fisher
Ernest J. Getto
Lawrence B. Gotlieb
Thomas E. Holliday
Barbara J. Kelley
Louise A. LaMothe
Yolanda Orozco
Dennis M. Perluss
John B. Sherrell
Mark R. Steinberg
Brian A. Sun

July 9, 1991

TO: Mayor Tom Bradley
City Council President John Ferraro
     and Members of the City Council
Chief of Police Daryl F. Gates

Ladies and Gentlemen:

It is our privilege to present the report of the
Independent Commission on the Los Angeles Police Department.

Since our Commission began its work early in April
1991, we have conducted a comprehensive investigation into the
use of excessive force by the Los Angeles Police Department and
related issues. We have sought to examine every aspect of the
law enforcement operations and structure that might cause or
contribute to the problem. This report documents our findings
and makes recommendations for your consideration.

We have completed this report within a restricted time
frame because delay would not be in the public interest. We
would not have been able to do so without the full support and
cooperation from many areas of local government, including the
entities which each of you heads. Nor would we have been able
to do so without the unprecedented volunteer efforts of lawyers,
accountants, and other experts acknowledged in our report.

Suite 1910   400 South Hope Street   Los Angeles, California 90071-2899   Telephone (213) 622-5205   Facsimile (213) 622-7318

Exhibit 1

(Continued)

July 9, 1991 -- Page two

      We commend our recommendations to your earnest and prompt consideration. It is our conviction that, if faithfully implemented, they will help to avoid a repetition of the abhorrent Rodney King incident and others like it.

      Providence destined Los Angeles for greatness as a City. It is in your hands to help fulfill this destiny by promptly addressing the reforms recommended in this report.

                  Respectfully,

Warren Christopher
Chairman

Mickey Kantor

John A. Arguelles
Vice Chairman

Richard M. Mosk

Roy A. Anderson

Andrea Sheridan Ordin

Willie R. Barnes

John Brooks Slaughter

Leo F. Estrada

Robert E. Tranquada

cc: District Attorney Ira Reiner
     City Attorney James K. Hahn
     Members of the Police Commission

PR REPLACEMENT AT METRO COLLEGE* (A)

You are Steve Cady, a 27-year-old Army public information specialist who completed his service commitment several months ago. You have an undergraduate degree from a leading public relations program. You spent one year as a general assignment reporter on a large city daily before going into the service.

Upon receiving your honorable discharge you were interviewed for several public relations positions. You consider yourself fortunate in securing a job in public relations at Metro College as assistant to the director of public relations, Donald Bock.

You were interviewed for the vacancy on Bock's staff last month when you met with Bock, President Angus Euclid, other officials of the college, and members of Bock's department. Two weeks ago you received a letter from the president offering you the position, effective January 1, and you quickly sent in your acceptance.

You are looking forward to the job with anticipation. Metro College seems an ideal spot for you at this moment in your career. Located in the midwestern city of Metro, the college is essentially an undergraduate, coeducational, private institution of 2,100 students,

---

*All names, places, and dates in this case are disguised.

with a limited number of master's degree programs. Metro College has been in existence 45 years. It draws 40 percent of its students from a radius of 40 miles around Metro and the remaining 60 percent chiefly from four neighboring midwestern states. The college offers 30 major degree programs, including an Urban Affairs program and some unusual "career-oriented" majors. It is on a very modern campus built in the past ten years by virtue of two successful fund drives by Metro industries and residents. Although its varsity sports program is limited, Metro maintains one of the country's finest small college basketball teams and numbers among its alumni three Little All-American basketball players.

Of the 2,100 students at Metro, approximately 58 percent are male, 8 percent African-American, 40 percent Catholic, 40 percent Protestant, and 20 percent Jewish. Approximately 70 percent of the residents of Metro are Catholic, and 5 percent are African-American.

Exhibit 26–1 is an abbreviated organization chart showing some of the key people on the staff and faculty of Metro College.

Yesterday, Tuesday, December 10, you received an unexpected and rather shocking telephone call from President Euclid. He informed you that Don Bock had been seriously injured in a two-car crash, and it was uncertain when, if ever, he would be able to return to work.

"I know you didn't expect to come to work for us until January 1," said the president, "but I'd like you to get here immediately and take over Don's work until we know more about his condition."

"Of course," you said. "I'll be there tomorrow."

"Good," said the president. "I'll get out an internal memorandum advising everyone that you will be handling Don's work for the time being. I'm very grateful."

It is now 9:00 a.m. on December 11, and you are seated at Bock's desk. His secretary has set in front of you various memoranda, messages, letters, etc., which were in Bock's action file or had arrived with yesterday's mail.

Bock's secretary had also advised you that the president's weekly general staff meeting is scheduled for 10:30, and you're expected to attend.

You are to indicate your reactions to each of the memoranda, messages, letters, etc.; your reasons for said reactions; and what you propose to do about each item.

Bock had scribbled the following note to himself at the bottom of the memorandum in Exhibit 26–2: "Make sure to get out a return memo to Johnson giving my decision by December 12 at the latest."

Bock had scribbled the following note to himself at the bottom of the letter in Exhibit 26–4: "Damn! Must talk to Rose at the earliest opportunity."

Bock had scribbled the following at the bottom of the letter in Exhibit 26–5: "At long last, a major media break! Make sure to give Travis the royal treatment."

Bock had scribbled the following note at the bottom of the memorandum in Exhibit 26–8: "This is a tough one, but they're all tough. Must make sure I get to this by Friday, December 13."

Exhibit 26-1
**Organization Chart
for Metro College**

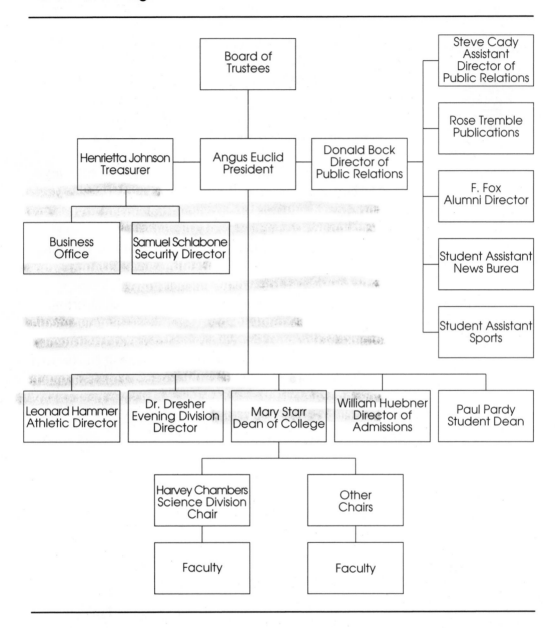

Exhibit 26–2
Memorandum

November 26, 19—

From: Henrietta Johnson, Treasurer
To: Don Bock
Subject: Revised equipment budget request

As you know, we delayed the decision on approval of equipment requests for the current academic year in order to ascertain the effect of actual fall enrollment on the college budget.

Fall enrollment figures, which have now been tabulated, indicate that we will be $75,000 short of anticipated tuition income. The president has therefore decided that all equipment requests should be trimmed accordingly.

You have submitted the following requests:

Item	Number	Description	Approximate Cost
1	1	Copier	$1,400
2	~~1 Cancel~~	~~Laser Printer~~	~~$1,600~~

The president has suggested that you decide which one of the above two budget items you prefer. We are trying to put the budget into final form before mid-December, and I would appreciate your decision by December 12.

Exhibit 26–3
Telephone Message

From: Ted Baxter, Sunday editor of the *Courier* and *Call-Bulletin*
Time: 10:00 a.m., Tuesday, December 10

Message: Mr. Baxter said that the long feature you sent in last week looks very good to him. He's scheduling it for this Sunday's entertainment section. He needs identification of the people in the three pics that accompanied the story and would appreciate it if you got back to him before noon on Wednesday, because he has a deadline to meet.

Ask the secretary to take care of this.

Exhibit 26–4
Letter

23 Wills Drive
Metro, State
November 28, 19—

Mr. Donald Bock
Director of Public Relations
Metro College
Metro, State

Dear Mr. Bock:

I am writing this at home tonight following the staff meeting you held today, at which you informed us that you have hired a young man named Steve Cady to be Assistant Director of Public Relations.

As you know, I have been a loyal member of the staff of this college for the past 12 years, and I have always felt that hard work and loyalty will be rewarded by those in the position to make such reward. I must speak frankly and say that I was shocked to learn that no consideration was given to those of us on the staff when it was decided to establish a new position in the department.

I know that I have only a high-school diploma, but I am sure you are aware that I have now accumulated 68 hours toward my Metro degree and that I have been in charge of college publications for the past eight years. I had hoped that when the opportunity arose for promotion to a new position, due consideration would be given to the aforementioned facts. For the sake of the college, I hope that the active role I have taken in the past two years in the Metro Women's Liberation Movement had not been held against me when various people were being considered for the new position.

When the opportunity arises, I hope you will allow me to present my case to you. I also hope it is not too late to alter the decision that has been announced. If I do not hear from you by Friday, December 6, I shall assume that the decision regarding young Mr. Cady is final. In such case I would like you to consider the week of December 9 my last week of service with your department.

Sincerely yours,

Ms. Rose Tremble

Call Rose see if you can set up an appt to talk to her.

Exhibit 26-5
Letter

TIME, Inc.
23 North Wacker Drive
Chicago, Illinois

December 3, 19—

Mr. Donald Bock
Director of Public Relations
Metro College
Metro, State

Dear Mr. Bock:

I'm very glad we've been able to firm up the visit to your campus of Peter Travis, one of our bureau men, and his research assistant.

As I advised you on the phone, we're preparing a cover story on today's college scene. We're trying to cover the entire college spectrum, ranging from large urban universities to small, church-affiliated colleges. Metro will be one of ten institutions that we intend to treat in some depth as being representative of the broad middle group of private colleges.

Travis and his assistant will be arriving on December 12 and staying at the Metro Sheraton. He'll get in touch with you shortly after arrival; you can expect him to stay in Metro for several days. We appreciate your cooperation.

Sincerely yours,

Rachel Dorris
Chief of Bureau

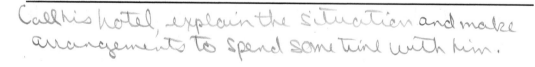

Call his hotel, explain the situation and make arrangements to spend some time with him.

Exhibit 26–6
Telephone Message

From: Sam Schlabone
Time: 4:30 p.m., December 10

Message: Mr. Schlabone said he's learned through his contacts that the sheriff's department, the city police, and the state police have a dozen John Doe warrants and will be making a pre-dawn drug bust on Durham Hall [a men's dorm with 110 residents] at 4:00 a.m., December 12. Schlabone wants you to know that the president has been informed of the bust. Schlabone said there is no way he can head off the police. He seemed very agitated.

Prepare a statement for the press.

Exhibit 26–7
Memorandum

December 9, 19—

From: Dr. Harvey Chambers
To: Donald Bock
Subject: Publicity for Dr. Reid

Dr. Reid received some exciting news today. He's been invited to deliver a paper at the annual meeting of the East Asian Studies Conference in East Lansing, Michigan, on February 14. Dr. Reid's papers will describe the 10-year study he's completed on the East Asian titmouse. We in the division think this would be of real interest to readers of the Metro *Courier*. I hope you will have one of your people follow through on this.

Schedule to cover at a later date.

Exhibit 26-8

Memorandum

December 6, 19—

From: Angus Euclid

To: Don Bock

Subject: Board of Trustees Action on Contraceptive Request

As you know, the Executive Committee of Student Government met with me last month to submit a request that we dispense through the Student Health Center a full range of birth control information and birth control devices. I promised to submit this request to the Board of Trustees, and in turn the committee agreed to say nothing publicly, pending action by the Board of Trustees.

The board is scheduled to meet here on campus Wednesday, December 18, and I shall submit the student request at that meeting. I have no way of judging at this time what the board's decision will be, but I feel we should be prepared in advance for steps we shall take regardless of whether the decision is positive or negative.

I would therefore appreciate hearing from you on how you would handle this rather delicate matter—what your office will do if the decision is positive, and what your office will do if the decision is negative.

Please get the above to me sometime this week so we can have time to discuss your proposals and suggestions.

Formulate drafts both negative and positive replies.

Exhibit 26-9
Memorandum

December 6, 19—

From: Business Office
To: Donald Bock
Subject: Status of mail account

    Ms. Johnson has asked us to evaluate the status of the various account numbers assigned to the major offices of the college and to report how each stands.

    All of your accounts, with the exception of one, seem in good order at this point. Account #415.6, Postage, now shows a deficit. You were allocated $1,150 for this account number, and you have already spent $1,250. As you know, the $1,150 has been allocated to cover your postal expenditures until June 30. *This office must take something from its account to balance the budget.*

cc: Ms. Johnson

Exhibit 26-10
Telephone Message

From: Main post office, Metro
Time: 2:00 p.m., Tuesday, December 10

Message: The main post office called and said that we've put insufficient postage on the letter from the president that we're sending out to all parents. As you know, this is the special letter we're mailing to notify parents that tuition next year will be $11,000. It also contains the supplemental material demonstrating why we have to raise tuition by $950. We sent the letter out under the regular first-class rate, but the post office says the letter is over weight and requires double the normal first-class rate. They're holding the 2,100 letters until they hear from us.

Request approval from President's office for additional funds.

Exhibit 26-11
Telephone Message

From: Paul Spellbinder
Time: 4:00 p.m., Tuesday, December 10

Message: Paul (editor of the college weekly) called to remind you that he's holding space on the front page of this week's issue of the *Clarion* for that story you promised him about the tuition increase. He wanted me to remind you that his deadline is 9:00 p.m. tomorrow. If he doesn't hear from you by then he'll probably run with a story citing "informed sources."

Call Paul, see what the story says.

Exhibit 26-12
Memorandum

From: Dean Starr
To: Don Bock
Subject: Who's Who Among Collegians

The attached seems to be a project that would provide some good exposure for the college. It doesn't seem to fit into any of the other offices of the college, so I'd like you to handle it. Keep me informed.

cc: President Euclid
Attachment: Letter from *Who's Who Among Collegians*

Exhibit 26–13
Letter

Who's Who Among Collegians, Inc.
380 Madison Avenue
New York, NY 10022

November 28, 19—

Dean Mary Starr
Metro College
Metro, State

Dear Madam:

We are instituting this year an exciting and meaningful search for the outstanding young collegians of America and are inviting your institution to take part in this new program.

Each year, we intend to select the outstanding leaders—men and women—on American college campuses. A quota has been set for each institution invited to participate in this valuable new program, said quota to be based on the number of full-time students enrolled.

Each college and university taking part in the program will be asked to nominate for *Who's Who Among Collegians* leaders who have demonstrated their excellence in academic, athletic, and extracurricular affairs. Nominations will be forwarded to us for final decision and approval. Those who survive the final judging will be enrolled in that year's honor list of America's top college students. They will also have their pictures and a short biographical sketch included in our annual volume of *Who's Who Among Collegians*.

We would appreciate learning whether or not you will officially accept this invitation to take part in our nationwide selection process. We have taken the liberty of considering that your reply will be affirmative. We are including you among the list of institutions in the program and have reserved 20 places for your nominees. We would like to suggest at this time that you try to complete your selections and send us your list of nominees with pictures and short biographical sketches by December 13.

Sincerely,

John Paul Jones
President

Call and inform them we are honored but unable to participate this year due to unforseen circumstances,

PR REPLACEMENT AT METRO COLLEGE* (B)

After reading the memoranda, telephone messages, and letters that you (Steve Cady) found on Bock's desk when you reported to work at 9:00 a.m. on December 11, you decided to take immediate action in regard to some of the material. This delayed you to the extent that you were 15 minutes late for the president's general staff meeting, and it was with some embarrassment that you tried to slip into a seat at 10:45. The president, however, spotted your entrance and cut short his remarks to welcome you to the group.

"This is Steve Cady," he told the 20 members of the general staff. "We all know and are sorry about Don Bock's unfortunate accident, and I know I speak for all of you when I wish him a speedy recovery. Meanwhile, however, I think we're extremely fortunate in having with us, two weeks earlier than expected, the young man who will be serving as Don's assistant. As I told all of you in the memo I sent around yesterday, Steve will be handling Don's work until we learn more about the extent of Don's incapacity. I appreciate the fact that you've joined us at such short notice, Steve, and I know you will receive full cooperation from everyone on the staff. Welcome to Metro, Steve."

---

*All names, places, and dates in this case are disguised.

You acknowledged the president's remarks with a nod, and the meeting proceeded. As it moved along from one subject to another, you took notes of the discussion with special care to note items and issues that seemed to fall within your jurisdiction. You had hoped to make a quick exit at the end of the meeting, but when it adjourned at noon the president made a special point of inviting you to lunch. Thus you didn't get back to your desk until 2:00 p.m. Awaiting you were another set of messages and the morning's mail. You spread them out with the notes you had taken at the morning's meeting.

You are to indicate your reactions to each of the messages, memoranda, letters, notes from the meeting, etc.; your reasons for said reactions; and what you propose to do about each item.

Notes from Morning General Staff Meeting

President spoke briefly—seemed almost as an afterthought—about student problems today. Mentioned as one of them the problem of drugs on campus . . . said this is a problem on all campuses, and he assumes ours is not much different from other campuses . . . suggested we all keep this in perspective and don't overreact about occasional busts and things like that . . . didn't mention anything about a specific bust . . . reaction on the part of the group was one of mild interest, nothing more. *Find out what schools drug policy is, inform the public.*

Hammer (director of athletics?) said the last black basketball player on the varsity team resigned yesterday and gave as his reason alleged racism on the part of Coach Norville Fletcher . . . big game Friday against arch-rival Salem College. He expects Black Student Union to be picketing our field house . . . I have lots of questions about this; must check with Hammer and

Fletcher soon, get details about the situation ... what about coverage by local paper and school paper? *Contact EEOC representative of the school,*

Director of Admissions (Huebner?) reported what was taken to be encouraging news ... under the newly instituted guaranteed early admissions program, the college currently has acceptance for next fall from 540 incoming students. Last year's total freshman class was 760. *School needs a program to encourage enrollment.*

Henrietta Johnson reminded the group that budget request forms were distributed some weeks ago and that all budgets for the academic year, which starts July 1, are due back in her office this coming Friday. *See if you can arrange an extention*

Hammer announced that all teams invited to play in the annual Metro Holiday Basketball Tournament to be held on campus January 2–3 had accepted invitations. He said that Bock was supposed to have submitted to him by today the text for the citation to be given to the coach of the New York Knickerbockers, who is being inducted into the Metro Hall of Fame at the final game. It was assumed that Bock hadn't submitted the text, and it was agreed that I would write it today so that the citation could be sent to the printers in time for the presentation. *Get bio on coach to submit citation,*

Above item reminded Euclid that the statewide Friends of the United Nations are holding their annual meeting on campus December 27–28. He's supposed to welcome them at 10:00 a.m., December 27, in Lawrence Auditorium with a five-minute address. Euclid said that he assumes that Cady will write an appropriate address for him and have it on his desk Thursday. Everyone laughed. Big joke! *Talk to Euclid, let him know you will review his draft.*

Business manager said that faculty will take off for Christmas intersession right after they give exams, but we are to remind staff people working for us—secretaries, clerks, etc.—that they're off from 12 noon December 24 until 8:30 a.m. December 26 and from 12 noon December 31 until 8:30 a.m. January 2. *Memo circulated to affected workers.*

Business manager said that the only parking lots to be kept open and clear of snow during Christmas intersession period will be lots A, B, and F. *Memo circulated*

. . . .

A Visit and a Telephone Call

About 2:45 p.m., as you were reading, reflecting about taking action on the items on your desk, your secretary announced that Chuck Wilson of the Black Student Union was here to see you. You told her to show him in; when he entered you introduced yourself and asked him to have a seat.

"I guess you want to talk about the conference you're holding," you said. "Well . . ."

The intercom buzzed. Your secretary said it was Michelle Watts of the *Bulletin*, and you told her to put the call through. You explained to Watts that you were Bock's new assistant and had come on the job two weeks early because of Bock's accident.

"Sorry to make life rough for you the first day on the job, but we've learned you've got a hot potato on your hands, and the city editor suggested I do a story about it," said Watts.

"Oh," you said. "What's that?"

"We understand that your student government has requested that the college start offering through your Student Health Service birth control information and contraceptives for all students who ask for them," said

Watts. "This is the sort of story that is sure to interest our readers, so I'm checking it out with you."

Pick up the conversation at this point. When you are finished, you should continue the conversation you were having with Chuck Wilson.

Right now I ~~have no comment~~ cannot confirm that, however let me call you back as soon as I get a confirmation.

Chuck, Give me as much information as you have, a list of all the students and faculty involved so a complete investigation may be conducted by our EEOC representative.

(oops)

Exhibit 27–1
Telephone Message

From: Chuck Wilson, Minister of Information, Black Student Union
Time: 11:00 a.m., Wednesday, December 11

Message: He'll be in to see you at 3:00 p.m. today to talk to you about coverage for the one-day statewide conference of Black Student Unions, which our BSU group is hosting this year for the first time. Said he's particularly interested in getting coverage of the opening speech, which is being given at 10:00 a.m., December 27, in Lawrence Auditorium. *I'll be more than happy to give my support.*

Exhibit 27–2
Memorandum

December 9, 19—

From: Dean Starr
To: Don Bock
Subject: Who's Who Among Collegians

My secretary reminds me that I sent you a memo on December 2 with an attached letter from Who's Who Among Collegians, Inc., and asked you to handle it. If I recall correctly, they gave us some sort of deadline, so I'm wondering what action you've taken or what your recommendation is. Please let me hear from you soonest.

cc: President Euclid

recommend that we not participate this year.

Exhibit 27–3
Memorandum

December 6, 19—

From: Angus Euclid

To: Don Bock

Subject: Letter from Greater Metro Women's Association

How about taking care of this?

Attachment: Letter from Greater Metro Women's Association

Exhibit 27–4

Letter

GREATER METRO WOMEN'S ASSOCIATION
8134 N. Main Street
Metro, State

President
Metro College
Metro, State

Dear Sir:

We are an umbrella association for a wide variety of women's organizations in the greater Metro area. As president of the GMWA, it has been my aim this year to make GMWA a real resource to our associated members. I am therefore writing to ask the assistance and cooperation of the college in a joint venture.

Specifically, I would hope that the college would co-sponsor with GMWA a one-day course or conference dealing with the practical aspects of public relations. My thought at the moment is that this would consist of a morning session, afternoon lunch with speaker, and afternoon workshops, culminating in a final assembly devoted chiefly to questions and answers.

I thought we might schedule the proposed one-day conference for early spring. Of course, this is predicated on your interest and cooperation. I would appreciate hearing from you or a designated representative, and I hope your reply is in the affirmative.

Sincerely yours,

Ms. Agnes Morehead,
President

PS: I forgot to mention this in my letter, but we have 48 organizations affiliated with us. They represent a total membership of 1,250 women. My rough guess is that we could expect between 150 and 200 women at the conference.

Ask Rose if this is a pet project she would consider taking.

Exhibit 27–5
Memorandum

December 6, 19—

From: Paul Pardy
To: Mary Starr
Subject: Request from Gay and Lesbian Alliance

The attached letter from the Metro Gay and Lesbian Alliance seems to have been sent to me by mistake. I assume it was meant for you. By the way, do we have any policy on this sort of thing?

Attachment: Letter from Gay and Lesbian Alliance

Exhibit 27–6
Memorandum

December 6, 19—

From: Dean Starr
To: Don Bock
Subject: Request from Gay and Lesbian Alliance

As you will note, Dean Pardy has referred to me the attached letter from the Metro Gay and Lesbian Alliance, and I am taking the liberty of forwarding it to you. This is one of those things that don't seem to fit into anyone's niche of responsibility, but it does seem to have definite public relations implications. I'm sure you will have some sound ideas on how to handle it, and by all means let me know your conclusions.

Attachment: Letter from Gay and Lesbian Alliance
            Memo from Paul Pardy

Exhibit 27–7
Letter

4 Prospect Street
Metro, State

December 5, 19—

Dean
Metro College
Metro, State

Dear Sir or Madam:

I am writing to you as president of the Metro Gay and Lesbian Alliance to request use of your mini-gym for a dance we plan to hold on Friday, January 10.

We note that the college has been hospitable enough to open its doors at various times to other organizations in the city of Metro; we hope this spirit of graciousness extends to a group such as ours.

We can assure you that we are a mature and responsible organization, with a constitution. Our membership is made up of people from all walks of life, including some professional people and a couple of students on your campus newspaper.

Our organization is perfectly willing to pay any rental that the college may charge for the use of its mini-gym for one evening. We are also willing to defray the cost of any special security you may want to have on hand for the occasion. We do not feel that such security would be needed, however.

We would appreciate hearing from you at your earliest convenience. We certainly welcome the opportunity to discuss this request with you.

Sincerely yours,

Sherman Capote, President
Metro Gay and Lesbian Alliance

Contact the department of building maintenance to determine who would allow and coordinate hall/room rentals.

COUNSELING FIRMS AND AGENCIES

MARTIN ASSOCIATES PITCH HOSPITAL ACCOUNT

In the two years following the incidents described in the two Metro Transit Review Commission cases (see Cases 24 and 25), Paula Martin's public relations agency added two full-time professionals and a full-time secretary to the staff as a result of increased business. Two of the new clients were from the city of Pendleton, 50 miles south of Metro, and Martin was therefore not surprised when she received a phone call one Thursday from Thomas White, administrator of Heywood Hospital in Pendleton.

word of mouth

"Although we've never met, I've heard some very positive comments about your agency," White told Martin. "We here at Heywood have decided to retain a public relations firm, and I'm calling to inquire if you'd be interested in being included among those we're considering."

I'm sure we would be interested," said Martin, "but of course we'd want to know details before committing ourselves."

"Of course," White said. "Time in this case is very important. Would you be willing to come down here tomorrow at 10:00 to meet with us?"

After checking her calendar, Martin agreed to the meeting but asked White to fax her that morning all available material about the hospital. In about a half hour she received via fax a brochure for patients entitled "Your Hospital," produced 10 years ago; a three-page, mimeographed list of rules and regulations for non-medical employees; a mimeographed employee newsletter, last published three years ago; and a four-page, mimeographed Annual Report, dated the previous year and signed by White and directed to the Board of Trustees.

Paula Martin spent the afternoon reading the above material, making numerous phone calls to people she considered knowledgeable about Pendleton and its three hospitals, and reviewing information sent to her via fax. From these sources and from a quick visit she made to the Metro public library, Martin learned the following about the three hospitals:

Heywood

80-year-old, 300-bed voluntary hospital ... moved to its present site 30 years ago ... 100 doctors on active medical staff and total of 1,000 employees including nurses ... no interns or residents ... emergency department manned around the clock by a paid medical and nursing staff ... 20-member Board of Trustees ... accredited ... situated in West Pendleton, considered the best section of the city, right on the edge of a low-income area populated mainly by Hispanic residents ... main building, constructed in 1962, is three stories high ... a $3 million School of Nursing building, which includes classroom and living quarters for 90 nurses, completed three years ago ... complex on spacious lot of land (40 acres) sufficient for present and future parking and for expansion of buildings when and if needed.

Paxton

No interns or residents ... limited emergency room manned during the day by medical staff who are in the hospital at the time and at night on a rotating call basis among the doctors . . . oldest hospital in the city . . . situated on a small plot of land (two acres) in the middle of South Pendleton, two miles from Heywood . . . four stories high with limited parking facilities and no room for expansion . . . a friend who knows Pendleton told Martin that Paxton has long held the reputation of being the "elite" hospital of the city, even though it is now overcrowded and in need of extensive physical rehabilitation.

Borkum-Brown

No interns or residents . . . emergency department manned around the clock . . . most modern hospital in Pendleton . . . located in the middle of South Pendleton on a 20-acre plot of land across the road from Pendleton's 90-acre, two-year community college . . . accredited . . . main hospital unit is five stories high with a new three-story $2 million extended care facility adjoining the main building . . . 15-member Board of Trustees.

Martin's friend also told her that the three hospital administrators have cordial relationships and meet at intervals to coordinate activities of mutual interest. There is, he says, a certain amount of rivalry among the medical staffs, each considering itself superior to the other two. Room and other charges at all three hospitals are similar, with some slight variations. Wages for non-medical personnel are highest at Borkum-Brown, due chiefly to the fact that these employees were organized a year ago by a national union. According to Martin's friend, the union recently started a drive to organize non-medical employees at Heywood and Paxton, but it has not yet sought an election at either hospital.

Along with the material faxed by White were some

clippings of news stories from the Pendleton paper dealing with the Patterson Report.

According to these stories, Dr. Anthony Patterson, a nationally known hospital consultant, had made an extensive study of the Pendleton hospital situation. In a report issued two weeks ago, Dr. Patterson recommended that Borkum-Brown, Paxton, and Heywood merge within ten years into one hospital at the Borkum-Brown site by adding two large wings to Borkum-Brown's present plant. Dr. Patterson, according to the news stories, recommended that a proposed new Paxton Wing be completed in five years and a proposed new Heywood Wing be completed within ten years. None of the news stories reported who had sponsored the report, nor did they cite any reasons advanced by Dr. Patterson for recommending consolidation of the three hospitals. The first accounts of the Patterson Report were carried in main lead stories in the newspaper. These were followed several days later by editorials lauding the recommendations and urging their approval by the trustee boards of the three institutions. The editorials said that the merger would eliminate costly duplication of services, would provide superior medical service for the entire community, could lead to affiliation with a medical school, and many other economies.

The most recent clipping reported that the trustee boards of both Paxton and Borkum-Brown had endorsed the Patterson Report recommendations, and that it was expected that the Heywood board would meet soon to make its decision.

any truth ?

. . . .

Martin's Visit

Following her arrival in Pendleton on Friday, Paula Martin was given a tour of the facility, introduced to various department heads, and returned to White's office for a final talk. Sitting in during the interview was Charles Finney, vice president of a local bank and president of the Heywood Board of Trustees.

White—whom Martin judged to be about 60—informed her that he has been administrator of Heywood for the past 25 years. She judged from his remarks, manner of speaking, and general attitude that he was in almost total command of the hospital. He seemed definitely a no-nonsense type of person; his clean desk and crisp responses in numerous phone conversations during her interview confirmed this assessment.

"I have always felt that the most important task of a voluntary hospital is to serve the public in the most efficient manner," he stated. "In trying to achieve this goal, I've tried to have Heywood provide the best medical care and service at the lowest possible cost. I understand from my fellow administrators in Pendleton and in other cities that public relations can be of value to a hospital, but I didn't think we could afford it. Last year we set up a public relations office staffed by one of our nurses who had taken some marketing and writing courses at our Pendleton Community College, but Mr. Finney and some other board members have convinced me we need experienced public relations counseling and assistance. We have already interviewed two other agencies, one in advertising and one in marketing, but at the suggestion of good friends, we asked you to come here today. We'd like to get your thoughts on how to handle what seems to be some pressing public relations problems and also get your ideas and thoughts about future public relations programming."

White nodded to Finney, who picked up the conversation.

"Mr. White," said Finney, "has sent you news stories about the Patterson Report, so you know that the boards of Borkum-Brown and Paxton have endorsed the recommendations and that the local newspaper has also urged approval by the three hospitals. This has placed us in a very difficult position for these reasons:

"1. As a voluntary hospital, we feel we should chiefly serve the needs of our immediate community.

That community is among the Hispanic residents living near us.

"2. We have a fine location here with sufficient space for future expansion. In addition, of course, we recently completed our School of Nursing building and are quite proud of it and of the fact that it's the only school of nursing in Pendleton.

"3. Unknown to anybody except our board, Mr. White, and our chief administrators, our board recently approved a projected capital fund drive whose goal will be to build a much-needed addition to our main building and a new enlarged emergency room facility. We have been planning these two additions for the past year, have architectural plans all set, and had intended to publicly announce the drive last week. We suspended this announcement when the Patterson Report came out.

"4. We have strong reasons to suspect that Dr. Patterson's recommendations are exactly what John Stuart wanted them to be. Stuart, you see, is president of the nonprofit Pendleton Health Planning Board, and he also happens to be president of the Paxton Board of Trustees. His paid job is general manager of Pendleton Manufacturing, our largest employer. The newspaper stories have never mentioned this, but it was the Pendleton Health Planning Board that engaged Dr. Patterson to do his study, and everyone connected with Pendleton hospitals knows that Paxton has been seeking a merger with Borkum-Brown for years now.

"5. In the past two weeks we have been subjected to intense but conflicting pressures. Leading citizens—many of whom have been large contributors to all three hospitals—have called me and other Heywood trustees, urging us to endorse the Patterson proposal of merger. However, leaders among the Hispanic-American community—and I might add that this community has become increasingly militant in recent years—have strongly urged us not to merge. They predict large-scale protests if we leave our present site.

"6. Our board has not yet taken action on the recommendations of the Patterson Report, but we will make our decision at a meeting scheduled for Monday. We feel this is a very difficult decision with definite public relations ramifications, and we would appreciate your advice and counsel before making this decision."

"Could I ask two questions at this point?" Martin asked.

"By all means do so," Finney replied.

"First," Martin asked, "what is the general sentiment of your board in regard to the consolidation proposal? Second, I noticed that the news reports about the Patterson Report did not cite reasons why Dr. Patterson proposed consolidation. What are the reasons for proposing this merger, and are they in the report?

"Regarding your first point," says Finney, "I'd say that most, but certainly not all, members of our board favor rejecting the merger, but I want to assure you we have an open mind on the subject. I also want to assure you that we want your honest answer, not an answer that you think will win the public relations account for you.

"As to the reasons, they are set forth in the report. I imagine they were not mentioned in the news stories because of space limitations. In any case, they are as follows: There is a definite trend throughout the country toward an organized approach to health care. Consolidation of all three hospitals would save the community money by having one hospital complex instead of three separate hospitals. The community would avoid costly duplication of services and expensive special equipment. A single complex could provide better medical care at less cost and would more likely be able to keep up with the latest advances in the hospital field. Finally, a complex could more easily lend itself to affiliation with medical schools, bring in interns, residents, and training programs for staff people.

"I think it's important to point out that even if the

Patterson Report is accepted by all three hospital boards, it will be almost a decade before Heywood is added to the Borkum-Brown complex. Regardless of what action is taken on the merger proposal, we at Heywood recognize the need to retain a public relations agency to develop a public relations program and be responsible for its implementation."

"What do you want to do at this point?" Martin asked.

"Well, as a first step," Finney said, "we'd like to know what questions you have in mind right now. These could be about the immediate problem of the Patterson Report, about Heywood and/or the community, or perhaps about the relationship between Heywood and your agency if you are given the account. Either Mr. White or I will be glad to answer them. The only restriction I will put on you is in regard to time, so please restrict your answer to the five or six questions you consider most essential. And while you're at it, tell us exactly why you're asking each question. In that way, we'll get a good idea of how you tackle a public relations project and problem."

The two men excused themselves for 10 minutes in order to make some phone calls and give Paula Martin time to formulate her questions. When they returned, she asked six questions and explained why she was asking each one. They gave her thorough, informative answers to each question.

"We have one final request," Finney then said. "As you know, the hospital board is meeting Monday. We would like you to meet with the members at that time. We'd like you to spend the time between now and the Monday meeting developing a memorandum and presentation to the board. Part 1 should consist of your advice and counsel as to the stand we ought to take in regard to the Patterson Report and its proposed consolidation. Include your reasons for your counsel, and frame them within a public relations context. By all means be as explicit as you feel necessary, and also explain in some detail *why* you suggest the action you propose to take.

"Part 2," Finney continued, "should consist of an explanation of the public relations program you would propose for the hospital, detailing the steps you would take in carrying out the program. I expect you would want to include major short- and long-term objectives, strategies, themes, programming possibilities, media and means to be utilized, and any other points you feel appropriate. You should be prepared, of course, to answer any questions board members may want to ask."

Recognizing that her meeting with the two men was about to end, Paula Martin quickly considered the wisdom of raising at this time the matter of compensation for what she had been requested to do. In effect, she recognized, she was expected to come up with sound public relations counsel for Heywood's immediate and long-term public relations problems, and thus far no mention had been made by either White or Finney about being paid for her work.

Martin decided not to bring up the matter of compensation, figuring she would include it in her memorandum and presentation. She spent the weekend preparing the memorandum, and when she met with the Heywood board Monday she made her presentation and answered questions from the board members. It was an interesting session.

That's Not How It Works in Our Business*

You are leading the new-business presentation to a big Japanese electronics producer, and it has been going well. The company is looking for a new firm in the United States and everything you say, including details of some of your experience in appliances, seems to click.

After 45 minutes you have covered your firm's credentials, related experience, and ways of doing business. Although you're not the biggest firm the prospect will meet, you're about to present two points of distinction that certainly will help them to decide in your favor.

The first is that one of your employees, Sheree Wilks, has lived in Japan for several years and speaks the language fluently. When Sheree breaks into their native tongue at the very end, the Japanese laugh and congratulate her.

The other winning proposition is that you, the president of the firm, announce that you'll be leading the account team. You say you wouldn't have been at the presentation otherwise, because in your firm, the people who present are the people who work the business.

There are smiles all around and the clinchers seem to have made the difference. Shortly after the prospects have left, however, you get a call.

"They liked you," says Scott LaRue, the one American among the four visitors. "But they wondered if they might look at another account team. Frankly, that would make you more competitive."

You're crushed, but you do understand. The fact that both you and Sheree Wilks are women just doesn't cut it with the Japanese.

I'd work, give them my best shot and if they didn't want it, Oh well Their loss.

"Tell them that's not how it works in our business," says a furious Wilks when you tell her. And you listen carefully because you really can't cave in on a sensitive issue like this in front of one of your best workers.

On the other hand, this is business, this is your company to run, and this is a hot prospect. You know in your heart that it does often work that way in our business.

Back in your office you call LaRue and announce . . .

HARASSMENT AT CLAHAN?*

Clahan Public Relations and Advertising is a diversified public relations, advertising, and marketing agency located in a midwestern city with a population of 152,000. The agency, which is well established and has an excellent reputation, was founded 27 years ago by E. Kenneth Clahan. It is an agency known for effective, creative, and, when necessary, hard-hitting programs. Their accounts range from tourism and hospitality to corporate and nonprofit. It is *the* agency in the area.

The agency has a secretary-receptionist, two graphic designers, two writers, five account executives, three advertising buyers, one account supervisor, a vice president (Dean Clahan), a president, and currently two paid interns and an assistant account executive.

Susan Claire, 26, was delighted that she had been hired as an assistant account executive at Clahan, because she knew of its excellent reputation and felt it was a great place to launch her new career. There was an added reason for feeling lucky to have the position: it was the summer of 1992, a recession was in progress, the job market was tight, and a number of her fellow graduates were having trouble getting jobs.

---

*All names, places, and dates in this case are disguised.

Susan was several years older than the average college graduate. She had started college in another state but dropped out for a few years to work as a secretary. She then returned to college for a degree in public relations. Moving to a new city and the new job seemed like a wonderful break for her. Bright, alert, and creative, Susan Claire was a young woman with excellent manners and a friendly, open nature.

Time passed swiftly for Susan on her new job. She put in a lot of hours, but far fewer than when she was taking five, three-credit courses and working 35 hours a week to pay the bills.

In her first month at the firm, Susan became involved in two major special events. She was surprised at how much work was involved in even the simplest event and the incredible detail that each special event plans book entailed. It was easy to understand why Clahan had won its excellent reputation; they covered all the bases and every possible alternative. It was fun working in an organization like this and especially with the account supervisor, Bill Myers. Susan was amazed at how much of each project he remembered and how he was able to discuss any phase of the various projects in the office. When she talked with the account executives who headed the accounts for which she was developing special events, they confirmed that Bill carried it all in his head. But, they warned her, "Always make sure that you have everything in writing. He wants it all in black and white. He may seem friendly, but don't ever forget he's 100 percent business."

Clahan had the reputation of choosing its employees very carefully, and several of the current staff had joined the firm either as interns or as their first job. Clahan was in many ways the training ground in the area. Its alumni were in all the major agencies and most of the smaller ones. It was a professional agency and— as Mr. Clahan had himself told Susan when she was interviewed—they expected everyone to behave professionally. It was a friendly place to work, at times a bit casual but always with the priority of getting the job done well.

During the month Susan had been working at Clahan, she had gotten used to coming in on time and staying late. No one watched the clock here, but they did keep close track of the time sheets. She was in her fifth week at the firm when Dean Clahan, 35, son of and heir apparent to E. Kenneth Clahan, dropped by to question her about some of the entries she had made on her time sheet. He indicated a couple of errors and suggested ways that she could avoid them in the future.

"Don't let this bother you," he said, putting his hand lightly on one shoulder. "I'm sure you'll catch these next time."

It was a friendly conversation, one of the longest she'd had with anyone at the agency.

Just over a week later, Dean stopped by to see how things were going. Again, he was friendly and helpful. Leaning slightly against her, he looked over her shoulder at the work she was doing and at the layouts of a poster for one of the special events. After a few comments on the poster, he asked if she would care to join him for a drink after work at Ray's Place, a nearby bar.

Susan thought quickly. He was single. She was single. Ray's Place was a very public place, centrally located, a block from the office. He seemed like a nice person, but he was the boss's son, and she remembered that it was best not to mix one's professional and personal lives.

"I think I had better pass today," Susan said. "I have a lot of work to do, and I'm not at all sure when I'll be done."

"Oh, that's no problem," said Dean. "I'll wait, if you want."

When Susan suggested taking a rain check, Dean said, "Okay, I'll ask you again sometime."

Susan thought that he seemed nice enough, but it

was probably better this way. About 8:00 p.m. she was able to work through a bothersome logistical problem on a charity fair that Mrs. Clahan and the mayor's wife were chairing. She left the office and drove home, excited about the progress she was making and the opportunities available at Clahan.

Three days later Dean stopped by her cubicle again, this time to tell her that her time sheets were just fine and reminding her that profit is based on what one can do against time.

"That's the mark of a real pro: doing your best when there's not really enough time to do a job," he said. Then he added, as if it were an afterthought: "Hey, how about that rain check you promised me? What about tonight after work?"

Susan had planned to work late again because she had a deadline to meet, so she said, "I've got a lot to do, and I'll be working quite late tonight. Maybe another time would be better."

"Well," said Dean, "I've got a lot of stuff to do, too. Let me do what I have to do and then I'll check with you later."

At 7:30 p.m. Dean dropped by and renewed his invitation. Susan couldn't quite figure any way to reject it, so she said, "Okay, in 15 minutes. But just one drink, right?"

"Sure, right," said Dean, and they had their one drink when they got to Ray's Place. Susan found it pleasant to relax after a long day, making small talk centering on work at the office.

"Hey," said Dean suddenly, "let's have another, order dinner, and you'll still get home early."

"I'm afraid I can't," Susan said. "It's a nice offer, but I have some things I have to do at home. This has been pleasant, but one drink is enough." Dean protested but finally acquiesced.

A week went by. Susan's first special event took place and was a great success. In fact, Mr. Clahan even dropped by to congratulate her on the fine work she was doing.

"I wanted you to know that we're very pleased with your work," Clahan told Susan. "Bill Myers tells me you've done highly professional work on the first special event, and he has interesting plans for your part in other projects coming up soon. His first evaluation of you is very positive. You can be proud of it. We certainly are, so do keep up the good work."

Later that same afternoon, Dean came by and, after complimenting Susan on her work, asked, "How about stopping by at Ray's and then having dinner?"

"Sure, why not," said Susan, still elated from the elder Clahan's praise. "How about 6:30?" Dean said that would be fine and told her he would drop by at that time.

The early evening hours at Ray's Place went by swiftly. The drinks and food were good and the conversation was casual, nothing special. They had seen some of the same movies, seemed to agree on which were good, bad, or indifferent. They found they liked the same music. After dinner, Dean suggested that they go dancing, but Susan declined. After coffee, they split up and she drove home. A couple of hours later, she got a call from Dean. They talked awhile, and he suggested dancing. She declined again. He suggested coming by for a drink. Again, she declined. She said she was tired and said good night.

The following night there was another similar call at about 11:00 p.m., this time with Dean suggesting that she drop over to his place, have a drink, and listen to some new CDs. Three nights later came another late call, a bit more pressing, suggesting that he could drop by her place.

Definitely troubled and uncertain by this time, Susan tried to take stock of the situation. If it were just any guy, she thought, she would have said "bug off," but how do you say this to the boss's son and ignore the fact that this was a recession? Susan felt she needed some advice, so she decided she would mention the situation to Karen Swicki, one of the five account executives in the firm and the only other woman on the professional staff. Swicki, whom Susan judged to be in her thirties, was a divorced woman with a daughter, age six. The two women had lunched together several times, so Susan brought up the situation the next time the two did lunch.

"I don't know how to say this, but I thought I'd ask an opinion about a personal matter," Susan said. "It's in regard to Dean. He's been very helpful and quite attentive . . ."

"So I've noticed," Swicki broke in.

"Oh," said Susan.

"Look," said Swicki. "This is none of my business, but I've been through this sort of thing before at the agency. All I can say is, take care of it before it goes too far."

Swicki looked like she was going to say more, but at that point another staffer from Clahan joined them, and that ended the conversation about Dean.

It did not, however, end Dean's attention to Susan. Upset by his continued calls, Susan decided she should have a talk with her former professor, Dr. Morgan Brooks, an understanding, usually helpful woman with a world of experience to share.

They met and Susan, a bit embarrassed, said, "I really hate to bother you with this, and I should be able to handle it myself, but I don't know what to do." She told her story.

"When he comes to see you in the office, or on that one date, does he ever touch you?"

"Not exactly," said Susan.

"What do you mean, 'not exactly'? Has he ever put his hands on you?"

"No, I mean, yes, once, the first time when he touched me lightly on one shoulder," said Susan. "But when he drops by my cubicle, which is every day now, he seems to make a point of looking at my work and moving in very close, and I haven't done anything to encourage him."

"Does his body touch you when he leans over?"

"Yes, just a little the first time, but a lot more lately," Susan said.

"In my opinion," said Dr. Brooks, "this is a clear case of sexual harassment. Dean is not just another guy, he's Clahan's son, the heir apparent in the firm where you work. He's taking advantage of his position to force his attentions."

"But what can I do about it?" Susan asked.

You have to decide what you want to do. As you already know, mixing business and personal relationships just doesn't work. The question seems to be, how do you deal with this? In this state there's the State Commission on Human Rights, and of course there are the courts. You may not want to go that way, but in any case you should run through what you think are your alternatives. Mull them over, and if you want to, we'll discuss them."

The two left it at that for the time being.

Step 2: Let Dean know you are not interested in him. She should not have went out for a drink in the first place.

Step 1: Document, document, document.

Step 3: Tell Dean you feel this is harassment and if it continues you will notify your supervisor.

Step 4: Act on it if necessary.

HILL AND KNOWLTON AND CITIZENS FOR A FREE KUWAIT

The New Account: No Time to Waste

Shortly after Saddam Hussein's Iraqi armed forces invaded Kuwait on August 2, 1990, a recently organized group, Citizens for a Free Kuwait, retained the Hill and Knowlton counseling firm to represent them. The contract letter was signed on August 20 by Robert K. Gray for Hill and Knowlton (H&K) and by Dr. Hassan A. Al-Ebraheem, president of Citizens for a Free Kuwait (CFK). It stated that "as counsel, H&K will: (a) advise Client management on public affairs aspects of Client's policies and procedures; (b) develop for Client's approval and implementation, a program designed to achieve Client's communication objectives; and (c) provide professional staff services as may be required to assist Client in the implementation of its program."

An H&K executive spelled out the above generalized goals four months later as follows: "Our mission is complex in all of its parts but it is simply defined: to assist these Kuwaiti citizens from all walks of life in helping the American people to understand them and weigh the legitimacy of their cause."

As required by the Foreign Agents Registration Act (FARA), H&K registered the CFK account at the Justice Department, listing 119 executives throughout the United States working on the CFK account. Among those signing the registration papers were 20 senior vice presidents, 18 vice presidents, 19 account executives, and President and CEO Robert L. Dilenschneider. Lauri J. Fitz-Pegado, a senior vice president, was selected to be the account supervisor. A Phi Beta Kappa graduate of Vassar College, Fitz-Pegado was formerly with the U.S. Information Agency and with Gray & Co. before it was absorbed by H&K.

"Hill and Knowlton, in conducting a multi-faceted PR campaign for Kuwaiti interests that may lead the U.S. to war in the Mid-East, has assumed a role in world affairs unprecedented for a PR firm," stated *O'Dwyer's PR Services Report* in a long, detailed front-page article in its January 1991 issue. "H and K has employed a stunning variety of opinion-forming devices and techniques to help keep U.S. opinion on the side of the Kuwaitis, who demand the complete ouster of the invading forces of Iraq."

The "devices and techniques" were many and varied. They included distribution on college campuses of thousands of "Free Kuwait" T-shirts and bumper stickers; press conferences featuring reports of torture and other abuses by Iraqi forces; meetings with editorial boards of key media; a "National Prayer Day" and a "National Free Kuwait Day"; and creation and distribution of scores of video news releases. H&K also provided assistance at a congressional hearing and assisted in organizing a photo exhibit of Iraqi atrocities in Kuwait that was presented to the UN Security Council.

In its story, O'Dwyer's notes that at the bottom of each press release H&K distributed for CFK, this statement appeared: "Hill and Knowlton, Inc. Washington, D.C. has circulated this material as the international counsel for the principal noted above. Hill and Knowlton, Inc. is registered pursuant to 22 U.S.C. Sec. 612 with the Department of Justice, where its registration statement and this material are available for inspection. Registration does not indicate approval of this material by the U.S. Government."

See Exhibit 30–1 for the listing of activities H&K provided to the Justice Department for the period through November 10, 1990. According to its filing with the Justice Department, reported *O'Dwyer's,* CFK paid $5,640,000 to H&K ($2.9 million in fees, $2.7 million in expenses) in the first 90 days through November 10. A new contract was reportedly signed November 1 for a six-month period.

"Despite all the PR on behalf of the overrun country," stated *O'Dwyer's,* January 1991, "the U.S. public remains deeply divided over whether American blood should be spilled to restore Kuwait to its former rulers.

"A *New York Times*/CBS News poll in December showed that 48 percent of Americans want the President to wait before taking any action if Iraq does not withdraw by Jan. 15, while 45 percent favor taking of action."

One event at which H&K provided assistance on behalf of CFK was a hearing held by the congressional Human Rights Caucus on October 10, 1990. Cochairmen of the caucus were Representative Tom Lantos (D) of California and Representative John E. Porter (R) of Illinois. The most riveting and shocking testimony was given by a 15-year-old Kuwaiti girl who identified herself as "Nayirah." She tearfully told the caucus, "I just came out of Kuwait. While I was there, I saw the Iraqi soldiers come into the hospital with guns. They took the babies out of the incubators, took the incubators, and left the children to die on the cold floor. It was horrifying." (In the press release distributed after the testimony, "the babies" was cited as "15 babies." In arranging for Nayirah's appearance, H&K provided media training for her and shot a video news release of her testimony.)

President Bush, who reportedly watched Nayirah's testimony on CNN, brought up her story in at least 10 subsequent speeches, telling one group that Iraqis "scattered the babies like firewood." In debate in Con-

[handwritten margin note: any proof of her story?]

[handwritten margin note: VW to Cadillic]

gress over the war resolution, six senators cited the incubator charge as one reason for support of the war.

On November 29, 1990, the UN Security Council approved a resolution authorizing the use of force if Iraq did not withdraw from Kuwait by January 15, 1991. On January 12, both houses of Congress approved the use of force if Iraq did not withdraw from Kuwait. When withdrawal did not take place, Operation Desert Storm began with the Allied air attack on Iraq on January 16. During the period February 23–27, U.S.-led coalition forces retook Kuwait, and the war ended with the cease-fire on February 28, 1991.

The Postwar Reverberations

The chief executive officer at H&K during the period in which the agency handled the CRK account was Robert Dilenschneider, but in September 1991 he was succeeded by Thomas Eidson. Although the CFK account had been terminated at the end of the Persian Gulf war, H&K's new president and CEO found the agency faced with reverberations concerning the Kuwait account a few months after he took over as CEO.

On the first anniversary of the Persian Gulf war, readers of the *New York Times (NYT)* were asked, "Remember Nayirah, Witness for Kuwait?" This was the headline over an op ed page article on Monday, January 6, 1992. The article, written by John R. MacArthur, publisher of *Harper's Magazine* and author of an upcoming book entitled *Second Front: Censorship and Propaganda in the Gulf War,* recapped Nayirah's assertions about babies being taken from incubators and left on the cold floor to die.

After noting that the congressional Human Rights Caucus cochairmen had explained that Nayirah's identity would be kept secret to protect her family from reprisal in occupied Kuwait, MacArthur wrote: "There was a better reason to protect her from exposure: Nayirah, her real name, is the daughter of the Kuwaiti Ambassador to the U.S., Saud Nasir al-Sabah. Such a pertinent fact might have led to impertinent demands for proof of Nayirah's whereabouts in August and September of 1990, when she said she witnessed the atrocities, as well as corroboration of her charges. The Kuwaiti Embassy has rebuffed my efforts to interview Nayirah."

Asking the rhetorical question of what made Nayirah so believable that no one at the caucus took the trouble to check out her story, MacArthur stated that one reason might lie in how she came to the attention of Congressmen.

"Both Congressmen have a close relationship with Hill and Knowlton, the public relations firm hired by Citizens for a Free Kuwait, the Kuwaiti-financed group that lobbied Congress for military intervention," MacArthur continued, then stated that H&K housed the Congressional Human Rights Foundation in its Washington office and that CFK donated $50,000 to the foundation following Iraq's invasion of Kuwait.

MacArthur said that because they were not sufficiently skeptical about the incubator story, the news media and Congress deserve censure. As for Representatives Lantos and Porter, concluded MacArthur, "Their special relationship with Hill and Knowlton should prompt a Congressional investigation to find out if their actions merely constituted an obvious conflict of interest or, worse, if they knew who the tearful Nayirah really was in October 1990."

MacArthur's letter did not prompt a congressional investigation, but it brought forth prompt responses from those cited by the *Harper's* publisher, as well as the entry of others into a subsequent battle of words concerning the caucus, H&K, and CFK.

On Monday, January 6, the same day the MacArthur article ran in the *NYT*, Kuwait's ambassador to the United States issued a statement whose lead sentence read, "The implication of today's *New York Times* op ed article by John MacArthur that my daughter Nayirah somehow gave false testimony to Congress last

year is totally false." The ambassador said that Nayirah was in Kuwait at the time she stated, that her
testimony of the events she witnessed has been verified,
and that he, the ambassador, insisted that only her first
name be used because of the danger to other family
members who remained in Kuwait. "The fact that Nayirah is my daughter does not taint her eyewitness testimony and any suggestion that we tried to manipulate
the hearing is outrageous," he stated.

On Tuesday, January 7, in her regular advertising
column in *The Wall Street Journal (WSJ),* Joanne Lipman led off with this sentence: "Hill & Knowlton, the
large public relations firm, just can't seem to straighten
out the messiest problem it has ever faced: its own."
Without naming MacArthur as author, Lipman stated
that "A column on the opinion page of yesterday's *New
York Times* accused Hill & Knowlton of helping its client, Citizens for a Free Kuwait, spread false tales of
Iraqi atrocities, which all but prodded the U.S. into
war." Lipman said that H&K insists on the truth of
Nayirah's testimony, which Lipman described as "allegations . . . that Iraqi soldiers yanked hundreds of Kuwait newborns out of incubators and left them on the
floor to die." The rest of Lipman's long column recalled
H&K's work done on behalf of the National Conference
of Catholic Bishops, the Bank of Credit & Commerce
International, and the Church of Scientology. She also
cited the change in leadership at H&K and detailed
criticisms of H&K by other public relations executives.

In a January 7 three-page memorandum to H&K
staff, CEO Thomas Eidson refuted the charges made in
MacArthur's *New York Times* article. Eidson said that
the firm had used proper procedures regarding the presentation of witnesses at the caucus hearing and told
the staff that he was proud of them and the firm for work
on the account, which he said was consistent throughout
with the highest standards of the public relations profession.

One week after Lipman's column appeared in the *WSJ* and Eidson sent his memorandum to H&K staffers, the *New York Times* set forth its views in a January 15 editorial headed, "Deception on Capitol Hill." The lead sentence read: "It's plainly wrong for a member of Congress to collaborate with a public relations firm to produce knowingly deceptive testimony on an important issue. Yet Representative Tom Lantos of California has been caught doing exactly that. His behavior warrants a searching inquiry by the House Ethics Committee."

Citing that part of MacArthur's letter revealing Nayirah's identity and her testimony, the *NYT* said that the issue "is not so much the accuracy of the testimony as the identity and undisclosed bias of the witness." The editorial noted that Nayirah's testimony "was arranged by the big public relations firm of Hill and Knowlton on behalf of a client, the Kuwaiti-sponsored Citizens for a Free Kuwait, which was then pressing Congress for military intervention." The editorial noted that Representative Lantos said that the fact that Nayirah is the ambassador's daughter did not alter her credibility. "That doesn't wash," said the editorial. "Had her identity been known, her accusations surely would have faced greater skepticism and been questioned more closely."

The editorial also raised questions about what it termed "the dubious financial dealings of the House caucus system," and it said that "until recently, for example, Mr. Lantos and Mr. Porter headed the Congressional Human Rights Foundation"; the Foundation rented space in H&K's Washington office at a reduced rate; the CFK gave $50,000 to the Foundation sometime after Iraq's invasion of Kuwait; and the "Foundation has financed Caucus travel, including trips by Mr. Lantos and his wife."

Tom Eidson wasted no time in responding to the *NYT* editorial in a letter dated January 15, 1992, which appeared in the paper on January 17.

"At no time has this firm collaborated with anyone to produce knowingly deceptive testimony," Eidson wrote. He stated that Nayirah was inside Kuwait when Iraqi forces invaded and she volunteered under an assumed name to work at Al-Adan Hospital. Eidson added that this was confirmed by the U.S. Embassy in Kuwait City.

Eidson said that the charge that Iraq soldiers removed newborns from incubators was conveyed to the UN Security Council by the head of the Kuwait Red Cross, Dr. Ibraheem Behbehani. Eidson quoted Behbehani as telling the Council: "Under my supervision 120 newborn babies were buried the second week of the invasion. I, myself, buried 40 newborn babies that had been taken from their incubators by soldiers."

Stating that it was common during the Iraq occupation for many to protect their identity, Eidson added that "Nayirah's credibility should no more be questioned than if she had been a doctor or teacher."

Eidson charged MacArthur with making "spurious allegations" about H&K's assistance to the Congressional Human Rights Foundation and said he is not entitled to undermine "causes and actions with which he does not agree through character assassination and insinuation."

In concluding, Eidson said: "I would ask if fundamental journalistic principles were served when no one checked the veracity of Mr. MacArthur's allegations with anyone at our firm prior to publication of this article."

In a January 24 letter, which ran in the *NYT* on January 27, John MacArthur took issue with Eidson's comments about Dr. Ibraheem Behbehani, head of the Kuwait Red Cross. Stated MacArthur: "Surely Mr. Eidson knows that Dr. Behbehani long ago retracted most of his testimony about infant deaths at that Nov. 27, 1990 hearing. Dr. Behbehani has told Middle East Watch he can't back up the story about the 120 babies whose burial he allegedly supervised. As for the 40 newborns he said he personally buried, Dr. Behbehani admitted to ABC News, 'I can't tell you if they were taken from incubators. . . . I didn't see it.' "

··

"60 Minutes" and "20/20" Spotlight Nayirah

Two popular TV programs, "20/20" and "60 Minutes," ran segments in mid-January about CFK, H&K, and Nayirah. Commenting on the reports in its January 22 issue, *Jack O'Dwyer's Newsletter* stated that "Hill and Knowlton took a heavy shelling from ABC-TV's '20/20' and CBS-TV's '60 Minutes' for its role in promoting the Persian Gulf war."

The CBS segment, entitled "Nayirah," was narrated by Morley Safer. In his introduction, Safer told the audience that in times of war, it has been often said, the first casualty is truth. "Certain buttons," said Safer, "must be pressed to get Americans to support a war in a place millions have barely heard of." Safer said that "one image touched American hearts and minds, and that image was that of a 15-year-old Kuwaiti girl identified only as Nayirah."

The camera flashed back to the October 10 congressional Human Rights Caucus hearing and to Nayirah's tearful testimony about Iraqi soldiers taking babies out of incubators and leaving them to die on the cold floor. Citing an Amnesty International report claiming 312 babies were killed when Iraqi troops pulled them from their incubators, Safer then stated that "an embarrassed Amnesty retracted its report." Andrew Whitley of Middle East Watch, on camera, said he agreed there were Iraq atrocities, but no evidence was found of the killing of babies taken out of incubators.

After stating that Nayirah was no ordinary witness, Safer cited her real identity and said it was revealed by John MacArthur while researching material for his book about the Gulf War. Representative Lantos, who was next shown being interviewed, said he never has a personal knowledge of what a witness tells the caucus.

"I haven't the faintest idea at this stage whether she (Nayirah) was telling the truth or not," he said.

In a voice-over, Safer said that one can only speculate on the effect of "the mysterious Nayirah's testimony. We can say for certain it was part of a massive campaign by the public relations firm of Hill and Knowlton to, in their words, 'Get Kuwait's story out.' Others might call it the selling of the war."

Before introducing his next interviewee, Safer said that Hill and Knowlton insisted on reading a prepared statement before answering questions. Lauri Fitz-Pegado then read the following from a TelePrompTer: "Hill and Knowlton has been accused of everything from helping to start the war against Iraq to orchestrating false testimony before a congressional committee, and I want to say as forcefully as possible these allegations are absolutely, unequivocally untrue."

Following a statement by Sheikh Saud Nasir al-Sabah (Nayirah's father and the Kuwait ambassador to the United States) that if he had wanted to lie he would not have chosen his daughter to do so, Safer in voice-over declared: "Lying was not the issue, but buying was. Hill and Knowlton was paid $10.5 million by something called the Citizens for a Free Kuwait, which Hill and Knowlton and the Kuwait ambassador claimed was separate from the government of Kuwait." In responding, the ambassador stated that "They paid that much money to a public relations firm because they are concerned citizens who happened to be in this country when the invasion took place."

Safer followed this up by stating that a document filed by CFK at the Justice Department reveals "there were a number of private contributions—$20 from a citizen in St. Louis, $1.50 from a doctor in Baltimore, $100 from Nashville—and then, at the bottom of the list, a rather large donation, $11,852,329, from the state of Kuwait."

Asked about the funding, Fitz-Pegado said that H&K's client was CFK, and the checks for the services came from CFK. "I have no information about the source of their funding," she told Safer.

The funding, said Safer, had one purpose: "to get a lethargic American public to support the intervention and a war against Iraq."

In his concluding comments, Safer said that the United States would most likely have gone to war without the testimony of Nayirah. "The troubling part of the story is the belief by the public relations industry that, with enough access, enough money, and knowing which buttons to push, war can be marketed, just like soft drinks and toothpaste," Safer said.

More Responses

In a long letter carried in the *New York Times* on January 27, 1992, Representative Lantos referred to MacArthur's op ed article of January 10 as part of the "grand campaign to rewrite the history of the Persian Gulf war." After citing a list of Saddam Hussein's violations of human rights and aggression against Kuwait and its people, he summed up MacArthur's contentions as "revisionist history."

The congressman stated that when the caucus decided to hold a hearing on Iraqi human rights abuses, it sought individuals who could provide eyewitness accounts and "among several individuals brought to our attention" was Nayirah. Representative Lantos explained and supported the reasons for not making her identity public, stated that she was a more credible witness because she was the ambassador's daughter, and said her account took a few minutes of a hearing lasting several hours.

Regarding the caucus and H&K, Representative Lantos said that "the suggestions of some special relationship with the public relations firm Hill and Knowlton is absurd." He cited hearings held on human rights abuses in other countries and said these are held "without regard to whether those countries are represented by any law firm or public relations firm."

H&K's Tom Eidson was cited at length in a multipage update in *O'Dwyer's PR Services Report* of February 1992. After recapping highlights of the "60 Minutes" segment on Nayirah, the story by *O'Dwyer*'s staffer Kevin McCauley reported key comments made by Eidson in his letter in the January 17 *NYT*. He also added information that was not in that letter, and McCauley quoted him extensively.

"All we did was to put forward a witness as requested," Eidson told the magazine. "We verified her story as much as we could during a wartime situation and we informed the Caucus of her true identity. Now this seems to be a responsible position for an agency to be in."

According to McCauley, Eidson minimized H&K's role in the Nayirah appearance and said the young woman wrote her own testimony. "It is painful for me to see H&K having dirt kicked upon it because we put forward the witness, told the identity of that witness and did nothing more," he told the magazine. McCauley also wrote that Eidson discounted the fact that CFK was funded almost entirely by the Kuwait government.

"They didn't break down where the various funding sources would come from," Eidson said. "The Citizens hired us, were running it, funding it, and I am not ashamed. Quite frankly, I'm quite proud of the straightforward, honest reporting and hard work that was done by H&K."

An April 1992 Spring Conference of the Counselors Academy of the Public Relations Society of America (PRSA) provided Eidson with another opportunity to explain his firm's handling of the CFK account. His speech, carried in the June issue of *O'Dwyer's PR Services Report,* focused on changes in society that are important to public relations professionals. Among the changes cited by Eidson was what he called "a growing emphasis on sex, scandal and superficiality among even our most respected news media.''

To illustrate his point, Eidson reviewed details about the Nayirah appearance at a hearing of the congressional Human Rights Caucus. He told his audience that H&K had recommended to her family that her real name be used, but the decision was made not to do so because she had relatives still in Kuwait and because Congressman Lantos said it was all right to use only her first name.

Eidson said Nayirah's story ''was challenged in a *NY Times* op ed piece by a man named John MacArthur,'' whose book about the Gulf War is soon to be published. Stating that he does not ''fault an author for using an op ed piece to become better known,'' Edison condemned what he called ''Mr. MacArthur's flagrant disregard of the elementary rules of accuracy and fair play.''

Eidson charged that MacArthur's article was ''rife with character assassination and insinuation,'' contained inaccurate statements, and was ''totally lacking in facts that might support his sensationalized conclusion.'' Further, said Eidson, at no time did MacArthur attempt to verify any information with the caucus, H&K, the U.S. ambassador to Kuwait, or any Kuwait government official working at the time in the Kuwait government.

Regarding the *NYT* and the *WSJ*, Eidson said one would expect the *NYT* to attempt to check facts or even provide H&K the chance for simultaneous rebuttal. The *WSJ,* contended Eidson, did ''even worse'' because it ''accepted this fervored piece of emotional journalism as fact, incorporating it into another story, again without checking the information or providing counterbalancing facts. In our view, mine specifically, both the Times and the Journal failed to meet their basic journalistic responsibilities by publishing articles without checking the facts.''

May 1992 brought to the 15,000 members of the PRSA a letter from their elected president, Rosalie A. Roberts. In it she summed up a statement sent out to the media following the "60 Minutes" January 19 segment on Nayirah.

"When '60 Minutes' stated that public relations people believe they could sell 'anything given enough money, time and access to the media,' PRSA sent a strong statement to the media, standing up against the blatant swipe Morley Safer took against all who practice public relations," the president wrote. She continued: "Our statement said, 'The role of public relations is to help organizations—even individuals and governments—exercise fully, however controversial the subject might be, their basic right to free speech.' Right or wrong, the recent news about Hill & Knowlton shows that public relations is now perceived in a strategic planning and management mode. Public relations helps all parties create relationships, even those involved in controversial issues. It is part of the American process of bringing issues and ideas to the court of public opinion."

The PRSA president said, "Hill & Knowlton has responded to questions concerning its Kuwait program and has addressed several chapters. . . . If you still have questions, I'd suggest you contact Hill & Knowlton.

John R. MacArthur's book, *Second Front: Censorship and Propaganda in the Gulf War*, was published by Hill and Wang in June 1992. In one chapter, the *Harper's* publisher dealt with Nayirah's appearance at the caucus hearing, H&K's involvement in the hearing, and the UN Council discussion in late November.

After citing Nayirah's statement about Iraqi soldiers and babies in incubators, MacArthur said that the hearing was "an unqualified success" for CFK and H&K. In the fall, MacArthur said, H&K "was busy selling it (the baby incubator story) to anyone who would listen. Following the success of the congressional Human Rights Caucus hearing, the eager press agents took their baby atrocity campaign to the eminently mediagenic locale of the United Nations Security Council chamber. . . . Rarely in the history of the U.N. had the Security Council permitted the sort of dog-and-pony show that H&K presented on November 27—via the exiled government of Kuwait—to illustrate the depredations of one country on another."

MacArthur described the audiovisual presentation by CFK/H&K as "slick and effective," and he said that the videotapes were interspersed with live witnesses, one of whom reiterated the baby incubator story.

"The next day," MacArthur continued, "the major media failed to mention Hill and Knowlton's involvement with the hearings, and their news reports converted the claims of the 'witnesses' into 'testimony.'

"Had they made inquiries, the U.N. reporters might have discovered that five of the seven witnesses at the U.N. that day—coached by the Hill and Knowlton team led by Lauri Fitz-Pegado—had used false names without saying they were doing so. Nayirah, in publicly maintaining her anonymity, had used the cover of trying to protect her family in Kuwait."

The lead review on the front page of the *NYT* Book Review section on Sunday, July 5, 1992, was a combined review of MacArthur's book and *Hotel Warriors,* a book about correspondents reporting the Persian Gulf war. Michael Janeway, dean of the Medill School of Journalism, Northwestern University, was the reviewer.

In reviewing MacArthur's treatment of the Kuwait baby incubator story, Janeway identified the author as the person "who blew the whistle on the public relations firm of Hill & Knowlton, retained by the Government of Kuwait to mobilize anti-Iraq feeling, an effort he compares to World War I propaganda about the beastly Hun's massacre of Belgian babies."

In a long paragraph detailing the main points of MacArthur's summary of Nayirah's caucus hearing appearance, Janeway noted that these points in the book were an expansion of those cited by MacArthur in his *NYT* op ed article. Summing up that section of his review, Janeway wrote: "Hill & Knowlton, the Kuwaitis and our embassy in Kuwait have all protested Mr. MacArthur's reporting. Mr. MacArthur himself agrees that the Iraqis (and Allied bombing) killed many innocent civilians, including babies in hospitals. What cannot be denied is the element of shameless deception in the public relations campaign on behalf of Kuwait (since the teenager claiming to have witnessed atrocities had other interests)."

The rest of Janeway's review dealt primarily with MacArthur's analysis and critique of the handling of the Persian Gulf war by the Pentagon public affairs department and by the media.

Epilogue: Media Reviews

During the time H&K had the CFK account and after the account terminated, public relations media and professionals expressed their views on how the account had been handled. Some of these views, cited in no particular order of importance and not to be considered a scientific representative sample of the views of the community of public relations professionals, are presented here for review and discussion.

In a long article in its January 1992 issue on H&K's handling of the CFK account, the monthly *inside PR* said it was not surprising that few competitors would comment on the record about H&K's work on the Kuwait account. "Opinion appeared to be equally divided between those who had watched the agency's troubles with a feeling of 'there but for the grace of God go I' and those who felt Hill & Knowlton had overstepped the bounds and misled the public," the magazine stated. It quoted an unnamed Washington agency head as declaring:

Whether the committee knew who she was or not, the public did not, and public opinion was crucial to the decision to go to war. As for the fact that Hill and Knowlton housed the Human Rights Foundation, that was not smart. Regardless of whether there was any impropriety, the appearance of impropriety was certainly created, and somebody should have been smart enough to see that coming.

Another unnamed Washington PR person was cited as follows: "The slogan for the whole effort was Free Kuwait. The fact is the last thing Citizens for a Free Kuwait wanted was a 'free' Kuwait. They simply wanted the old dictatorship restored. Is that misleading?"

Alfred Geduldig, consultant to the industry, commented as follows:

It seems that they have gone beyond what is fit and proper for a public relations agency by trying to draw the nation into war. The techniques Hill & Knowlton used were time-honored propaganda techniques that have been used for centuries: charges of cruelty and particularly the claim that your enemy is murdering infants. Agencies have to consider the consequences of their actions, and in this case the consequence was that America was drawn into war.

John Budd, president of the Omega Group public relations consulting firm, observed that "unfortunately, the public relations programs that make news and set the agenda are those conducted for high visibility clients by large agencies. That means these companies have a responsibility to the industry to act in an ethical fashion."

Reacting to the observation that H&K contends that all parties are entitled to professional counsel in the court of public opinion just as they are in a court of law, Budd said:

> Everyone ought to be entitled to representation, but you have to develop your own standards. If you want to be seen as the public relations equivalent of an ambulance chaser, that is your decision. Most people in this business, however, are not for rent to anyone who wants to hire them.

The monthly *inside PR* suggested that in drawing conclusions about recent high-visibility cases, public relations professionals should consider these questions:

> To what extent should every viewpoint, no matter how controversial, be entitled to representation; to what extent should PR firms be responsible for ensuring that the information they disseminate on behalf of a client is accurate and truthful; and where is the dividing line between propaganda and public relations?

At two different times in the first six months of 1992, *Jack O'Dwyer's Newsletter* ran editorial commentary critical of the name and the funding of the Kuwait account.

In its January 22 commentary following the "20/20" and "60 Minutes" programs, the weekly publication, discussing the "so-called 'Citizens for a Free Kuwait' account," said that " 'Citizens' is a false name that should never appear anyplace but in a footnote or in a parentheses. The U.S. public did not begin to know the truth about the Kuwait Government War Promotion account (the accurate name) until October of 1991— long after the war was over."

As to funding, the newsletter observed that "while H&K worked on the $11 million+ account the public was only told it was funded by a group of wealthy Kuwaitis." O'Dwyers said that months after the account was filed with FARA it was learned that the Government of Kuwait paid more than $11.8 million to the account "while 78 individuals paid $17,861, including one woman who gave $1. The $17,861 equals 15 one-hundredths of one percent of the total."

In its May 20, 1992, issue, *Jack O'Dwyer's Newsletter* editorialized about "the re-emergence of the use of 'fronts'—a hoary technique that discredits the PR industry." The weekly said that "Citizens for a Free Kuwait" was a front for the Government of Kuwait. (The newsletter also said that the " 'Coalition to Protect Communities and States' Rights,' a client of Burson-Marsteller, is a front for gambling interests who want to curtail the spread of American Indian casinos.") The technique, said the publication, "poses a severe threat to PR."

After stating that H&K argues that it didn't know that the more than $11.8 million 'Citizens' account "was 99.85% funded by the Government of Kuwait," the newsletter observed: "Plain common sense would indicate that members of coalitions should be identified as well as their contributions. If a coalition has 100 members but one of them funds 99.9% of it, the public should know this."

In its March 1992 issue, the newsletter's sister publication, *O'Dwyer's PR Services Report,* ran a long article citing critiques of H&K's handling of the Kuwait programs carried in January by "20/20" and "60 Minutes." The lead read: "Hill and Knowlton in mid-January was faced with what many PR people would regard as their worst nightmare—coverage in the same week by two of the most watched and hard-hitting TV shows."

The publication said that some thought Fitz-Pegado did "a good job" and was "forceful," while others thought she was "unyielding . . . defiant . . . arrogant." Because she was shown reading from a TelePrompTer, said the publication, some thought her credibility was "greatly compromised." Other comments cited by the publication follow:

> New York counselor Richard Weiner said that since H&K was being paid $11 million and war was at stake, it should have investigated Nayirah's claim before using it and spiked it if there was any doubt.

> A counselor in Texas who watched both shows said he feels Nayirah "was put up to it" and that H&K should have investigated but "all that H&K could hear was the sound of $11 million talking."

> Robert Irvine, of the Institute for Crisis Management, said H&K violated a major crisis rule by not checking a key fact—whether or not babies had been wantonly murdered by Iraqi soldiers as charged. "The fog of war rose a few months earlier than the American public realized," he said.

O'Dwyer's PR Services Report noted that when Fraser Seitel, former senior vice president and Director of Public Affairs at Chase Manhattan Bank, addressed the Westchester/Fairfield chapter of PRSA on January 23, H&K's PR for Kuwait was the number-one topic.

"Almost all of the 35 members present thought H&K and PR had been given a black eye by the programs. Some thought the PRSA ethics board should launch a probe to show that PR can keep its own house clean," *O'Dwyer's* states.

O'Dwyer's story on the reactions of PR professionals to the two TV news shows ended with remarks Eidson made in a telephone interview with the magazine. These are the points he made:

- H&K verified Nayirah's claim "to the very limited ability we had during the war." Dangerous conditions, he said, impeded research.

- Eidson said H&K told the congressional caucus of Nayirah's identity, and he noted that she testified under oath.

- Defending the account name, Eidson said that hundreds of U.S. and Kuwaiti college students and citizens worked on behalf of CFK, and "it was truly an across-the-board effort."

- Finally, as to the Kuwait government's providing more than 99 percent of the funds for the account, Edison said the agency was dealing with a group of "independent business people" who did not "break down what their various funding sources were."

Exhibit 30-1

H&K Describes
Kuwaiti Work to
Justice Department

"On behalf of the foreign principal, registrant provided counsel on a national media program, strategic planning and message development. Registrant assisted foreign principal in coordinating interviews with national print and broadcast media outlets and contacted media on various national programs and events including: National Free Kuwait Day, National Prayer Day, hostage letters release and visit of various Kuwaitis.

"Registrant also developed and disseminated press/information kits for distribution to the media, members of Congress, universities, local, state, and federal government officials and the general public. Registrant implemented strategy for building support for foreign principal at state and local level, contacting the offices of governors and mayors to encourage proclamations/resolutions. Registrant also contacted community, business, academic, and elected leaders to encourage participation in public rallies and to join a network of supporters for the freedom of Kuwait.

"Registrant provided general monitoring of congressional activities with regard to Persian Gulf crisis, including coverage of congressional debate, committee action, and public statements of members. Registrant contacted congressional members and staff, chiefly of leadership offices, and Senate Foreign Relations and House Foreign Affairs committees, to provide information relative to Kuwait.

Mailings Made to Congress

"Registrant drafted and disseminated mailings to Congress on foreign principal organization, background of Persian Gulf crisis, human rights issues, economic issues, and similar matters.

"Registrant arranged appointments with congressional members and staff to explain principal's viewpoint, and generally accompanied foreign principal to these meetings. Registrant responded to requests for information and assistance from members and staff of Congressional committees and caucuses.

"Registrant also provided information to Administration officials regarding foreign principal.

"Registrant assisted with electronic media services in Saudi Arabia and arranged satellite feeds and provided footage to United States media. Registrant produced media advisories to broadcast bureaus located in Saudi Arabia; assisted with the Kuwaiti People's Congress in Jeddah, and provided media support and counsel.

Many "Grassroots" Efforts

"Registrant coordinated various grassroots efforts including a National Free Kuwait Day rally at universities across the country, a National Prayer Day, a National Student Information Day and the preparation for national speaking forums. Registrant drafted, distributed and disseminated media advisories and press releases announcing Kuwait information day; National Free Kuwait Day, Organization of Women for a Free Kuwait; appearances of resistance fighters, and Islamic Art Tour promotion.

"Registrant coordinated media training workshops and presentation training workshops for foreign principal for press conferences and media interviews; monitored television broadcasts; produced nightly radio program, and coordinated media summaries for daily distribution to foreign principal."

Source: Reprinted with permission of *O'Dwyer's PR Services Report,* January 1991.

Reprint for Discussion

PR Credibility Demands Objective Ethical Rules *
Harold W. Suckenik

Public relations, if it is to gain the stature of a profession, must have a set of objective standards that the public can understand.

At present, there are only subjective standards, which leads to the regular trashing of PR in the media.

For instance, Hill and Knowlton has been criticized recently for taking on the "Citizens for a Free Kuwait," the National Conference of Catholic Bishops, and the Bank of Credit and Commerce International accounts.

Some firms said they would never represent such clients although their reasons for this remain entirely subjective, i.e., the reasons for their rejections were not publicized in advance.

This gives them the option of actually taking one of the above clients. I am making no judgment here as to whether H&K did anything wrong in representing the above clients.

Most PR people believe everyone has the right to PR but that no PR firm is required to take any particular client.

The criterion for selection is thus subjective. The PR person who has a subjective standard is not being professional since there is no way for an outsider to tell what that standard is.

Here are some objective rules that the PR industry or individual PR firms or practitioners might consider adopting.

*The article by Harold W. Suckenik is from his column on PR and Legal Issues in the July 1992 issue of *O'Dwyer's PR Services Report*. The rejoinder by Anthony Franco appeared in the September 1992 issue. Both are reprinted with permission of the publisher, Jack O'Dwyer. © 1992 by *O'Dwyer's PR Services Report*.

But they must be adopted in advance, not *ex post facto*.

?
- I will not represent a client who is controversial.

 • I will not represent a client who is not truthful with me or with the media.

 • I will not represent a client who takes a position opposed to my personal beliefs (e.g., a cigarette company).

- I do not believe that governments should propagandize their own or other citizens and therefore will not represent a domestic or foreign government.

 • I will not represent a client who wants to conceal his or her real identity.

 • I will not represent a client who does not allow me to disclose that I represent this client.

ok
- I will not represent a client whose name is misleading as to the source of funding or motivation of the group.

ok • I will not represent a client whose message is contrary to the fundamental beliefs of the U.S., e.g., is either racist, discriminatory or exclusionary.

Enforcement Needed

The above are only samples of objective ethical standards. The public is well aware of such standards that exist in the legal and medical professions.

For instance, everyone knows that all defendants have the right to legal counsel no matter what the offense. People also know that doctors are at least supposed to do "no harm."

The above professions have a responsibility beyond making money. At certain times their practitioners must do certain things that have absolutely nothing to do with money making.

In setting up objective ethical standards, PR should do research among its audiences to ensure that the problems of these audiences in dealing with PR people are faced.

For instance, if you asked reporters what they see as PR's biggest ethical problem the answer would be "availability."

Just getting PR people to come to the phone on a controversial story or getting PR people to make their clients available are the biggest problems reporters face in dealing with PR.

Oftentimes . . . the top PR person at a company is absent or "in a meeting." Lower-level staffers can only field questions.

Those listed as press contacts on releases are often not there when called. Some ethical standards for PR people that the press would write are as follows:

- I will not take on as a client someone who refuses to meet the media face-to-face.

- I will speak directly to the media myself when possible and will ensure that knowledgeable PR pros are available when I am unable to do so.

- I will list several contact names on releases both at the client and the PR firm and ensure that representatives are present.

- Neither I nor my clients will obstruct or dodge the media.

Research among the public is also needed. The problem with some of the association PR codes in existence (which are enforced almost entirely in private and which are little known to the public) is that they don't address the needs of the press and public.

Some PR people feel that the basic ethical guideline for PR is that it represents the right of an individual to have his or her story told in the forum of public opinion.

This raises the question of the numerous other times when so-called PR is involved in the dissemination of information.

What about internal communications, when a PR professional is functioning in an arena where there is no automatic check on the truthfulness of something by inquisitive media?

"PR" has expanded recently into a wide range of communications techniques that provide no opportunity for questioning by the media or anyone else—advertising, sales promotion, special events, booklets and pamphlets, to name a few of these techniques.

Since PR is such a rapidly changing field, an ongoing commission or board is probably needed to keep up with current practices and make judgments on a case-by-case basis.

· ·

Letters

I have refrained for the last several years from writing letters of this nature, but your contributing editor Harold Suckenik's article, "PR Credibility Demands Objective Rules," (July issue) prompts me to write the following.

Among his drips of wisdom about our profession, he lists what he terms "objective rules" PR practitioners should consider adopting. For the most part, Harold makes some interesting suggestions. But he leads off his list of suggestions with "I will not represent a client who is controversial."

Now, I assume that Harold is still a practicing attorney and may—and I emphasize *may*—represent a defendant or two. He says this one (along with the others) are objective ethical standards adopted by the legal and medical professions—hogwash. The legal profession represents murderers, rapists, Dr. Kavorkian ("Dr. Death") and others. Are they not controversial? If the legal profession followed what he is

asking PR people to do—not to represent the controversial—
you could kiss your profession goodbye, Harold.

I'm sorry, Harold, love-hate relationships that the legal profession so altruistically defends itself in defending the "controversial" sometimes occurs in our field, as well. My advice is to stick to legal causes affecting PR—counselor—or practice what you and your colleagues preach.

Anthony Franco, President
Anthony M. Franco, Inc., Detroit

Dear Mr. Franco:

Professions other than PR, e.g., lawyers, doctors, certified public accountants, are licensed by the state and, therefore, have their ethics legally mandated. Also, there are severe penalties for violations, e.g., disbarment.

Also, lawyers are officers of the court. For example, in New York State an attorney's signature alone is sufficient to issue a restraining notice or witness subpoena.

You have misunderstood the thrust of my article: since PR is an unlicensed profession, i.e., lacking governmental authority, it needs to have clearly articulated ethical standards that are widely accepted within the profession and generally known to those outside it.

Harold Wm. Suckenik
Contributing Editor, *O'Dwyer's PR Services Report*

A LETTER FROM PETER GANTOR*

One October morning Robin Gras, vice president of public relations for a large national organization and a former officer of the Public Relations Society of America, received the letter in Exhibit 31–1 from Peter Gantor. Gras recalled him immediately as a very sincere young man who had been a member of the Pinacle Group's public relations department several years ago and had left to take a better-paying position with a Chicago firm. After reading the letter Gras decided to think about it for a day or so and then respond to it.

*All names, places, and dates in this case are disguised.

Exhibit 31-1
**Letter from Peter
Gantor**

Brentwood and LaBella
Fernwood Towers
Los Angeles, CA 90038
(213) 859-6240

October 2, 1992

Robin Gras
Vice President, Public Relations
The Pinacle Group
Farmington, CT 06032

Dear Robin:

Greetings. It's been some time since we last communicated. Let me quickly bring you up to date.

As you can see from the letterhead, I'm now working for an advertising agency in Los Angeles. I'm a senior advertising copywriter and an all-purpose PR person. In fact, I'm here to establish a PR arm for the agency. It's a great opportunity—and one hell of a tough job. That brings me to the major reason for this letter. I need the opinion of someone in the profession I respect.

Building the PR credentials of this agency means selling public relations to clients who have thus far avoided it. It also means educating agency management (the president and the creative director). It's a frustrating task. Both individuals agree they want a PR arm for its profitability, but both also admit to knowing little or nothing about the profession. (Profession is my word, not theirs.)

The president goes a little further. He openly states he doesn't like PR and doesn't trust those involved with it. His reasons are simple: he doesn't understand it, can't explain it, doesn't know how—or if—it works, can't justify it to the client, and so on. He tells me this to my face and that I can't count on him for support in front of the client (he says he'll openly shoot me down because, after all, he knows more about what the individuals will readily accept than I do), then follows up by saying he wants to see more PR activity.

The creative director, in the presence of the president, agrees with the president. In private, he tells me to work around the president. Then he follows up by stating PR people are ineffectual pessimists unwilling to face reality. Maybe he's right (in my case). That's one of the things I would like your opinion on. But before you can develop one, you need to know a little more.

My creative director claims that he is a realist. The first thing you should know is the creative director's distinction between a realist and a pessimist. The best way to explain is to provide a brief example.

An insurance company (mobile homeowner's insurance) wants to sell 500 mobile homes that it has repossessed. A realist finds an interesting slant for nationwide publicity based on those 500 repos. (For example: "Insurance company turns mobile home dealer to liquidate 500 repossessed units in Texas.") A pessimist, on the other hand, recommends *not* designing the campaign around the announcement that this company has 500 repos it wants to unload because of the possibility of negative public reaction. Rather, there are other vehicles and other publicity approaches that do not highlight the repo thing.

Frankly, I told my creative director that I could not, in good conscience as a public relations professional, recommend touting in publicity my client's wish to sell 500 repossessed mobile homes, because it's detrimental to the company's professional image. Insurance companies make their profit from investments. These homes represent over $10 million in bad investments. This company also has a guaranty corporation. They insure the mortgages at the time of sale. This so the bank will give the mortgage in the first place, so the home will be sold, so that (hopefully) the insurance company will write the homeowner's policy.

Insurance companies are not on the list of consumers' most respected corporations to begin with. Some people think they run a kind of legalized protection racket. They raise their rates indiscriminately, and when you have a claim, they no longer know you. So we haven't got the best consumer attitudes to start with. Now we're going to publicize nationally that we threw 500 people out of their homes. Why? Because they couldn't pay the mortgage? Or because they didn't pay their insurance? Does this insurance company somehow get a lien on your home when they insure it? Granted there's no connection between insurance and repossession. But I can foresee all kinds of fears and misconceptions developing in the public's mind as a result of this type of publicity. I feel that the questions I presented above are just a few of the possible reactions.

My creative director's reaction to my reasoning was: "Hell, that kind of thinking went out 15 years ago." He went on to say that I should've faced reality. The people were evicted for a reason: they couldn't pay the mortgage. The reality is that a lot of people lost their jobs. Repo is not a bad word: it's the real business world. Further, he says, it's an interesting story: What happened to the people that they lost their jobs, where did they go, what are they doing now? So, he says, the insurance company would not be thought of badly for evicting people from their homes. (That, he says, is an old conservative view.) Rather, it's a hell of a story that the papers will use, and the homes will get sold.

I said that we shouldn't stir up a hornet's nest when the homes could be sold using other techniques. He responded by saying my basic way of thinking was wrong, that 90 percent of all PR people he ever knew found ways to avoid doing things because of the problems that might result, rather than going ahead and accomplishing the short-term goal efficiently.

I told you it was frustrating. I can't help but wonder if he's right. My better judgment tells me no. But I do wonder if I was overreacting about public sensitivities.

I'd like your opinion. I know you'll hit me with the truth—no sweet answer just to make me feel better. If I'm wrong, I need to know that so I can adjust my thinking, philosophies, and approach. If I'm thinking soundly, I need to know that, too.

No

Am I wrong to assume that as a public relations practitioner I should be keenly aware of the negative ramifications of any program or policy? That I should actually try to anticipate the problems and formulate means of avoiding and/or handling them? The key, I think, is *look*. I look very hard for any possible cause of negative public reaction before I design a campaign. Then I design a campaign to overcome or avoid their flare-up before the fact.

You see, I was told that if I can't stop looking for and finding problems or potential problems, I should get out of the PR profession. I had always thought that *was* my profession: isolating and anticipating areas for negative public reaction and endeavoring to achieve public acceptance. Maybe my head is on backwards. I know what my convictions tell me, but I'm not beyond realizing that I may have formed the wrong convictions.

Anyway, whatever the case, I want to get a seasoned professional's opinion—if not to confirm my convictions, then to alter my course. If I'm wrong, I want to correct it. If I'm right, I don't want to turn myself into a Hollywood publicity agent at the beckoning of my boss.

I've taken enough of your time. And thank you for fighting your way through this letter. I'm looking forward to hearing from you and trust all goes well.

Sincerely,

Peter Gantor

Why did the agency hire you?

Reprint for Discussion

*A Real Look in the Mirror **

Frank W. Wylie

Most mornings practitioners look in the mirror to check the closeness of the shave, or the artistry of the makeup. Only then do we set off for whatever the world will bring.

Let's take the same type of careful look at who we are and what we do. It might suggest some much needed changes in our behavior.

We might discover that we are world-class students of our navel, asking ourselves the same few questions over and over, and repeating the very same answers. In many ways, we are myopic.

Every year the birds fly south, the salmon swim up river, and public relations lemmings undertake the umpteenth annual, holy grail search for a new definition of public relations. What hours we waste, what a spectacle we make!

We debate rather endlessly whether we should call ourselves communication or public relations people. If we choose the former, we relegate ourselves to a lower status in the eyes of management—which has not, for the most part, deigned to accord "communicators" a top executive status. Besides that, many of us do more than just communication. The best of us are accepted, sometimes revered, for our ability to analyze trends, predict their consequences and make policy recommendations that keep our clients or company at the leading edge of progress. Others deny the term "public relations" as the inclusive title and, in the process, have developed well over 100 other terms to describe what we do. Then, we have the gall to

*Reprinted with permission from the January 1992 issue of the *IABC Communication World,* monthly publication of the International Association of Business Communicators.

A REAL LOOK IN THE MIRROR
305

say that the public does not understand what we do. Small wonder: We've confused them too long, too thoroughly. If we would settle on one term, and spend our time doing our jobs well, people would know how we can be helpful . . . and that is more important than them knowing what we do.

I suggest we accept "public relations" as the term, stop trying to redefine it, and let our actions provide the necessary definition of our work.

Where Should PR Be in the Curricula?

Another of the annual time-wasting arguments is: Where should public relations be taught? There are advocates for many loci, but suffice it to say, the government defines where it fits. It voted for *journalism* and that's where most programs are. However, their location is the minor consideration and does not merit our fuss or argument.

The real issue is: Is it being taught well? And, even if it's being taught well, what can we professionals do to help make it better? What can we do to provide worthwhile guest lecturers, tours of our firms, days with a professional, and more affordable events? What can we do to create worthwhile currency to the faculty so that they are teaching relevancies to their students? What about summer, or semester break, fellowships so PR faculty can learn what is going on in public relations? But, even this is a bit presumptuous.

Colleges and universities expect faculty to arrive with a Ph.D., know the field, and be about 26 years of age. Where, you ask, is the professional experience? The perception is correct. Many faculty do not have it. Others have experience that is thoroughly out of date. We can help a lot, if we will help them become leading-edge current. We must.

Let's give the cooperative approach to improving PR education our highest priority. If we hope to have a good future, we must take responsibility for the training of those who succeed us, and who will probably face tougher problems than we have yet known.

Management Can Practice PR—If It Has To

As we look at ourselves and our business, let us take note of the fact that almost every week a person not trained in PR is assigned to supervise the public relations function. The usual review of such a happening is phrased this way, "Oh my, another management doesn't know what PR is all about." Balderdash. For the most part management knows exactly what it is doing and, more often than not, does it well. If they don't put a PR person in charge of PR, it is usually for one of two reasons: Either no one has demonstrated how PR can help the firm achieve its objectives, or the available people don't know enough about the company, the industry and the societal climate of the day. Let's stop charging the error to the management. Let's start figuring out why we were found wanting, and work to make sure that we are so good that we can't be overlooked or bypassed.

> **Employee Communication Often Ego Massage**
> Internal communication has been, perhaps always will be, hampered by egos. Often management is too unwilling to make the hard decisions. At other times, they see internal communication as a slathering of good news and 'ataboys. They want to be loved, but often do little to deserve that love. In contrast, the tradition of internal communication is that often the less competent were chosen for internal . . . while the most competent were chosen to interact with the public and media.
>
> Fortunately, management's judgment often was flawed. Some superb people found their way into internal communication and did miracles. Those early, but very important pioneers, are the angels and saints in our heaven.
> Professor Frank W. Wylie
> California State University, Long Beach

We can start with our own professional development. How many of us are really current, know all the facts and technologies that we should, know all the nuances of the changing society in which we live? How many of us give top priority to our own professional development? Do we just think about it or do we do it? Do we take the time that is necessary to learn what we ought to know? Do we expand our skills beyond that of the communication technician or technocrat? Do we stretch ourselves as much as we stretch and stress those who work for us? If you pass this mirror test, you are either a very rare person or are practicing self-delusion.

If we look in the mirror and see "the communication business," we shortchange our firms and clients, and ourselves. We are in the business of anticipating problems and creating planned programs to deal with them. We are in the business of improving and expanding understanding and of changing behavior. We are charged with winning approval, and of strengthening and maintaining the host of relationships which are essential to our current and future success. We must enable our organization, or clients, and their publics to arrive at a consensus of understanding, and do it before anyone else does. Even, or perhaps most importantly, in problem solving we must demonstrate special skills: We are the people who have the strategic skills to address the *now* problem and, simultaneously, to set in motion the actions which will avoid a recurrence of the problem in the future. It is not enough to fix something; it must stay fixed.

Let's Clean Up Our Act

At some point, and I suggest now, we must start to clean up our own act. A look in the mirror will reveal that we tell wondrous stories about the virtues and values of accreditation. But we don't promote or publicize it. We have not educated management or human services to realize that accreditation has meaning and value. We don't include it in our advertisements or search requirements. All of our organizations must accept the premise that accreditation is something that must be earned, and re-earned on a continuing basis. If we treated our firms or clients as we have treated accreditation, we would have been fired, or would have lost the account.

Similarly, we boast often of the great virtues of our codes of ethics, but we fail to enforce them in any manner which would develop public understanding or approval. If we are serious about codes, we must begin to enforce them. We must become the source for media on what is and what is not acceptable in public relations practice. We must address the hard questions, not just the easy ones. We must provide judgments on hypothetical cases so that practitioners and media will have and share effective guidelines.

No business has a monopoly on flacks, fakes and phonies, but we have had, still have, what seems like a disproportionate number of them. Consider the damage they've done, the counterbalancing that we now must do. The water is muddied; the environmentalists are mad. We must address and satisfy the public's expectations for improvement. And we must do this promptly, demonstrating what we can contribute to the world beyond our own self interest. We can't just do well; we must make up for a lot.

PR as a Profession Is Arguable

Look into the mirror again and recite the fruitless arguments about whether public relations is, or is not a profession. Fact: It isn't. A profession has four basic characteristics: (1) a generally accepted course of readily available graduate study, (2) government-administered examination for access to the license, or certified, profession, (3) required continuing education requirements, (4) local and national organizations which monitor and, when necessary, censure. If it is possible to license physicians, certify brain and heart surgeons, surely it is also possible to do the same for public relations people. Let's stop hiding behind the facades of flag-draped, freedom of speech misconceptions and decide if we really want to be a profession. If IABC and PRSA decide we do, we can. And, if we are not serious about being a profession, let's stop wasting time talking about it and wishing that the inept, incompetent and unscrupulous will go away. Without a police power, they stay and complicate our existence, postpone much progress.

There are many things that we are, perhaps even more that we are not. But as we become more self-critical, let us always remember that we have been privileged to pursue that which is probably the most exciting, most intellectually challenging, and most satisfying craft that ever existed. It is good, perhaps great, but we can and should make it better.

Shakespeare's advice in "Hamlet" would work well for us: "This above all: to thine own self be true."

Look hard in that mirror. Look honestly. And then let us change, work together, and progress.

A SEARCH FOR PUBLIC RELATIONS COUNSEL* (A)

About four years after Monarch Laundries went public, Merton Sachs, 64-year-old head of the firm (which had been founded by his father 40 years before) told Vincent Puleo that the board of directors had approved Puleo's recommendation that the firm engage public relations counsel.

"Your memorandum, the Auger study, and Professor Levin's report convinced the board," Sachs told his 32-year-old executive assistant. "Let's get on with it, Vinnie, before they change their minds."

Puleo nodded in agreement. The board seldom overrode a Sachs recommendation, but both Puleo and Sachs knew that the $200,000 first-year figure they had budgeted for public relations counsel was a bit high for some of the older board members who had little understanding or knowledge of public relations. He had been wise, Puleo reflected, in authorizing the Auger study and the Levin report; he had little doubt that these had been important factors in the board's decision.

Puleo also reflected that he was fortunate to have a boss like Merton Sachs. Although Sachs was twice as old as Puleo, he had high regard for the younger man's capabilities. An increasing share of the management of

---

*All names, places, and dates in this case are disguised.

the firm had been turned over to the younger man. The two made a good team. Merton Sachs was wise in the ways of the linen service field and wise enough to know that a bright young man can often teach an older one new tricks. Puleo was bright but not brash and smart enough to know that a wise old man can often teach a young man much about patience and restraint.

The Auger study, designed to explore the hospital linen service market, was completed in November by the nationally known Auger Marketing Research Corporation at a cost of $40,000. It involved depth interviews with 100 carefully selected hospital administrators and board of trustee members in the Northeast regarding their hospital-owned linen services and their judgment about the relative merits of four leading linen service firms (including Monarch). The report by Professor Austin Levin, a leading marketing authority, had cost the firm $18,000 and reflected Levin's opinion that the Monarch "systems" approach represented a new dimension in the field of hospital linen services. In fact, Levin had predicted that if Monarch did not achieve "spectacular success" in moving into the national hospital linen service market, it would only be because Monarch had not marketed itself properly.

At the time of the study and the report, the linen service industry was divided into numerous small and medium-sized fiefdoms. Most firms restricted their operations to the city in which they had their plant, though a few venturesome firms operated on a regional basis with plants in several cities. Monarch, with sales of $50 million and 600 employees, operated out of its main plant headquarters in Albany, New York, with additional plants in Springfield and Worcester, Massachusetts. Most of its customers were large industrial and business concerns, but in recent years it had moved into the hospital linen service field.

After making detailed studies, Sachs and Puleo were convinced that the potential national market for hospital linen services, particularly utilizing their "systems" approach, was greater than existing linen services business. They had in turn convinced their board of this potential market, but they hesitated to set up new plants and "go national" before firmly establishing new customers outside their present orbit of operations. The only steps the two had completed were a commissioned 22-minute, slide-sound presentation explaining Monarch's "systems" approach to hospital linen services; preliminary discussions with a woman (age 30) whom they considered hiring as the firm's public relations director; a budget of $200,000 as the top figure for outside public relations counsel; and board approval to contract for said counsel.

······································

Hackiss Recommends Three Firms

Prior to getting the board's approval, Puleo had had preliminary discussions with a six-person public relations firm in Albany. He had rejected it, however, because he felt the firm lacked sufficient know-how and would be too "provincial" for the task. He had also had discussions with a New York advertising agency with accounts in an allied field but had rejected it also. He sensed that the firm was primarily advertising-oriented rather than public relations–oriented. With Sachs's approval, Puleo contacted an old college friend, Peter Hackiss, now director of public relations for a large New York City medical supply concern.

Hackiss visited one afternoon with Sachs and Puleo, read through the Auger study and the Levin report, viewed the slide-sound presentation, and suggested three counseling firms: Rice Associates; Dresher-Placebo Associates; and Hammer and Rogerstein. The first two firms, said Hackiss, were among the 15 largest counseling firms in the country, and the third was among the 10 largest. Hackiss said that all three had excellent reputations, well-known national clients, and were just about the right size for Monarch. (The latter point was made in response to Puleo's concern about size. As he explained it: "We're probably small peanuts, and we don't want to get 'lost' among the many large accounts handled by the giants in the public relations field.")

Hackiss's contact at Rice Associates was Joan Costa, a 36-year-old account executive who had gone to the same school as Puleo and Hackiss and whom Puleo knew by name but had never met. Costa and Hackiss had been friends for many years. Costa, Hackiss knew, had been with a Chicago public relations counseling firm for ten years and had joined Rice Associates one year earlier.

Hackiss's contact at Dresher-Placebo Associates was Glenn Dresher, a 54-year-old veteran counselor who was known nationally in the profession for his years of active work in the Public Relations Society of America. Hackiss and Dresher had been friends for many years.

The Hammer and Rogerstein contact was Bernard Apfel, a 47-year-old executive vice president of an aggressive, marketing-oriented firm and also a longtime friend of Hackiss.

With the consent of Sachs and Puleo, Hackiss telephoned Costa, Dresher, and Apfel and explained to each that his good friend Vincent Puleo was seeking public relations counsel for Monarch. Each was apprised of the fact that Puleo wanted to come to New York City for initial talks. They were told that Puleo would be having such talks with three counseling firms, though none of the three was told the others' names. Hackiss very briefly outlined the nature of Monarch's work, said the firm had budgeted up to $200,000 for counseling, and asked if the counselor was interested. All three replied affirmatively, and Hackiss set up appointments: the morning of March 6 (10:00 a.m.) for Rice Associates; the afternoon of March 6 (2:00 p.m.) for Dresher-Placebo Associates; and the morning of March 7 (10:00 a.m.) for Hammer and Rogerstein.

In setting the appointment with Hackiss, Glenn Dresher asked Hackiss if Monarch had done anything in the way of public relations. Hackiss mentioned the Auger study and the Levin report. Dresher said he had worked several times with the Auger firm, had a high regard for them, and knew Levin's reputation as well. He asked Hackiss for copies of the two reports before the meeting, and Hackiss in turn relayed the request to Puleo. The latter thought this was a good idea but he decided to show the slide-sound presentation at each of the three meetings as a briefing for the Monarch "systems" approach. He then sent similar letters to Joan Costa, Glenn Dresher, and Bernard Apfel confirming the appointment date and asking to have available a carousel slide projector, a stereo slide tape unit, and a screen (Exhibit 32–1).

On March 1 Puleo got a telephone call from Joan Costa acknowledging receipt of Puleo's letter and confirming the date. Costa said her firm would have available the projection material Puleo had requested. She suggested lunch together after their discussion, which Puleo accepted.

On March 2 Puleo received confirming letters from Glenn Dresher and Bernard Apfel (Exhibits 32–2 and 32–3). In discussing the coming meetings with Sachs, Puleo voiced the thought that it might be a good idea if Sachs went with him to New York.

"Our two judgments about the people I'm going to meet would be much better than just my judgment alone," Puleo pointed out. "This is going to be an important decision for the firm, so if you can free yourself I think it would be worthwhile if you went along with me." Sachs was in agreement, and Puleo notified the three contacts that he would be accompanied by Sachs.

Rice Associates

Promptly at 10:00 a.m. on March 6, Puleo, accompanied by Sachs, announced himself at the offices of Rice Associates and asked for Joan Costa. Costa came out into the outer reception room and introduced herself to Puleo, who in turn introduced Sachs. They went into a small room attached to Roger Rice's office, outfitted like a den with leather chairs, guns, and trophies, where similar introductions were made with Rice and another staff member named Stanley Joffrey. The latter was referred to by Rice as a vice president of the firm.

"We've cleared our entire morning for you, Mr. Sachs," said Rice, "so why don't the two of you tell us about your problems while we listen."

Sachs deferred to Puleo, who sketched in the linen services industry, the Monarch firm, and its "systems" approach. Questions, when forthcoming, came from Rice, with both Costa and Joffrey maintaining a respectful silence. After about a half hour Puleo broke off and suggested the slide-sound presentation.

"Joan, go out and make sure the equipment is set," Rice told Costa, and after Costa left the room, Rice quickly sketched the nature of Rice Associates and its clients. When Costa returned to say that the equipment was set, Rice suggested that she make sure a carafe of water and glasses were available. Assured by Costa that they were available, Rice ushered the group into the firm's conference room where the presentation was shown. After another hour's give-and-take, during which time Rice addressed his remarks mainly to Sachs, Rice suggested lunch. The private club to which he took them was nearby, so the group walked over: Rice walking with Sachs and the other three behind.

At the conclusion of lunch, Puleo said he'd like to have a written proposal from Rice Associates by March 24, and Rice said this would be done. Sachs and Puleo then went to their meeting with Dresher.

On the way over in a taxi, they discussed the morning session and found they were in general agreement. Rice, they felt, impressed them as a successful corporation executive who was somewhat pompous and overbearing with his associates. Though Puleo didn't mention it to Sachs, he also felt that Rice had treated Joan Costa like some third-rung clerk. They were both of the opinion that Rice didn't have too clear a conception of their "systems" approach and that some of his questions indicated he had not really studied the material Puleo had sent to Costa.

Though Joffrey hadn't said much during the morning's discussion, the two considered him to be a New York "sharpie," as Puleo put it.

. . . .

Dresher-Placebo Associates

Although Sachs and Puleo arrived at Dresher-Placebo Associates sharply at 2:00 p.m., they had to wait 15 minutes before Glenn Dresher came out to meet them. Following introductions, he brought them into his corner office and introduced Tricia Bushinger, executive vice president, and Ralph Nolan. The latter was not identified by title.

Dresher's office was smartly done in the best decorator style; it was large, comfortable, and very well furnished. Puleo noticed three PRSA Silver Anvil awards, and Dresher explained the accounts for which they had been won.

Dresher handled most of the discussion, addressed his remarks to both Sachs and Puleo, and quickly demonstrated to them an intimate understanding of their firm and its problems. He complimented Puleo for the material sent on ahead and praised the slide-sound presentation when it was run in the firm's conference room.

Following the presentation of the film, Dresher took about a half hour to outline the way his firm operated. He cited some "case studies" the firm had handled and indicated that Nolan would probably handle the Monarch account under the close and direct supervision of himself and Bushinger. Puleo had the somewhat uncomfortable feeling that Dresher considered the matter closed and the account his.

"Is this it?" Puleo asked finally. "What about a written presentation and plan?"

"We don't operate that way," Dresher replied. "A certain chemistry works in relationships like ours. As we get to know you better, to know your problems and your people better, we'll develop definite plans and set objectives. We know we can do a real job for you. You know we're good, or you wouldn't be here. All you need to do now is to agree you want us to work for you; we'll draw up a simple contract letter and get to work."

After a few minutes of further discussion, Puleo pointing out that he and Sachs were considering several counseling firms, it was agreed that Puleo would let Dresher know Monarch's decision by March 27, and the meeting ended.

At dinner with Sachs that evening, Puleo admitted that he had been very impressed with Glenn Dresher, and Sachs agreed. Both felt that Dresher exuded a great deal of confidence in his firm's ability to do the job for Monarch, seemed to have a sound grasp of Monarch's approach, and had an impressive list of clients, which included one in a field closely related to theirs.

"As for a plan, or rather nonplan, maybe that's the way things are done in public relations," Sachs mused aloud. "In a way, you know, that's the sort of approach we've been taking with our systems approach. We can't seem to get it down on paper the way we want it, so we more or less ask prospective clients to take us on faith. We tell our clients that we're good, take us and we'll show you, and that's what Dresher says to us."

Hammer and Rogerstein

Sachs and Puleo were on time the next morning for their 10:00 a.m. appointment. Bernard Apfel met them at once in the outer reception room and brought them into his office to introduce them to Bill Francher, a vice president.

The office and the pace at Hammer and Rogerstein, both Sachs and Puleo noted, differed considerably from the firms they had visited the previous day. Whereas Rice's and Dresher's offices were as large, spacious and decorous as Sach's own office back in Albany, Apfel's was as small, cluttered, and busy as Puleo's. When the group went down the hall to the conference room, Sachs and Puleo also noted much hustle and bustle in the halls.

The conference room was in use.

"Wasn't I supposed to have the conference room?" Apfel asked one of those present, and when advised otherwise, he laughed at his own error and brought the group back into his own office. After hasty improvisation, the equipment was set up and the slide-sound presentation was viewed. Apfel complimented Puleo on the film; then he and Francher asked questions concerning Monarch. Francher, in particular, had an excellent grasp of Monarch's problems and its "systems" approach. When Apfel had to answer his telephone, which rang several times during the morning, Francher carried the conversation along. Everyone by this time was on a first-name basis. At one point Apfel excused himself to "go out and give my secretary some instructions about the calls I got."

When Apfel returned, he discussed the nature of his firm and showed some brochures the organization had produced. He cited some of the work the firm had done for major clients whose names were household words.

Before leaving, Puleo told Apfel that he would like to have the Hammer and Rogerstein proposal by March 24. Apfel said they'd be pleased to work with this deadline.

Puelo and Sachs discussed their impressions of Hammer and Rogerstein on their way out to the airport. Both liked Apfel's friendly, sincere approach and had been very favorably impressed with Francher's astuteness regarding Monarch. Although the hustle and bustle of the office routine had at times interfered with their discussions, they felt that the firm was on the move at all times. They were favorably impressed with the Hammer and Rogerstein work they had seen. At the same time, they worried that the firm was so large and so busy Monarch might not get the attention they felt it needed. In parting, they agreed to hold back final judgment until the March 24 deadline.

The first of the three firms to be heard from was Dresher-Placebo Associates on March 10. Puleo, at the New York Hilton with his wife for a weekend of playgoing, received Dresher's telephone call transferred from Albany. Dresher asked if a decision had been made; Puleo replied that he was still awaiting letters and proposals from the other two firms. Dresher said he would be getting a letter off to Puleo early the next week. Puleo got the impression that Dresher was much interested in the Monarch account, and he said he'd be glad to hear from Dresher the following week.

Follow up

The Rice Proposal

On March 16 Sachs received a one-page letter from Rice (Exhibit 32–4), which Sachs in turn passed along to Puleo. The letter was accompanied by a 15-page brochure describing the structure and operations of the Rice organization, a short flier describing the Rice approach to financial public relations, and a 10-page proposal outlining "A Sales Promotion Plan for Monarch Laundries."

The Rice proposal described the firm's program as a joint effort of Rice Associates and Monarch, which would include sales aids, advertising, publicity, and public relations. The program recommended the following order of priorities:

1. Sales development within the areas served by the Albany and Massachusetts plants

2. Establishment nationally of an understanding of the Monarch system among hospital administrators

3. Careful consideration given to the introduc-

tion of this system in the Albany and Massachusetts plants

4. Future geographic expansion and necessary investment to be guided by the results of the Sales Promotion Program

Thirteen steps were then detailed under the heading "Method of Operation." These included an evaluation based on personal observations of sales problems and the company posture; selection of an effective name for the Monarch system and development of a striking insignia; preparation of a selling brochure; assistance in automating and strengthening the slide presentation; preparation of a sales letter to be sent with the brochure to selected hospital administrators served by the Monarch plants; preparation of a letter to be sent to 30 groups considering co-ops; a series of ads to be prepared and placed in *Hospital* magazine; a meeting with the American Hospital Association to arrange to make the brochure available to its members; preparation initially of at least two articles for placement in national professional journals and use of reprints for follow-up to inquiries; supplying a booth for the August convention of the American Hospital Association; setting up a National Advisory Council; scheduling of Rice representatives for appearances before hospital groups; and preparation of an annual report, semi-annual report, and dividend enclosures.

Under the heading "Budget," Rice Associates stated they would carry out the program for a total of $190,000 for the year. Of this total, $150,000 would cover the cost of all services including counsel and supervision by the principals of the firm and the actual time spent on the program by Rice staffers. Out-of-pocket expenses were estimated at $40,000, and these expenses would be fully itemized and billed at net cost.

The Dresher Letter

On March 17 Puleo received a four-page letter from Dresher (Exhibit 32–5) underscoring Dresher's reasons why his firm could execute an effective program for Monarch and suggesting that they proceed on the basis of a $12,000 per month fee, plus expenses.

On March 18 Puleo received a brief note from Apfel saying it would take a bit longer for his organization to send along its informal proposal (Exhibit 32–6). On March 22 Sachs received a brief note from Apfel thanking him for visiting Hammer and Rogerstein and noting that the proposal would be going to Puleo in a few days (Exhibit 32–7).

In a discussion with Sachs on March 24—the date Puleo had named for submission of proposals—Puleo mentioned that he was perturbed by Hammer and Rogerstein's delay.

"If this is an indication of how they operate, I don't like it," Puleo said. However, the two agreed to wait a few days for the Hammer and Rogerstein proposal to come in. On Tuesday, March 28, Puleo received a call from Bill Francher, who was very apologetic about not getting off the prospectus and who said he had just returned from London and would get the proposal to Puleo by Monday, April 3, and possibly by Friday, March 31.

The Hammer and Rogerstein Proposal

The proposal, in the form of a detailed, single-spaced, eight-page letter, was dated March 31 and arrived on April 3. It was addressed to Puleo, signed by Bill Francher, and started as follows:

Dear Vinnie:

The more I think about Monarch's problem, the less complicated it gets. Perhaps I'm oversimplifying, but here is how the question looks to me:

1. The care, feeding, and financing of hospital

linen services is a constant source of irritation, frustration, and expense to hospital administrators, their staffs, and their boards.

2. Monarch offers proven solutions to these problems.

3. But not enough of the right people know about Monarch or its service.

4. Because they don't know, they're trying to handle the problem in a variety of ways. The most serious of these in terms of Monarch's future is the movement toward cooperative linen services. This movement is taking hold very rapidly.

5. Unless Monarch can find some way to break this momentum by interposing its own story, a good part of the market will be lost. Monarch must present administrators, staff people, and board members with what Austin Levin terms "the fifth alternative." And it must do this fairly quickly.

At this point the proposal outlined target audiences; stated that the Monarch story has to be developed, dramatically and precisely, on paper; observed that Monarch has to establish itself as the authority with the answers in a creditable manner widely circulated; and concluded that the public relations effort must have continuity and follow-through.

Detailing the "tools" to achieve the above-mentioned goals, the proposal described nine "projects" for telling the Monarch story and four main ways of reaching the financial community. The projects were: a basic position paper; a research job of listing target audiences, market by market; preparation, through personal interviews, of successful Monarch case histories and placement of articles about such satisfied clients; development of by-lined articles by Monarch executives; design and carrying out of an interview survey to identify viewpoints and problem areas among specific audiences and reporting of the results through appropriate publications; sponsorship of seminars as a wedge for market-by-market promotion; a concerted effort to get prospective customers to visit hospitals served by Monarch and also to visit Monarch's refurbished plant; development of important speaking dates and appearances; and use of reprints for a very low-pressure direct mail campaign. In conclusion, the letter made the following points:

> That's how the mission looks to us, Vinnie. Both the hospital-directed work and the financial relations program could mesh wonderfully together, and the total effort could be exciting and meaningful. We'd love to do it for you.
>
> Our professional fee is $150,000 annually. This covers the "people" side of the budget in New York, which would be a center of the whole activity.
>
> The "things" part of the budget—publications, photography, travel, telephone calls, etc.— we can only estimate at this point. If you budgeted $30,000–$40,000 for the year, I'm pretty sure we'd be well covered. (With the exception of petty-cash items, disbursements from this fund are only made with your prior approval.)
>
> Finally, it would be great if we could set aside a kind of "war chest" of $8,000–$10,000 so that we could have on-the-spot support for your market-by-market program (both hospital and

financial) from our regional offices. We can turn the regional office people on as we need specific support, and turn them off again when a promotion is wound up. They can handle things like seminar arrangements, advance publicity, newspaper, radio and TV interviews, and so forth.

So the total cost should be in the neighborhood of $188,000–$200,000 for the year. We would want a firm six-month agreement, cancellable either way thereafter by 60 days notice.

Bernard and I are delighted that you gave us the opportunity to think about this. I believe we could make a real contribution. If, as you deliberate on your final choice, you'd like to meet the account team that would be doing your work here in New York, we'd be delighted. So much depends on the chemistry between the particular people involved. I'll be off to London again on Tuesday, but Bernard will be calling you midweek to see if there's anything else you need in the way of information, people, or back-up.

All good wishes,

William Francher

P.S. Since time is so short, I'm taking the liberty of sending a copy of this letter directly to Merton. Some additional copies of our Visual Report and our current client list are enclosed.

On April 3 Puleo wrote to all three counseling firms acknowledging receipts of their letters. The following day, he met with Sachs to discuss a decision on retaining one of them as counsel for Monarch.

In discussing Rice Associates, Puleo and Sachs were in agreement that they felt neither Roger Rice nor Stanley Joffrey was their "type" of person and that Rice seemed too conservative in its approach and programming. Puleo said he thought the Rice proposal was adequate but not particularly outstanding. Sachs, who said he had merely glanced through it, agreed with Puleo's estimation.

Both Puleo and Sachs agreed that Dresher was their kind of man and would do a hard and effective sell for them. At the same time, they were bothered by the fact that he hadn't really set down a program on paper. As Sachs phrased it: "'Faith is important, as I said the other day, but $144,000 worth of faith is a hell of a lot of faith."

Both Sachs and Puleo agreed that Francher's proposal was realistic, imaginative, and to the point. It had impressed them, but they were bothered by the fact that it had come in late, and they saw this delay as a possible symptom of the treatment they might get from Hammer and Rogerstein.

"So," Sachs finally said, "what do we do now?"

Exhibit 32–1
Letter from Monarch
Laundries

I'm writing to confirm the meeting Peter Hackiss set up for us on (date) at (time) in your offices.

I'll have a short slide-sound presentation that should help give you a better idea of our story. I'll need a carousel slide projector, a stereo tape unit, and a screen. I'll carry the slides, tape, and sound synchronizer with me.

I'm enclosing two studies and our recent Annual Report to give you some background about us. Your reading of this material prior to our meeting should make the meeting more productive for both of us. Of course, I expect that the enclosed information will be kept in the strictest confidence.

I'm very much looking forward to our meeting next week.

Sincerely,

Vincent A. Puleo
Assistant to the President

Exhibit 32-2
**Letter from
Dresher-Placebo
Associates**

March 1, 1992

Dear Mr. Puleo:

I am looking forward to our meeting on Monday. We have a carousel slide projector, a stereo tape unit, and a screen on hand.

Meanwhile, we'll do our homework with the material you sent us.

Cordially,

Glenn Dresher
President
(PRSA Accredited)

Exhibit 32-3
Letter from Hammer
& Rogerstein

March 1, 1992

Dear Mr. Puleo:

We are looking forward to meeting you on Tuesday, March 7, at 10:00 a.m. in our offices, and we appreciate the material you sent us in advance of the meeting. It should help us in being better prepared and will certainly save all of us considerable time.

We have available the projection equipment you requested, and it will be set up for you.

Looking forward to the pleasure of meeting you.

Sincerely,

Bernard Apfel

cc: Peter Hackiss

Exhibit 32–4
Letter from Rice Associates

March 15, 1992

Dear Mr. Sachs:

We've spent an intriguing few days putting together the attached suggestions for you. Intriguing because we feel, as you do, that there is a great opportunity here, and because the task is just difficult enough to be challenging.

Although we have had neither the opportunity nor the time to explore in depth the reaction of hospital officials, a quick probe with some of our friends has shown a real need for your services. We have no doubt, on the basis of your success in the areas where you are now operating, that your system could prove to be the answer.

Please be assured that we are confident we can provide you with the material you need to carry out your sales campaign and can bring you national publicity at the beginning and, of course, to an even greater extent as your program progresses.

We have attached two copies of our recommendations, along with a copy of our firm's brochure and a flier on our corporate and financial departments. Please feel free to call me with any questions or for expansion of any of our suggestions. We are anxious to work with you.

Cordially,

Roger Rice

Exhibit 32-5
Letter from Dresher-Placebo Associates

March 16, 1992

Dear Vincent:

There are several reasons why I feel we can be most helpful to you in the development of the most efficient and productive public relations program.

You have obviously gone "first class" in the manner in which you sought out top professional people to help you in the management and understanding of your opportunities. We like to think that we are also in the top professional ranks. We are one of the most dynamic agencies in the field and are proud of the fact that we have been retained for many years by such clients as (name) and (name), and that we have recently been selected above all other agencies by such sophisticated people as (five well-known names listed).

In addition, many of our executives devote themselves to the betterment of our profession through leadership in the activities of the Public Relations Society of America (two examples listed).

We would bring to your program a team of people with deep dedication to the highest standards of professional practice.

Another asset is our extensive specialization, which means that we put at your disposal some of the country's most competent people in the areas of publicity, research marketing, financial relations, and government relations; and we provide the most comprehensive coverage of the entire country through our own large offices in New York, Chicago, and Dallas.

Third, we have extensive experience in test marketing and market expansion programs, currently working with such successful companies as (six national consumer product firms listed).

Fourth, we have considerable direct experience in the hospital field. One example is that we represent the (client named). Another is that, as Public Relations Chairman of the Westchester County Hospital Association, I have been intimately connected with hospital activities for a decade and have also been a speaker before meetings of the National Hospital Public Relations Association.

Fifth, we are heavily management-oriented. We serve as confidential consultants to the top executives of a great many successful corporations and trade associations. Since we enjoy a high degree of their confidence, we have a considerable insight into management processes and problems and have been able to be of help and assistance in many significant ways—a reservoir of experience that would, I am sure, be useful to you in the expansion of your business.

Sixth, we have evolved a comprehensive concept of what public relations is and how it would be most efficiently applied to business situations. We proceed on the basis of sound research and comprehensive planning.

The Auger study is a real contribution to an understanding of your situation and provides an excellent basis for meaningful programming. As it happens, we are involved in many situations with the Auger organization, such as (four organizations listed). We work well together and we have devoted much combined time to working productively together.

From a public relations point of view, it is significant that there is widespread lack of awareness of your better method of linen service that you provide (attributes listed). These factors all lend themselves to public relations techniques that will dramatically and convincingly capture the interest of your important "publics" and persuade them to talk business with you.

Vincent, we are extremely interested in helping you realize what is obviously a great potential for Monarch Laundries. This is a time of great turmoil and change in the nation's hospitals, and the revolutionary impact on individual hospitals poses a situation in which effective public relations can be highly profitable.

I believe that your program should "sell," first, your concept of service, then the specifics of the service itself, and, finally, but of equal importance, the quality and integrity of the company and its top management people. These are all areas in which we have had experience and success, and we are "raring to go."

I suggest that we proceed on the basis of a $12,000 per month fee, plus expenses. This fee will cover planning, supervision, and full staffing of your account, and I give you my personal assurance that we will do everything possible to provide the best program that experience and talent can make possible.

We work on a simple letter of agreement, containing a 90-day cancellation clause, and I'll be happy to send one along as soon as you have had an opportunity to make your decision.

We greatly appreciate your courtesy in giving us such a thorough briefing, and we look forward to what we earnestly hope will be a decision to select us.

My best to Mr. Sachs.

Cordially,

Glenn Dresher
President
(PRSA Accredited)

Exhibit 32–6
Letter from Hammer and Rogerstein

March 17, 1992

Dear Vince,

This note is just to let you know that it will take a bit longer than planned to send you our informal proposal regarding a public relations program for Monarch.

Bill Francher, who is writing the proposal, has had to make an unexpected trip to London, which has set back his timetable a few days. However, I expect that you will be receiving the proposal by the end of next week.

Thanks again for the briefing. It was, as you undoubtedly realize, extremely helpful.

Best regards,

Bernard Apfel

Exhibit 32-7
Letter from Hammer
and Rogerstein

March 21, 1992

Dear Mr. Sachs:

I just wanted to thank you for taking so much time to visit us. I am keenly conscious of the complicated requirements that are involved in a program for Monarch Laundries, but if I may say so, it does sound like a tremendous idea and one that is bound to succeed.

Our informal proposal will be going to Vincent Puleo within a few days. I hope you will have a chance to study it as well.

Meanwhile, thanks again for your time and patience.

Sincerely,

Bernard Apfel

A SEARCH FOR PUBLIC RELATIONS COUNSEL* (B)

In analyzing the proposals and the executives of the three public relations counseling firms (see Case 32), Puleo decided to utilize an elimination process to make his final selection. It was his opinion that Rice Associates rated third, and he suggested to Sachs that they eliminate Rice from consideration. Sachs concurred, and Puleo wrote a brief note to Roger Rice (Exhibit 33–1). Rice replied by return mail (Exhibit 33–2).

Puleo then telephoned Bernard Apfel and Glenn Dresher for appointments to visit each a second time, the former on April 18 and the latter on April 26. He received confirming notes from both.

In making the date with Apfel, Puleo sent his regards to Francher and said that he would be pleased to see him on April 18.

"I'll be glad to pass along your regards, but Bill won't be with us that day," Apfel replied. "Bill is our . . . well, he writes our proposals because he's so good at this sort of thing, but he won't be working on the account."

"Oh, I see," said Puleo. A moment's pause. "Well, anyway, we'd want to meet the people who will be working on the account. Okay?"

---

*All names, places, and dates in this case are disguised.

"Of course," replied Apfel, and he was as good as his word when Sachs and Puleo showed up on April 18 for the meeting. Two Hammer and Rogerstein staffers were present, whom Apfel introduced as Kathleen Sanchez, a group leader and vice president, and Mike Schmidt, an account executive.

Puleo judged Sanchez to be about 38 and Mike Schmidt about 30. In the ensuing conversation concerning Monarch, it seemed to Puleo (and Sachs later confirmed his impression) that Sanchez and Schmidt had had no more than a scant briefing about Monarch, the industry, or the firm's problems.

In preparing for the meeting, and for the later one with Dresher, Puleo had prepared a list of specific questions. Now he asked them of Apfel and in each instance got a quick, to-the-point answer (see Exhibit 30–3).

The discussion between Monarch and the Hammer and Rogerstein people lasted through the morning. About 12:30 Apfel invited the group to lunch at an exclusive private club. On the way over, Puleo walked with Schmidt and learned that Schmidt had worked six years for a small city daily and had joined Hammer and Rogerstein only four months earlier. An enthusiastic young man, Schmidt said he welcomed the chance to work on his first account.

Sachs, walking with Apfel and Sanchez, learned that Sanchez had been with Hammer and Rogerstein for 12 years; prior to that time she had been a newspaper reporter and director of public relations for a hospital. Sanchez impressed Sachs as being astute and quick.

When Sachs and Puleo returned from New York, they received letters from Apfel, which they immediately acknowledged (Exhibits 33–4 and 33–5).

In setting up the April 26 visit with Dresher, Puleo asked that the account executive slated for the Monarch account be present, but Dresher was alone in his office when Sachs and Puleo were ushered in. Dresher, responding to a question from Puleo, said that Ralph Nolan would handle their account when it came to Dresher-Placebo Associates, and he was available if they wanted him. Puleo said this probably wouldn't be necessary since Dresher hadn't thought it was necessary. Sachs, Puleo, and Dresher discussed the account by themselves. Puleo asked Dresher the same questions he had asked Apfel, and Dresher's replies were as quick and to the point as Apfel's had been.

When Sachs and Puleo returned to Albany that evening, Sachs asked Puleo which firm he preferred: Hammer and Rogerstein or Dresher-Placebo Associates.

"I'm satisfied we've explored this sufficiently," Sachs said. "Let's make our decision tonight."

Puleo agreed. "It's a tough one, but it could be worse," he said. "I think either one will do a fine job for us. Frankly, my brain tells me Dresher-Placebo Associates, but my gut tells me Hammer and Rogerstein."

Exhibit 33-1
**Letter to Rice
Associates**

April 19, 1992

Dear Mr. Rice:

I'm sorry to tell you that we've decided to retain the services of another agency.
The decision was not an easy one for us to make.

We enjoyed meeting you and your associates, and we really appreciate the time
and effort you spent on us.

Sincerely,

Vincent A. Puleo
Assistant to the President

cc: Merton Sachs

Exhibit 33-2
Letter from Rice Associates

April 21, 1992

Dear Mr. Sachs:

We were disappointed indeed to receive your letter saying that you had selected another agency. We sincerely feel that you are on the right track and that your operation is bound to be successful. We would like to have been a part of it.

If at any future time you should feel like talking with us further, we would be only too happy to meet with you.

Cordially,

Roger Rice

Exhibit 33-3

**Puleo's Questions
with Answers by
Apfel and Dresher
(as Puleo Jotted
Them Down During
Discussion)**

Question	Apfel Answer	Dresher Answer
1. Who will be the account executive?	Mike Schmidt	Ralph Nolan
2. How will he work with us?	He'll practically be living with you for the first four months.	He'll become part of your family.
3. How will you work?	We sit down with you and jointly work out a plan.	We work out a program with your help.
4. How often do we see your people?	As often as necessary.	As much as needed.
5. Do your account execs change often?	No.	Of course not.
6. Will the account exec work just for us?	No. You'll have about half of Schmidt's time, but don't worry about this.	No. Nolan has other accounts, but don't worry, you'll get what you pay for.
7. Do we get scheduled reports?	You can get anything you want, but we lay out a plan and meet regularly to check it.	You'll have progress meetings with us.
8. How will we be billed?	Monthly in advance on basic fee, and monthly on expenses after incurred.	Same general reply.
9. Will we see vouchers?	If you want them.	In extraordinary detail, if you want them. In fact, not a penny will be spent without your approval.

| 10. How involved are you in the hospital field? | Not directly, but we're in related fields. | We had a hospital supply account, and now we have related field accounts. |
| 11. When do we start? | Today, if you want us to. | Right now, if you want. |

Exhibit 33–4
Letter from Hammer and Rogerstein to Puleo

April 18, 1992

Dear Vince:

    Notwithstanding the fact that your screening process is as tough as getting into Yale, it was good to see you and Merton Sachs again.

    At the moment we all feel somewhat talked out, but if there is anything further that you wish to know, please don't hesitate to get in touch.

    We are awaiting your decision with a great deal of anticipation; but win or lose, I want to express our appreciation for your interest in our organization.

Best regards,

Bernard Apfel

P.S. Since you were nice enough to speak favorably of our Photo Exhibit, I thought you might be especially interested in a booklet we've prepared. It's a compilation of articles by our senior people, and we're rather proud of them.

Exhibit 33–5

**Letter from Hammer
and Rogerstein to
Sachs**

April 18, 1992

Dear Merton:

Kathleen Sanchez, Mike Schmidt, and I enjoyed our get-together very much. We are all elated at the possibility of working with you.

There isn't much about us now that you don't already know, but if you do need anything else, please give me a call. Meanwhile, thanks again for your obvious interest in hearing us talk about ourselves.

We look forward to hearing from you.

Best regards,

Bernard Apfel

A SEARCH FOR PUBLIC RELATIONS COUNSEL* (C)

After a long discussion regarding the relative merits of Dresher-Placebo Associates and Hammer and Rogerstein (see Case 33), Sachs and Puleo agreed they both preferred to retain the Dresher firm. They so notified Glenn Dresher by telephone on April 27. Puleo then notified Bernard Apfel of the decision, and Apfel in turn replied (Exhibits 34–1 and 34–2).

At Dresher's suggestion, Sachs and Puleo—who were scheduled for another meeting in New York anyway—attended a strategy meeting in Dresher's office on May 2. Present were the two Monarch officials, Dresher, Tricia Bushinger, and Ralph Nolan. The meeting lasted all morning and extended through lunch. In the opinion of both Sachs and Puleo, it was very productive. Basic discussion centered around the public relations strategy to be followed in the immediate present and over the long run. Before the meeting ended, it was agreed that Nolan would come to Albany the following week to make a personal tour of the Monarch facilities there and to continue the discussion started at the New York strategy meeting. It was also agreed that the effective date of the Monarch–Dresher contract would be May 8. The contract itself arrived in Puleo's office on May 7,

---

*All names, places, and dates in this case are disguised.

when it was countersigned and a copy returned to Dresher.

When Nolan visited Puleo on May 11, he brought along Kara Tome, who was introduced to both Puleo and Sachs as a member of the Dresher firm. Puleo in turn introduced Ramona Stangel, the new director of public relations for Monarch as of May 1. Stangel, age 30, was the woman Puleo had been considering for the job for some time. She held a B.S. degree in public relations and had been assistant public relations director of a medical complex in Albany for eight years.

Nolan spent the entire day with Puleo and Stangel, agreeing mutually that Nolan's first job on the account would be to prepare a new brochure underscoring the Monarch "systems" approach as a "fifth option" to existing hospital linen service programs. Nolan told Puleo that he would put together a written plan and would get it to Puleo in the near future. It was also agreed that Nolan would immediately prepare the draft of a letter to be sent out to a specific target audience: administrators of hospitals that Puleo knew were considering co-op laundry programs.

Nolan's draft letter arrived in Puleo's office on May 16. It struck Puleo as a poor letter and disappointing effort. He returned it to Nolan with numerous corrections and suggestions for changes.

Nolan's Program

On May 20 Puelo received from Nolan an 11-page, double-spaced, typewritten "Promotional Program for Linen Systems for Hospitals." (Linen Systems for Hospitals was the suggested name Nolan had proposed for Monarch, as a coordinated but separate part of Monarch Laundries.)

The program listed four public relations objectives:

> 1. To create a strong new image of the company as the originator of a unique "systems" approach.

2. To instill in the minds of hospital administrators an appreciation of this unique "systems" approach.

3. To create confidence for the competence and quality of the company and its management.

4. To assist the company's sales force by preconditioning the market and providing tools that will help them sell the "systems" approach to prospects.

As a "sales objective," the program proposed to increase client hospitals in the company's present sales areas and to induce hospital groups throughout the United States that were contemplating the establishment of co-op laundry services to consider the Monarch approach instead. The program proposed four "devices and tools":

1. Selection of the name "Linen Systems for Hospitals."

2. Development of a new logo for the new name.

3. Editing and tightening of the sales slide presentation.

4. Preparation of two new sales brochures, one for local and one for national use.

Under "The Local Program," the proposal listed local and regional target publics and suggested the following "basic PR activities": creation of the sales brochures, preparation of articles for professional publications, news releases, and reprint mailings. Suggested supplementary activities included seminars for key hospital personnel, speaking engagements, and assistance in developing trade shows.

Under "The National Program," the proposal listed as the national target audience those hospital groups thinking of "going co-op." It suggested setting up a meeting of those hospital officials with Monarch officials, who would utilize the slide presentation, kits, and the new brochures. These groups might also be invited to tour the Albany and Massachusetts plants. Other suggested activities included a basic research study on the merits of co-ops versus Monarch's system, talks before major hospital administrator groups comparing the merits of co-ops versus the "systems" approach, articles in leading hospital journals analyzing the difficulties experienced by co-op groups, and an article in a major business publication identifying the company as the originator of the "systems" concept.

In discussion of the proposal with Sachs and Stangel, Puleo and the others agreed that it was somewhat better than the proposal put forth by Rice Associates, but certainly not as good as the one developed by Bill Francher of Hammer and Rogerstein.

Tome Takes Over

One week after receiving the proposed public relations program, Puleo got a telephone call from Tricia Bushinger of Dresher-Placebo Associates informing him that Nolan was no longer with the counseling firm; the account would be handled by Kara Tome. Puleo's reaction was an ambivalent one. He was not at all happy about having account executives switched on him, but, on the other hand, he had not been satisfied with Nolan's work. When Bushinger suggested that Tome get up to Albany as soon as possible, a date was arranged for June 7.

At the June 7 meeting—an all-day affair attended by Puleo, Stangel, and Tome—Puleo started to discuss aspects of the Nolan proposal, but Tome said that proposal was now "out the window" and suggested they disregard it. Puleo asked if there would be another proposal, and Tome said that, of course, she would set one up and submit it.

At Puleo's suggestion, it was agreed that for the immediate future Tome would concentrate on the brochures, a history of the corporation and biographical sketches of the leading executives, assignment of a clipping service, and the development of a logo for the company.

"What about the upcoming national convention of hospital administrators in Denver on August 15?" Puleo asked Tome. "Should we sign up for a booth, and will you develop it? Will the brochure be ready by then?"

Tome said they should definitely get into the Denver convention exhibition; there was plenty of time. And she would be glad to work on the booth.

Puleo received the first draft of the brochure copy on July 7 and rejected it outright as poorly conceived, poorly written, choppy, and in many instances ineffective in projecting the Monarch "systems" concept.

"It's as though she didn't even understand what our system is all about," Puleo told Sachs, and the latter agreed. Sachs also expressed perturbation over the fact that the firm had already paid $24,000 to Dresher and seemed to be getting little to show for it. Puleo agreed with Sachs, but suggested that it was perhaps too early to tell.

Telephoning Tome to express his strong disappointment with the brochure copy, Puleo said he was sending it back. He said he was also disappointed to find that Tome hadn't seemed to grasp what Monarch's "systems" concept was all about.

"To tell you the truth," Tome replied, "I didn't write the copy. We have a writer who handles such work, and I guess he missed a good deal. Don't worry, though, we'll work it over again, and I'll get it to you by July 20."

Between July 7 and July 20 Puleo had several visits with Tome when in New York on company business. On one of these visits he passed Glenn Dresher in the hall, and they chatted briefly. Dresher asked how things were going on the account, and Puleo replied "so-so." Dresher suggested they get together while Puleo was there, but he was tied up when Puleo finished chatting with Tome, and they didn't have a chance to talk further.

Puleo and Tome did have a chance to discuss work on the logo. At Tome's suggestion, it was being done by the one-man firm that had put together Monarch's slide-sound presentation. Puleo rejected the logo that Tome had approved, and Tome agreed with the one Puleo selected from others submitted. Puleo himself wasn't too satisfied with the logo, but he felt it was the best of the group he had seen.

On one of his visits, Puleo asked Tome what she had in mind for the Monarch booth at the national convention in Denver on August 15.

"Something like this," Tome replied, and she drew a quick rough sketch on a yellow scratch pad. Puleo said it didn't look like much to him, and Tome said she would of course rework it and submit it in a more polished form.

Tome met her July 20 deadline for submission of the second draft of the brochure. But this one proved as unsatisfactory to Puleo and Sachs as the first. Their chief objection was that the copy was too pedestrian—it didn't have "sparkle." In rejecting the copy, Puleo sent Tome a three-page letter containing detailed objections and suggestions for improvement.

Tome came through with a third draft on August 2, and this draft was accompanied by a three-page informal letter saying that Tome had personally handled the copy this time. Sachs, Puleo, and Stangel all agreed that the copy was an improvement over the first two drafts, but in their opinion it still needed rewriting, more sparkle, and a smoother flow of transitional material.

The letter itself summarized the status of work that

had been done to date and work immediately ahead, and in general followed the guidelines set down at the June 7 meeting.

By August 2 no work had been done on the Monarch booth, and at this point Puleo told Tome to forget the booth and turned over that project to Stangel. Puleo also decided that it was too late to plan to use the new brochure at the August 15 convention exhibit and decided he would use the old one he had on hand.

Discussing Monarch's relationship to date with the Dresher firm, Sachs told Puleo on August 7 that he was very unhappy about the state of affairs.

"We've paid them $36,000 so far, and what have we got for it?" Sachs asked. "If you ask me, I think you and Stangel could have done better on your own. Maybe we'd be better off . . ." Sachs let his thought drift off incomplete.

"I'm not satisfied either, by a long shot," Puleo replied. "On the other hand . . ." Puleo also let his thoughts drift off. He reviewed the situation in his own mind. He was definitely not happy with the type or amount of service he had received from Dresher-Placebo Associates. He could write a strong letter to Glenn Dresher. He could lay down the law to Tome. He could terminate the contract; in which case he might well consider placing the Monarch account with Hammer and Rogerstein. Finally, he could simply terminate the contract, period. But he knew his own public relations director was new and couldn't really be expected to do the sort of job that a New York City counseling firm could do. He himself was much too tied up in other administrative details to get personally involved in public relations. In fact, he was much too involved as it was. He really had a problem, he reflected wryly, as he locked his desk and went home to his family.

Exhibit 34-1
**Letter to Hammer
and Rogerstein**

April 27, 1992

Dear Bernard:

Easier letters I've written.

We've decided to have a go with another agency. I'm sure I must sound like an old fussbudget, but it sure was difficult to make a decision.

We found it easy to eliminate most of the original agencies we contacted. When we got down to the cream, it got tough. At any rate, for better or worse, we made the decision. This may be a hell of a thing for me to say, but if we should find that we made the wrong decision, you'll be the first to know.

Merton and I enjoyed meeting you and your people, and we sincerely appreciate the time and trouble you took with us.

My sincerest regards,

Vincent A. Puleo
Assistant to the President

Exhibit 34-2
Letter from Hammer and Rogerstein

April 29, 1992

Dear Vince:

We are disappointed but not downhearted. People who hit it off as well together as we obviously did have a way of getting together from time to time. I have no doubt that one of these days we will be talking to each other again.

Meanwhile, I want to wish you and your agency the best of luck. I honestly think you have a better mousetrap and with the right kind of publicity, public relations, and promotion you will sell it.

One final point: Since we are both going to be around for a long time to come, I would like to have the privilege of staying in touch with you from time to time to find out how things are going. I feel a proprietary interest in the future of Monarch, and want to keep abreast of what's going on.

Very best regards,

Bernard Apfel

PERSONAL/ PERSONNEL CONCERNS

AN INTERNSHIP AT WILSON-JONES*

Jane Daugherty, a public relations major at a western university, was beginning her first internship at a small public relations agency. Although she had gleaned a lot of information about the internships from her fellow public relations students, she was still a bit nervous. She had worked at a variety of jobs, and had been successful, but this was her first professional job. She had heard a lot about the importance of networking, so she realized she had to make a good impression on this job. It was, she felt, the key to everything.

Jane had been warned about the importance of first impressions by her internship class instructor, Professor Sophia Chase, who told her that the first two seconds of the job interview was the most important part. That's what she'd heard, over and over. As Professor Chase put it: When they form that first opinion of you, either you can build on a plus or you have to counteract a negative.

Agreeing with all of this, Jane prepped for her interview by talking with her public relations professors and with her public relations mentor. They all seemed to agree that a good, small agency was the best place to get a variety of experience. That was important to Jane.

---

*All names, places, and dates in this case are disguised.

After four years of working her way through college, she didn't want to be a glorified secretary.

When Jane made her initial visit to Wilson-Jones Public Relations, Advertising, and Marketing, her immediate impression was that they were sort of laid-back Californian. The firm itself was a combination of an advertising firm that had seen its billings decline, a marketing firm that had a reputation for being brilliant (and a bit wild), and a public relations firm that had always done well. Personnel consisted of nine professionals; two secretaries, one of whom was a receptionist; and two part-time clericals.

While waiting for her interview, Jane noted that when a phone call came in, the receptionist immediately addressed the callers by their first names. Not very professional, thought Jane. She observed that slacks and open-neck dress shirts were the uniform for men. Women wore tailored blouses and skirts or well-tailored slacks.

Jane, who had agreed to work Wednesdays and Fridays, started her internship on a Friday and decided that her suit—the one and only—would be the appropriate attire. Beige with a brown blouse seemed neutral enough, and she could shed the jacket if that seemed appropriate. Makeup and accessories got a careful double check. The mirror in the building lobby seemed usefully placed and provided a full-length verification.

As Jane entered the office she recognized several people whom she had met during her initial tour of the agency. All were dressed in blue jeans and casual tops. Had she not recognized the people, she'd have thought she had entered the wrong office. Her suit didn't play well at all. It was casual day, a common practice in the city where the firm was located. Jane felt awful. She had tried so hard to make the right impression, and now she was totally overdressed. Sheilla, the secretary/receptionist, sensed the problem and tried to solve it with a too-loud voice: "We forgot to tell you about casual day. It's our fault, not yours."

Feeling it best to drop the matter rather than respond to it, Jane asked if she could see Erica Wilson, the partner who had hired her. (Ralph Jones, the other partner, had run his own agency until the merger five months ago.)

"She's not in now, and it will be a miracle if she comes in this afternoon," Sheilla said. "You know how bad Friday traffic is."

Jane was surprised. She had assumed that the person who had hired her would be there to get her started. "Well, who else should I see if she's not here?"

"Why don't you just help me today?" Sheilla said. "We have two huge mailings to get out, and everyone seems to be on deadline. You can learn how things work here, and I can clue you in as we go along. That way you'll learn how this place works. I can give you a few tips that should be of help to you."

"But don't I have to report to someone?" Jane asked.

"Oh, you can report to me," Sheilla responded. "I know you're here and that you came early. I review the time sheets for everyone, and I can tell you one sure thing: No one remembers that you came in early, but they do remember if you stay late. So, okay, let's tackle the press kits. We'll be heroes if we get them out early."

Sheilla showed Jane where the press materials were and which ones needed to be recopied. When the switchboard buzzed, she excused herself.

Well, thought a disappointed Jane, it looks like this public relations internship is going to be Secretaryland Revisited: copying, collating, and stuffing. Jane thought of reminding Sheilla she was a public relations intern, but then she decided that might not be wise. She couldn't help but wonder if what was happening to her would have happened were she a male intern.

Deciding to get down to the task assigned to her by the secretary/receptionist, Jane made the necessary copies. Then she lined up the materials for walk-around collating. She noticed that the labels and envelopes were in separate piles, so she combined them and was ready to collate. That took time, because this was a national mailing and there were many more copies than anything she'd ever seen. She didn't notice the time and was surprised to find it was 12:45 when she finished assembling, stuffing, and getting the kits ready for mailing.

When Jane got back to the reception desk, Sheilla interrupted what was obviously a personal conversation to say that she'd be with her in a few minutes. Jane went to the cubicle that had been assigned to her, the one with a Mac. At 1:25, Sheilla said that she was going to take a late lunch, but first she'd explain the second kit. It was for a brand-new client.

Jane decided to skip lunch and grind out the second kit, remembering that it was important to get both kits out early. She thought it a rather impersonal place. People moved around a lot, but no one really stopped to start a conversation with her. Then someone stuck his head in and said, "Tell Sheilla I'm leaving for the day, but she can reach me if she has to." This was the first of several such messages. The place was emptying out. If others were still here and working, you couldn't prove it by her. But, she thought, maybe this is how agencies work.

Just as she finished the last kit, Sheilla reappeared. Jane explained that all the kits were ready. What else needed to be done to get them in the mail?

"Help me get them down to my car, and I'll take them to the post office so they can travel over the weekend," Sheilla said. "You've worked hard, so you can take off." It was 3:15, and the advice sounded good. Jane had errands to run, and this was the only blank spot in her weekend.

When Jane came to work the following Wednesday, she was greeted warmly by Erica Wilson, who said, "It was wonderful of you to help Sheilla get those kits out Friday. They are really important. Oh, I'm sorry I wasn't here to greet you on Friday. I had an important client meeting and a new business presentation. Then I crashed."

Wilson continued, "Let me explain how things work here. It's my agency, and you work for me. However, sometimes we get really crazy here, and you will have to help whoever needs it most. To keep them from pulling you apart, I'll tell you who to work with each day. If you have questions, come see me. If I'm not here, see Sheilla. She knows where all the bodies are buried."

"That sounds great," Jane said. "I like working hard and am anxious to get real-life experience in writing, client meetings, and strategy development—anywhere I can be of help."

Wilson replied, "You'll get it all, but you'd get more if you could spend more time with us. Two days a week is not a lot of time; not many projects can get wrapped up in a day. But I understand about school and your other job." (Jane made $6.00 an hour at the internship, and $9.00 to $11.00 at her waitressing job.)

A month passed. Jane sat in on one brainstorming session, and a couple of her ideas got mauled about but were included in the plan. She wrote and rewrote several releases. The Wilson-Jones style was different than the one she'd learned at school. They used lots of adjectives and wrote borderline promotional copy for some of their media contacts. Her professors had warned her against that, but it seemed to work here. They got back clips that clearly reflected what they'd written. It was a satisfying experience, but she noted that everyone was talking about a need for more agency income. It was tough to improve things during a recession. Everyone seemed tightly wired, and people snapped at each other a lot. But Jane was learning, and she decided that she was getting exposed to the way it really was.

This Wednesday was different. She sensed it when

she first came in. While grabbing a cup of coffee, she asked Sheilla what was going on.

"Well, Erica just did your first review, and I've mailed it to Professor Chase. You came off OK. It wasn't a rave, but it was solid. You done good. Be glad you have it. Things are lots different now."

"What's so different?" Jane asked.

Sheilla shrugged, rolled her eyes, and said, "Well, the agency has been doing a lot of work, but it hasn't made money. In fact, we've lost a lot. Now they've hired Marietta McWilliams to come in three days a week and get things organized. She's dynamite on wheels, very creative and tougher than stainless steel. You watch—heads will roll, and she'll roll them fast." Jane had no idea who Marietta McWilliams was, but she didn't want to ask and seem ignorant and uninformed about something she probably ought to know.

Sheilla's prophecy was sound—more proof of the wisdom of the secretarial network. On Friday four account executives, three men and one woman, got their notice between 8:00 and 9:00 a.m. By 11:00 they'd cleaned out their desks and left. Was this the profession that she'd worked so hard to enter? What kind of future was there for her when the older, more experienced people were getting laid off?

Shortly before noon, Wilson called Jane into her office. The intern thought that she, too, was about to be history.

"We've been working hard, but losing money," Wilson said. "I've hired Marietta McWilliams to come in and look at the agency to help me reorganize." Wilson paused. "I assume you know Marietta, don't you?"

Jane shook her head.

"Well, no matter. There certainly will be changes, but they won't affect you. You work for me, but I did want you to know that a lot of things are up for grabs."

It was a rude awakening. Jane was well aware that the recession had negatively affected the advertising and public relations fields, but she couldn't get over the firing of almost half the professional staff and the way it had been handled. She had worked with two of the four account executives and knew they were thoroughly professional, capable, and hardworking, yet they were now gone, just like that!

Jane made one attempt to impress Marietta McWilliams, but it didn't turn out as she expected. Given the job of writing a 400-word profile of a client, Jane spent eight off-duty hours on the assignment and referred briefly to this fact when she forwarded it to McWilliams for approval. It came back heavily edited and with a cover note: "Rewrite as per editing. We expect off-duty hours when a job calls for it."

Three weeks before the end of the term, Jane was told to see Professor Fleet, the PR Option Head. Her professors worked together, and shared notes on all the students, but Jane couldn't figure out what was up. She found out quickly.

Professor Fleet minced no words. Normally very soft-spoken and kind, he was obviously upset about something, and he got to the point immediately.

"I've had word about your internship from Marietta McWilliams," he told Jane. "She says that your writing is weak, you're an apple-polisher, and you're not really doing the job that needs to be done. She says that you're not up to par—far below the other two interns she's had from our program—and not a credit to the school."

"But I received a favorable letter from Erica Wilson, the head of the agency who hired me and to whom I report," said Jane.

"That's old news," said Fleet. "There's no yesterday in this business. This agency was too fat—losing money. They would have folded if they hadn't brought in McWilliams to straighten them out. She will, too, so if I were you I'd watch my step. Just remember, there are only weeks left in the term, so make your peace."

Professor Fleet slipped on his jacket and picked up

a batch of blue books. "I'm giving an exam; I have to go to class," he said as he rose to go.

A dazed Jane didn't know what, if anything, to say or do.

WOLFE GETS A JOB OFFER*

On Tuesday, June 6, when he returned home at about 7:00 p.m. after nine holes of golf on the Burnam College course, Professor Eugene Welk was advised by his wife that he had received a long-distance telephone call from Harvey Frost of Portland, Oregon. Frost had left a message asking Professor Welk to call back, collect.

As he put through the call, Welk recalled that Frost had graduated from Burnam about 12 years before with a B.S. in public relations, taken a hospital public relations job in Burnam (population 80,000), and a few years later moved on to the West Coast. There he became an account executive with the San Francisco office of one of the country's largest advertising agencies. Welk and Frost had kept in touch, and Welk knew that Frost had done very well for himself both financially and professionally since leaving the East Coast college. Welk wondered why Frost was calling, and after the usual pleasantries about family and such, he quickly satisfied his curiosity.

"I don't know if you read about it in the trade press," said Frost, "but three of us in the office here bought out the West Coast operation of the firm we've been working for and have been on our own for the past eight months."

---

*All names, places, and dates in this case are disguised.

"Oh?" said Welk. "How's it going?"

"Fine," said Frost. "We've kept the accounts, added some new ones, and are busy searching out new business. In fact, that's what I'm calling about. We've made a strong pitch for the Alaska travel account and hope to wrap it up on June 20 when we go up to Juneau for a final presentation."

"Did you say 'Alaska'?" asked Welk.

"Right, Alaska," said Frost. "If we get it, it will be a sizable account, probably billing between $400,000 and $500,000. It'll be concerned mainly with public relations but will include advertising, too. There's only one small problem, and that's why I'm calling.

"The people we're dealing with in the state development office and on the governor's staff insist that if we get the account they want us to station an account person permanently in Juneau. We've searched locally but haven't had much luck."

"I wonder why?" Welk said dryly.

"Look," said Frost, "Alaska may seem like snow, seals, and polar bears to you people out East, but it's not all like that. Juneau's washed by a branch of the Japan current, and its climate is mild compared to the interior. It's also the capital. In any case, if we get the right person we're willing to pay $22,000–$28,000, depending on experience and that sort of thing. All we ask is a two-year commitment, and we'll always have a good spot here in our Portland office if for some reason things don't work out. We've got a lot of business, and this would be quite an opportunity. So . . . do you know of any Burnam PR graduates who might fit the bill and would be interested?"

"Not offhand," said Welk, "but I'll make a few calls. I have in mind one or two grads who might do. Trouble is, you're out there and they're way out here."

"That *is* a problem," agreed Frost. "We don't have time to fly someone out here, and in any case it would be rather expensive. My thought is that if you recommend someone, I'll go by your recommendation. You've been in this field 25 years, and I know I can't go wrong following your recommendation. We could arrange to have the candidate presented on tape, and of course we could work up a bio and provide that to the client also."

Welk agreed to check with one or two PR graduates working in Burnam and to get back to Frost on Wednesday. That evening Welk called the two graduates. The first said he might be interested, but he knew his wife wouldn't want to resettle in Alaska. The second, Tom Wolfe, expressed immediate interest.

Wolfe, 22, had graduated with a PR degree from Burnam a year and a half before and was working as an announcer for a small local radio station. While at Burnam he had worked as a tour guide for a local wine producer, compiled a good but not outstanding academic record, and done well in all his public relations courses. Unmarried, he lived at home with his parents. His current salary was $14,000. He dated the field and had no steady girl friend.

After outlining to Wolfe what he knew about the Alaska position, Welk said he could call Frost the next day if Wolfe wanted to have his name put forward.

"At this point, I just want to know if you're interested," said Welk. "No sense in going any further if you're not."

"Well, this is all rather sudden, but why not?" said Wolfe. "Go ahead, by all means call."

The next day Welk called Frost and told him about Wolfe and his interest in being considered. In citing Wolfe's qualifications Welk spoke very affirmatively about the 22-year-old. In addition to citing his record, Welk stated that he felt that Wolfe had always shown a good deal of imagination and maturity and was a very responsible person and a good writer. Frost said that Wolfe sounded like the kind of person who might just fit the bill. He ended the conversation by telling Welk he would call Wolfe either that day or on Thursday.

Welk then called Wolfe and told him he could expect a call from Frost.

When Welk returned home from work on Wednesday evening, he received a call from Wolfe to say that Frost had not yet called. Wolfe also said that he had been thinking about the Alaska thing; he wondered if he could come over to the college at noon the next day. The two agreed to have lunch together.

"I've been doing a lot of thinking since I got your call," Wolfe said as the two sat in the college's student union. "On the one hand, it sounds like a great opportunity—yet on the other hand . . ." Wolfe's voice trailed off.

"Look," said Welk, "why don't you try to sort this thing out logically? You outline for me what you see as the negative and the positive aspects."

"Well, here's the way I see it," Wolfe said, "The first negative is the fact that it's thousands of miles away. Second, it's in Alaska. Third—well, third, this all seems a rather odd way of doing things. I mean, there must be something wrong with the proposition if Frost is willing to take me sight-unseen and pay me as much as $22–$28,000."

"It does seem unusual," Welk agreed, "but remember, Frost is in a sort of bind in regard to time. He's simply relying on me to do a sound screening job for him. I guess he feels I wouldn't recommend you unless I felt you could do the job."

"Yeah, I guess that's true," said Wolfe somewhat dubiously. "But it still seems strange to me. Anyway, it's bothering me. The other thing is, I don't know much about this outfit that Frost has."

"The same principle applies in reverse," said Welk. "I guess you have to rely on my recommendation to you that Frost has what it takes. He'd be a good man to tie yourself to at this point in your life. In any case, what about the positive aspects?"

"As I see them, the first thing is the salary. At the

very least, I'd almost double my current salary. In fact, I'd be making as much as most at our station. Of course, the cost of living in Alaska is very high, and that has to be considered. The job also sounds like a real challenge and would be a quick entry right into the public relations field. And if for some reason things don't work out, Frost does say that they'll always have a good spot open in their Portland office."

"Let me add a few points," Welk said. "Real public relations opportunities in a city the size of Burnam are rare. This means that if you really want to get into public relations you're probably going to have to make a move someday. With one and a half years of radio experience you've probably already maximized the benefit of your radio background. I mean, any more time you pile up at the radio station won't do much good when it comes to seeking a public relations job.

"Further, the job market for public relations people these last two years has been tight, and jobs at this salary for relative newcomers are rare indeed. What you feel about Alaska is important—I guess you look at it like a sentence to Siberia. There *are* people, you know, who see Alaska as one of the last frontiers of opportunity.

"The important thing, though, is not how other people see this but how you see it. The important thing is what you want to do with your life. In any case, don't let your judgment be swayed by my reactions.

"I am curious about one thing, though. Let's assume that Alaska wasn't involved and I told you that Frost had an opening for a junior account executive in his Portland office at $23,000. Would you take it if it were offered to you?"

"No, I don't think so," said Wolfe.

"Oh? Why not?"

"Well, although that's much more than I'm making now, expenses would be higher, and I really don't think it would be that much of an improvement."

"I see," said Welk.

The two chatted some more, but the rest of the conversation was mainly a rehash of the points they had already gone over. When Wolfe went back to work he was as uncertain as before.

Frost called Wolfe late Friday afternoon. He spoke to Wolfe for about 20 minutes; said he felt that Wolfe had the right qualifications for the Alaska job; told Wolfe about the status of his firm and the opportunities in it; said he would expect a two-year commitment if the account came through, and that room would be made for Wolfe in the Portland office if, for some reason, the Alaska situation didn't work out well; and offered Wolfe a beginning salary of $26,000.

Wolfe said he appreciated the offer, recognized the opportunity and felt he could do the job, but after careful consideration had decided to stay at the radio station in Burnam.

GETTING TRAPPED IN THE ROUTINE*

Beatrice Ayala, 26, had worked in a small but excellent public relations office as a secretary-assistant for three years. She had saved her money, taken courses at night at a nearby state university, and majored in public relations.

At last, with just 24 units left to complete her degree, she could afford to go to school full time and work part time (22 hours a week). As she thought about it, her classes now meant a lot more. This was the final drive to moving from secretarial to professional status. Also, the remaining classes were challenging; they required more research, longer papers and presentations, and very thorough preparation. Up to now school and the job had been manageable, but there wasn't much slack. She completed the courses with "A's" and one "B" grade, the latter grade lowered on a team project. She would have liked all "A's", but she felt she'd done well. Her professors did, too.

At the start of the final semester, her advisor asked her to think about what PR field interested her most and then come back a week later to discuss her plans for getting such a job. As she walked into the office, Professor Stevens greeted her warmly and, before she

---

*All names, places, and dates in this case are disguised.

sat down, said, "First tell me what field interests you most and then tell me why they should be interested in you. What do you have that the other applicants lack?"

Beatrice thought, this is like Case Study. The questions come out of nowhere, fast and serious. It's all bottom line, "hard ball," now. As she put down her backpack, she thought quickly and then replied, "I'm interested in working in nonprofit, because I like helping other people and because I believe that there is more opportunity there right now."

The professor smiled; his student had been listening. "And . . . ?" he said.

Beatrice had been through that before, too: the question and the open space. As time went on it got easier. Now, she was ready. She knew this would be tough, friendly but tough. She'd spent a lot of the weekend thinking about it.

"I've had three years of work in a small agency. I've done all the clerical things, and I know WordPerfect, Word Star, Aldus, Adobe, Lotus, and an account management program. I've worked with media and with nonprofit accounts. In a small agency you learn to do it all. I can make good presentations, I write well and fast, and I can do it in both English and Spanish. I'm used to hard work, I manage my time well, and I know how to get along with people. In addition, I am creative and have experience in preparing both text and design for client accounts."

Again Professor Stevens smiled. He'd watched her grow and was very happy with her progress. He spoke slowly: "Beatrice, that was a good response. I have an opportunity for you to try it out. I just had a call from Mary Robison at the local Girl Scout office. She has an opening. It's a good-to-excellent place to start in nonprofit. Mary Robison has a good reputation. She is well-known by both the media and other PR people and can help you a lot. She's new to the Girl Scouts, and she is putting together a regional PR office for them. She needs help and she needs it now."

The next morning, Beatrice made an appointment for an interview. She then went to the Girl Scout office in a nearby city and and told them she was a student and wanted to learn as much as possible about the Girl Scouts. Then she went to the library and continued her research. She also called two other professors and her former boss to learn more about Mary Robison. She was interviewed the next day and got the job, starting at $24,000.

She found the job busier and faster paced than she had imagined. Mary's assistant, Chris Joiner, was trying to prove how well she could do, perhaps to demonstrate that she should have had the job that Mary got. But Mary didn't seem to care much about being boss. She just wanted to get results in a hurry. Since her strong suits were newspapers, magazines, and management, and Chris was strong in broadcast media, they divided the work and went at it. There were several ongoing campaign projects; it was all work, no glamor, and no time for orientation. They all came in early and worked hard, fast, and late. Two months passed.

Beatrice was not pleased at how things were going. Oh, they were doing a great job, but in that busy office she was getting lost in the shuffle. She was back doing the clerical work, while the two older professionals were doing the important and creative tasks. It wasn't what she wanted to do, but it was a recession and she had a job that paid well. However, she knew she could and should be doing more of the real PR work.

When she reached the threshold of her frustration, she walked into Mary's office after hours to talk to her.

"Mary, I need to talk to you for a few minutes about something that is very important to me. First, I'm glad to be here. I enjoy working with you and Chris, and I think we make a wonderful team."

Mary responded, "I know that Chris and I are both pleased with you and feel you and we are making a real contribution here."

Beatrice said, "I agree that a lot of progress has been made. You are getting all sorts of good exposure for the Girl Scouts and are creating some excellent programs. But sometimes things are so busy that I wonder if you realize that for two months straight I have done almost nothing but clerical duties. I think I can make a bigger contribution than that."

"No, frankly, I wasn't aware of it," said Mary, seeming a bit surprised. "I came in here and we were in the middle of two major campaigns. I just dug in and went at it. Chris was good at broadcast, and I let her cover that while I covered the print and management side of things. There was hardly a moment to think. But let's think now about what you think you should be doing."

Beatrice replied, "I am good at writing; I relate well to the Hispanic community; and I know how to handle media calls, coordinate spokesperson interviews, and work well with unit communicators. I want to take on more professional responsibilities."

"I'm glad that you brought this to my attention," Mary said. "Sometimes it's easy to get too wound up in what's happening and not cover all the bases as one should. I assure you that I will make sure you do more interesting work from now on. Now, if you'll pardon me, I have to go to a dinner."

Beatrice was a bit startled by the abrupt ending to the conversation with Mary, but she felt that she had done the right thing in discussing her feelings about the way work had gone during her first two months on the job. Another week passed, and Mary didn't mention the subject. Beatrice became more unhappy.

On Friday after work she met an old friend, Dorie Mullins, for dinner. Dorie's world was going well. She liked her job, and had a great new relationship. She asked how Beatrice was doing and listened thoughtfully to the whole story. Then, she asked: "Well, what are you going to do about it?"

BRUCE CANFIELD IS GIVEN THE WORD* (A)

While working in his office one Friday, the writer of this case had an unexpected visit from Bruce Canfield, who was on a three-week vacation with his family and had stopped by for a brief chat. While bringing the case writer up to date on his professional career in public relations, Canfield told the case writer that he was still working in Detroit and very happy in his work.

The case writer knew that Canfield was 30 years old; upon graduation from college he had joined the New York public relations staff of the Tremount Corporation. Tremount, the case writer knew, had its corporate headquarters in Detroit and, in terms of corporate size, ranked 24th on the *Fortune* 500 list. The case writer was intrigued by Canfield's story of his public relations job experiences, and he asked Canfield if he would mind recalling it on tape. When Canfield agreed to do so, the case writer set up a tape recorder and later transcribed Canfield's remarks. They are reproduced as follows.

You may not remember this, but thanks to you I got that first job in New York City. You put me in touch with Tom Markson, who had also graduated from our college with a public relations degree, and who was in charge of the New York office of Tremount. It was a lucky break for

---

*All names, places, and dates in this case are disguised.

me because Markson had an opening on his staff—there were four professionals on the staff at that time—and he was willing to take a chance on me because you recommended me. Of course, I had to make a trip to corporate headquarters in Detroit, but they went along with Markson's recommendation and I was hired at $18,000. Not being married at the time, I figured I could make out on that salary, and of course I knew I was fortunate to get started in a position that would bring me into contact with the top media people in the country.

The job was great because it was right where the action was and because Markson proved to be a real friend rather than just a boss. Although, as you well know, I'm not the most polished writer in the world, I was also fortunate because I wasn't supposed to do much writing but instead was expected to work with media people making publicity contacts and placements. I was really good at that sort of thing. The company must have been satisfied, because they kept raising my salary. Within three years I was making $25,000. In the meantime I began going steady with this girl from Tarrytown who had a job in a hospital as a lab technician. We got married and moved into a rent-controlled apartment in Bronxville.

As I said, I was doing fine on the job in New York, but I wasn't surprised when I was told the company was going to transfer me to the headquarters public relations staff in Detroit; this was fairly standard operating procedure for them. My wife and I enjoyed New York and all that, but we weren't unhappy when the move came and I was transferred. They made me public relations manager of one of the company's product groups, gave me a $3,000 raise, and of course covered all our moving expenses. Within the next three years I became manager of stockholder relations, my salary went up to $36,000, and I bought a new house for $90,000 in the country where there was plenty of fresh air and room for our little Jonathan.

That stockholder relations job was not very exciting. I figured it was all part of the learning experience, even though there were times when I felt I was underutilized. I imagine I felt this way because there were 25 professionals on the corporate public relations staff, and we probably had more people in public relations than we really needed. In a way, that was a fortunate thing, because just about that time the economy went into a tailspin and so did the company's sales and stock. There were layoffs throughout the entire company, and of course that included public relations.

One day the vice president of public relations called a meeting of the entire staff and told us that anywhere from 20 to 30 percent of the staff would be cut. He said they would be evaluating everyone's performance and were looking for ways to cut costs because we were top-heavy. Sure enough, some staffers were transferred to other positions, some were simply let go, and some were given early retirement. When I looked around one day I figured out that, with the exception of three of us, the entire staff consisted of veterans with years of experience and special expertise, and I got very nervous.

In a way, I guess it was some consolation to know that the company considered us good enough to keep us on board. The other two were a very talented black fellow who was going to law school and a very bright, terrific writer, a woman. The three of us—all the same age—were the only young people left. They had let others go who had a lot more experience than we had, and we used to get together for lunch every once in a while to figure out what was going to happen to us. The Equal Opportunity Commission was putting lots of pressure on the company, on all companies of course, and I said to the other two: "I look around this table and see a black guy and a woman. I'm blond-haired and blue-eyed, and I know who's going where." We all laughed; we were very close friends, but none of us really knew what was going to happen.

Well, one day Charlie Perry, the manager of corporate relations and my boss, told me they had cut all the people they wanted to cut and that there was really nothing to worry about. However, I knew that my job was a premier job, and what with all the consolidation of duties I figured they might want to get a writer on the job who could write annual reports and that sort of thing and who could also work with security analysts. I was not especially skilled at that sort of thing, and I recognized that there were guys around who were just more talented than I was in that direction. So it didn't come as much of a surprise to me when Perry suggested we go out to dinner and have a little talk. What I mean is, the idea of having "a little talk" didn't come as a surprise, but the dinner did. Up to this time we had gone out to lunch occasionally, but never to dinner. This is going to be it, I thought, and I wasn't wrong.

Perry said the company had been under a good deal of pressure on two fronts: in the financial community and in media relations.

"You've done a good job in stockholder relations," he said, "but you're especially strong in media relations. As it happens, that's where we can best use you. We've got other people, as you know, who have had stronger backgrounds in finance than you do, but you are a standout on media, and particularly electronic media centered in New York. What we'd like you to do is to go to New York and run the office there. We really haven't had top performance at that end ever since we brought Tom Markson here to Detroit a few years ago. We'd also want you to work closely with Jeff Peters, manager of the whole northeast region of the company. He's considered one of our top management people."

"What about Paul Thiel?" I asked, referring to the man who then headed the New York public relations operation.

"We want to bring him here to Detroit," Perry said, and I saw by this that Perry had his game plan all set up. It's like a game of dominoes where one goes here, another there, and every move has to fit. I knew that if I balked, I would be creating some problems.

"Well," I said, "I have mixed reactions. I like it here and so does my family. The New York move seems like a challenge, but on the other hand I would be going back where I started six years ago."

I didn't say it, but it seemed to me that Perry was blowing up the move to make it sound real good for me. Instead, I asked: "What's the alternative, Charlie?"

"I'll be very frank with you," Perry said. "We've cut all the people we want to cut and we have a bunch of talented people we want to do something and so this is what we're offering you. We can use you best in New York and would like you there as soon as possible. Don't worry about selling your house, the company will buy it if you can't find a buyer. We'd like you to go to New York and find a place to live. Go next week. Take whatever money you need from the expense account, fly down with your wife, rent a car, do whatever you have to do, and come back and let us know where you're going to live and how soon you can get there."

It was clear to me there was no alternative in the company's plans, and so we ended the evening with me saying that I would be a good corporate soldier and would be delighted to go to New York to find a place to live. That was the easy part of it; the toughest part was at home. My wife was very good about it. She said, "It's your career, it's a decision you're going to have to make. I love it here, but if we have to move, we'll move."

I looked at four-year-old Jonathan and I thought, it's great for him out here in the country. It would be terrible to take him to New York. I also knew what I would become. My whole personality changes there, and I become very aggressive. When I go to New York on occasion, it takes me a day to get back to normal. My wife doesn't even like me when I get back from New York.

Anyway, we talked about all these things for a long time that night, but we went to bed agreeing that we would go to New York to look for a place to live. One of the things I had to do before going was to call the program chairman of the Public Relations Society of America chapter in Detroit and tell him that I couldn't handle the program I was responsible for a couple of months from that time. Frank Danforth, the program chairman, had a job as a public relations manager at Mavis Metals, which had its headquarters in Detroit and was 48th on the *Fortune* 500 list.

"I'm being shoved off to the New York operation," I said to Danforth. "I'm not especially happy about it, but that's the Peter Principle, or maybe you'd call it the Domino Theory. In any case, I don't expect to be around here long, so I didn't want to hang you up on the PRSA program at the last minute."

I guess I was overwrought and tired, and I think he sensed that something was wrong. He asked me a few questions that didn't quite register with me at the time.

"What do you do over there at Tremount?" he asked, and I told him. Then he asked: "How many years have you been with Tremount?" and other things like that. You see, we knew each other casually from PRSA meetings we had attended, but that was about the extent of it. Anyway, these were leading questions to gather information, but that didn't register on me at the time as I answered them. He finally suggested that we get together about the PRSA program so he could pick up where I left off, and we made a lunch date for the next day.

I met him the next day and gave him my file on the program. There wasn't much in it, because I hadn't done much on the program. He asked me more questions about my job at Tremount, what I thought about the strengths and weaknesses of the job, the extent of the job, my responsibilities, experience, and that sort of thing.

"Frank," I finally said, "I'm wide-awake now so let's lay our cards on the table. You're interviewing me and I realize that now, so what have you got?"

Danforth laughed. "We don't need any financial public relations people, but we do have a job here," he said, "and it's something you may not be interested in because it's an area in which you haven't had much experience."

Danforth then went into details about the position, which was in a three-person group in the public relations department that was concerned with gathering, coordinating, and dispensing information about energy and the environment as each of these related to Mavis Metals. He said that Mavis was a heavy energy user and was also heavy into the environmental area, but people weren't aware of what the company was doing. They had formed this group to make sure that everything done was coordinated through one agency. Danforth also said that I would be particularly involved in the areas of nonfillable beverage containers, litter, solid-waste management, and federal agencies concerned with these aspects of the industry.

When I told Danforth that I thought the job was very interesting, he said I should think about it. He asked me what I was going to do about the situation at Tremount, and I told him I was going to take my wife and family to New York to find out what it was going to take to live there. I knew there would be severe financial ramifications to consider.

"Well," he said, "you go find out about this thing. I want you to know that we are interviewing other people for this job, but you go ahead and find out the things you must find out."

The next day I took my family to New York. We left Jonathan with the in-laws in Tarrytown while my wife and I checked out various areas in the New York suburbs. We checked in New Jersey, Westchester, and even up in Rockland and Putnam counties. As you know, that could mean a daily round-trip commute of 2-1/2 to 3 hours, but we wanted to check all possibilities. We spent four days doing this checking, and although it was a chore we also found time to visit old friends, dine out, and see some plays. I didn't go near the New York office because I didn't want to. I knew the office people, and I could always get into the personnel thing later. What I was concerned about was living and financial matters.

By Thursday I had these matters pretty well firmed up in my own mind. I figured that, considering everything, if I made the move to New York I ought to get about 27 percent more than I was making in Detroit just to come out even with my present salary of $36,000. So I added another 5 percent, because Perry had given me to understand this would be a good move for me. I figured that a boost of 32 percent would just about do it. I had done my research, and knowing that the company doesn't move fast, I decided to call Perry and thus give him enough time to think about it and discuss it with whomever he had to discuss it. I therefore called him and told him what I thought and about the 32 percent.

"Well, Bruce," he said," I don't think that will happen, but let me check it out and see what the reaction is upstairs."

His answer was predictable; this was standard operating procedure. You know what I mean: "Yes, Bruce, you deserve 32 percent. I can't give it to you but let me check it out."

The one surprise was that he phoned me at my in-laws about four hours later.

"I've checked it out here, Bruce," he told me, "and they're prepared to make you an offer of 18 percent."

"Gee, Charlie," I said, "we're still pretty far apart, but I'm not very good at negotiating. You know I'm a candid individual, so I'll tell you frankly that I'm not very happy with that and I really can't hack it with just 18 percent.

"However, I don't want to argue with you, so I'll tell

you this: I have all the documentation with me about comparative livings costs and that sort of thing, cost estimates showing what I need to raise my child in New York and have a reasonable standard of living for my family. I'd appreciate it if you would think about it over the weekend, talk to the other people involved, and see if you can come closer. In fact, I'd like you to meet that 32 percent figure."

"Okay," said Perry, "but I don't know what they're going to do."

"Fine," I said. "I'll see you on Monday."

"Monday?" he said. "Aren't you coming back tonight or early tomorrow?"

"No," I said, "I'm coming back on Sunday. I still have some money left in my pocket, Charlie, so I'm going to spend the rest of the week here and I'll see you on Monday."

Perry didn't reply, but I now knew just where I stood. I now knew where they were coming from, which was at about 18 percent, and that they would probably come up to maybe 21 percent or maybe 22 percent. Meanwhile, on Friday my wife and I went to speak to a builder who had been recommended to us, and when we got back to my in-law's house I was told that Mavis had called twice and left the message that I should get back to them. The person who had called was John Friendly, assistant to Danforth at Mavis, whom I had met several times and knew to be a pretty savvy guy.

"Bruce," he said when I called, "we want this job filled and we want to make you an offer, a firm offer. If you feel you can't take it, we have another candidate who we think can handle the work. We can offer you $35,000."

BRUCE CANFIELD IS GIVEN THE WORD* (B)

When John Friendly told me that Mavis was making me a firm offer of $35,000, I knew that if I accepted the move to New York with Tremount, I would be able to get at least 18 percent more than the $36,000 I was then making with Tremount in Detroit. I also judged that Tremount might well go as high as a 21 or 22 percent increase. Up to this point in my conversations with the Mavis people, the subject of salary had not come up. So when Friendly said their firm offer was $35,000 I said: "John, that's less money than I'm making now," and when he asked how much I was then making I bumped it up a little and said: "I'm making $38,500."

"That's not what the job pays," Friendly replied, "but I'm going to put you on hold and talk to Danforth."

"Fine," I said while I held the line and my breath. He got back to me shortly.

"I talked to Danforth, and he said we can go as high as $37,000, but that's it," he said.

"John," I said, "I'll tell you this right now; I'm not going to try to hold you up, and I'm not going to try to hold Tremount up. As far as I'm concerned the job sounds like a real challenge. I really don't want to go to New York, and I'm not going to go back and play your

---

*All names, places, and dates in this case are disguised.

job against Tremount. I'm telling you I'll take the job, and I accept it right now on one condition: that I pass a physical if you'll set it up for Monday."

"Fine," Friendly said. "I'll set it up. Call on Monday and we'll tell you where to go and what time we've set for the physical."

I ran into Charlie Perry when I got into the office Monday, and I said that I would be out of the office that afternoon and would talk to him Tuesday. He asked what I had found out, and I gave him all the documents, showing the higher cost of living in New York.

"That's very convincing, very convincing," he said.

"I certainly hope so. I hope it's 32 percent worth of convincing," I said. Of course I knew I had the other job, but even if he had matched my 32 percent I would have left the company. However, as was his habit he suggested that we get together and talk about it, and we agreed that we ought to do so on Thursday because he was tied up until then.

I took the Mavis physical on Monday afternoon and they informed me on Tuesday that I had passed it. On Wednesday there was a big staff meeting of the entire Tremount public relations staff, but I deliberately did not go. Instead I typed out my resignation from the company, saying briefly that I had had a great experience, had learned a great deal, and was sad to leave after six years but had found an opportunity with another company in Detroit which I couldn't pass up. That's all I said. I didn't name the company, but I said I would be leaving two weeks from Friday. I gave the note to Charlie Perry's secretary shortly after the staff meeting started and said to her: "You'd better take this in to him, Sandy; it's not very good news and it makes me kind of sad, but you'd better take it in to him."

I waited in the outer office and in a few minutes Perry came out.

"Bruce, you handled this very well," he said, and

he repeated: "Yes, very well. Do you mind telling me who you're going with?"

"Not at all, Charlie," I said, "I'm going with Mavis."

"That's fine for you, I'm sure," he said. "We really do need you in New York, but we appreciate the fact that you didn't try to play us off against them."

And that was that. We parted on friendly terms, and two weeks later I started my new job at Mavis.

THE INTERVIEW*

George Williams, 39, had recently resigned a public affairs directorship because he didn't like the surroundings and didn't enjoy working with his former boss. He also thought that he could do better, for several reasons. Williams had built a good reputation in the field, he was active in the Public Relations Society of America at local and district levels, and he had a host of good contacts.

He was therefore not surprised that he had passed the preliminary interviews for a job with a Catholic university. He had met with Father Claude, who was in charge of public relations, and with Rochelle Fanchett, the development director. Now they wanted him to meet with the president. The job and university seemed intriguing. Williams was definitely interested—not committed yet, but interested. He had some reservations about Father Claude; maybe it was just that the good father seemed more traditional than any boss Williams had ever had.

When Williams arrived for the interview with President O'Malley, he was immediately ushered in, even though it was five minutes before the time of his appointment. O'Malley was friendly, courteous, acutely

---

*All names, places, and dates in this case are disguised.

observant, and he listened thoughtfully. Williams was impressed that here was a man who knew how to be in charge and to run things well.

The president started the conversation with a few observations about the current state of the faculty. As he put it, they saw the entire summer as a vacation rather than a time for intellectual renewal, scholarship, and study. He mused about the need for more scholarship and dedication to the task at hand. While talking about the size and development of the university, he mentioned the many demands that are placed on the president. He expressed the need for someone to relieve him of some of the ceremonial chores. "Our basketball team is very successful," he told Williams. "They're in a big tournament, and they want me to fly in to demonstrate the university's support for their effort. The coach called last night and again this morning. The director of athletics called, too. What do you think?"

"President O'Malley," Williams responded, "what would you do if your debating team were competing in a major national event? Would you rush to attend?"

"As it happens, they are, but I told them I couldn't get away just now," said O'Malley.

Williams did not break the silence.

O'Malley continued, "You're right, I guess that I should call the director of athletics and tell him I can't go." He buzzed his secretary and gave her that message. He told her to assure the athletic staff that he was supportive and wanted them to give his best wishes to the team before the game.

"We have another problem," said O'Malley. "Our student activities director invited one of the national officers from the National Organization for Women to come and speak at a rally on campus. I didn't hear about it until the afternoon of the day before. Several parents called my office and were very irate. They wanted to know what I was going to do about it. What would you have done, and why?"

"A few phone calls aren't the end of the world. They may not have much real meaning at all," said Williams. "Also, I don't believe that you should do anything. You didn't invite her, and you'd only escalate the problem if you got involved. However, you need to have a statement so that there is one clear message going out."

"All right, what should that message be? And, by the way, are you Catholic?"

"First, no, I'm not Catholic, but that shouldn't really be an issue," Williams replied. "I know your faith's tenets quite well, and I would know them better if I were to come here. Second, the statement would sound something like this:

> Student Affairs Director Marion Leggett acknowledged that Eleanor Smeal would be giving an open lecture at the university tomorrow, Friday, at 11:00 a.m. in the main lecture hall.
>
> When asked if Smeal didn't espouse different beliefs than the university, Leggett replied, "She probably does, but we let our students consider a variety of opinions on subjects. They have a sound Catholic educational background and have the ability to make sound, ethical decisions on any subject."

"You think you could contain it that way?" O'Malley asked.

"Yes, I do," Williams said. "Further, the person who caused the problem should be given the opportunity to work out the solution—under guidance, if necessary. Also, handling it that way gives an important message to a lot of people on campus."

O'Malley asked, "Do you think Father Claude is worldly enough and well enough versed in public relations to head that office of this university? I want this university to grow, to gain stature, and to play a bigger role in this community."

Williams liked this type of parrying, but he wasn't about to be trapped on a question like that. "I only met the man once; we talked mostly about the university and what I might do if I came here. Therefore, I'm not really in a position to answer your question now," he said.

"If you'd been here a month, could you answer that question openly?" O'Malley asked.

"I could."

"Would you?"

"I have loyalty to my boss. Who would that be?"

"Me," O'Malley said.

"Yes, I'd answer it frankly."

"I have some reservations about our sports information director," O'Malley said. "I never quite know exactly what he's doing, or whether he's worth what we pay him. Do you know anything about that?"

"Why yes, as a matter of fact, I do," Williams said. "A year ago I tried to hire him away from you, but he was too loyal. He's one of the top ten sports information people in the country. He does a great job for you with only a student assistant to help. You're lucky to have him. Hang on to him. He's a great asset."

After a few minutes of pleasantries President O'Malley ended the interview, saying, "We'll be in touch with you soon." Williams left thinking that he'd get the offer. Two days later he did, and it was for substantially more than he had been making at his last position. He wasn't sure, though, if he would accept it.

Reprint for Discussion

Personal Values, Not Rules, Guide PR's Choices *
John F. Budd, Jr.

The greatest problem in communications, George Bernard Shaw once observed, is the illusion that it has been accomplished. I was reminded of that during my research into this matter of ethics . . . of codes, regulations, guidelines, rules of conduct, of documents of unbelievable comprehensiveness, painstakingly constructed by legions of committees of our peers, in virtually every country where our craft is pursued.

This profusion of 'shall nots' makes Moses' Ten Commandments seem like a two minute television sound bite. It all suggests to me that life in Public Relations is dangerous to our health and will eventually kill us!

But will we behave any better in the interim thanks to this abundance of guidelines?

Do criminal laws and statutes deter thieves?

The Roaring Twenties American muck-raking columnist Drew Pearson once observed that he operated by the sense of smell. When something smelled wrong, that's when he got to work. So when I sniffed about on this subject of ethics I became more concerned about what we're not highlighting than what we so meticulously identify as 'no-nos'.

Many years ago a very wise technologist, with a long, storied career as vice president of research, explained to me why the United States had product quality problems not experienced by the Japanese. (He'd just returned from a VIP inspection tour of a number of Japan's newest plants).

* Reprinted with permission from *IPRA Review* (Vol. 14, No. 3, 1991), the quarterly publication of the International Public Relations Association, John M. Reed, editor. John F. Budd, Jr. is Chairman and Chief Executive, The Omega Group, New York.

In the U.S., he said, we focus on catching defective products *on the* production line—much of our state-of-the-art technology goes to improving the sophistication of the detection systems.

On the other hand, in Japan, their attention is all *upfront*—designing products and systems so there, literally, *are no defects* and, correspondingly, little need for detection systems.

It's a matter of attitude not adaption.

My approach to ethics in Public Relations is in this context.

I want to shed some light on those grey, ambiguous problem areas where there are no hard and fast, right or wrong answers. Yet the potential is there for some very troubling, if not unethical, conduct. There are a number of genuinely difficult situations (and I'll review some of them shortly) where there is enormous latitude for rationalisation, a flexibility that creates infinite 'wiggle room' for the quick of mind and short of conscience.

I hope to sharpen awareness of the ethical dilemmas that fall in this no-man's land between clear cut standards and subjective, personal judgements. I will cite no instances of honest vs. dishonest, or legal vs. illegal, but difficult instances where judgements can go either way. The criterion are not the published standards but the unpublished values each of us holds.

Socrates said 'that an unexamined life is not worth living.'

Let us therefore examine ours more carefully and, perhaps, more objectively, if not more honestly.

As I said at the outset, having read or dipped into the voluminous material on ethics, I am persuaded that the ethical practitioner cannot be defined in terms of rules. We can't pretend that ethical behavior can be created simply by the publication of regulations, codes of conduct or legalistic standards. No matter what the censure may ultimately be, it isn't the ultimate deterrent.

John Gardner, who in his writings and speeches has

done more to clearly define the mystic of leadership than anyone else, mentions 'trust' no less than ten times in his most current and searching literary examination of leadership.

Countless circumstances operate in our special world to diminish trust. Let me pose some scenarios that today exist. Some may be uncomfortably familiar. I suggest no right or wrong choice. You make the call—but ask yourself if your decision has the capacity to inspire trust in yourself by others?

Bait and Switch
....
Is it ethical to make a client proposal with senior staff, then assign to the account, young relatively uncredentialed staffers?

Selling the Sizzle Not the Meat
....
Is it ethical to tease the prospective client with 'suggestions' of high visibility results that are probably unrealistic? Not promises, mind you, but subtle references to *NY Times, Wall Street Journal, Time,* etc.

Churning
....
Is it ethical to create/make work to add up the chargeable hours? The unwanted press kit to be widely disseminated; the unneeded audit or survey.

The Sycophantic Syndrome
....
Creating extravagant paeans to the CEO in release material that will please only an audience of one—and strains credibility outside. Unethical or just unprofessional?

'You're the Boss'
....
Is it unethical to withhold critical judgement on statements in fear of 'rocking the boat'; or allowing yourself to be intimidated by legal counsel?

Producing Corporate Disinformation
....
Do you feel troubled when you issue what you know are half truths in an attempt to create plausibility and divert attention from other aspects of an issue? Is it justifiable on the basis of 'you're entitled to tell your side of the issue?' The facts may not be challengeable, but the intent can be.

About 'White Lies'

Is it ethical to dismiss a minor infraction of the truth to a necessary 'white lie?'

Creating a Semantic Curtain

The more difficult an issue becomes the greater the tendency to couch statements in carefully constructed legal language—totally undecipherable to an audience that has a legitimate right to know, e.g. business or financial press. Is it ethical?

All Head; No Legs

You write a headline on the story that dazzles the client with its self-serving adjectives and you tell him it's going to a high leverage media but you know they'll never use that headline. Is it ethical to lead the client (or your boss) astray like this?

There's a bit of Confucian teaching that fits here: it goes: 'Those who know the truth are not equal to those who love it!'

In getting myself up to speed to get my arms around this squishy subject—much like trying to put fog in a bottle—I boned up on some of the thoughts of my predecessor on this platform—Mr. Dimma. Let me tell you—I could have sold one year internships with him to some of my peers for a crash Masters course in Public Relations! I liked what he said, the way he says it, and how he thinks. When he said that 'rotten ethics and unrestrained greed blossomed in the go-go economy of the last eight years of the Eighties', I knew I had met a man I could relate to.

But the issue goes deeper than the arrogance of an Ivan Boesky who, in 1985, told students at Berkeley that 'everyone should be a little bit greedy.' And was lustily cheered!

It centres on the impact, sometimes insidious, of the domineering presence of 'the bottom-line.' Any businessman's genuine sensitivity to such qualitative values as social responsibility is in reality restrained by economics. He has a more limited range of options than his critics generally recognise or concede. He cannot be arbitrary about choosing. Profit *is* the test of his success, . . . not '*a*' test but '*the*' test. This is the foundation of his corporation's existence and the source of resources to be applied to *any* social responsibility.

This is not to say that executives are myopic about money. Time and time again business demonstrates its willingness and its creativity in contributing to society.

But I am suggesting that economic pressures tend to minimize contemplativeness when faced with those uncharted grey areas of ethical dilemmas where almost any answer can be made to fit our conscience.

. . .

Whether it marks a coming of age or not, Public Relations is itself big business these days—$8 billion annually—and it is increasingly more public than private in ownership.

I do not argue that private Public Relations entrepreneurs are an ethical breed apart from the CEOs of publicly owned Public Relations consultancies.

(Personally, I feel that public ownership is an egregious mistake that has unleashed as many ills as flew from Pandora's Box when Epimetheus unwisely opened it— some of which fall into the ethical conundrum category.)

What I am suggesting is that public ownership introduces us to the new world of temptation.

All men are honest it is said, until they are faced with a situation tempting enough to make them dishonest!

Public ownership and the ascendancy of quarterly profits over such qualitative values as creativity, innovation and client service, introduces us to choices that bear a punitive penalty.

I can't prove this but I have to believe that somewhere in the troubled environment that has seen from 60–70 per cent of earn-outs established in the process of the purchase of entrepreneurial firms, terminated prematurely, that part of it stems from a fundamental conflict of interests— to the pressures to make financial judgements rather than instinctive ones. The *Financial Times,* in a revealing piece on the trouble with earn-outs, pointed to the irresolvable clash between *what* is in the best long term interests for the company against *what* would boost short term profits—and the size of earnings.

We develop our ethical principles from religion, history, family, school and peers. They are an amalgam of diverse, subjective, sometimes inconsistent, experiences, and they are constantly going through direct and indirect examination by each of us.

Public Relations practice rests squarely on a moral base. Let's not get caught up in an Aristotelian debate on any of the issues I raised.

Sociologist Bob Jackall suggests that we begin by accepting our own instinctive sense of what is right to justify trust. We will then intuitively make decisions that reflect integrity, unimpeded by monetary pressures. We have a special responsibility because of our role as counsellors. Here, an old adage should set our focus. It says: 'A good example has twice the value of good advice.'

Guiding executives through the mist of grey ethical dilemmas requires considerable fortitude and sophistication. We must be familiar with, and comfortable with, the philosophical underpinnings of ethics.

Unlike the academic preachings, I do not suggest that you dose yourself up with heavy reading—Sophocles, Joseph Conrad, Tolstoy, Dostoevsky—unless you have a yen for that sort of old best-seller pedantry. There are a number of real-world books on the subject that will sharpen your sense quite adequately.

Twenty years ago Chief Justice Earl Warren called for the development of 'professional counsellors in ethics'. Counsellors who could offer sophisticated guidance in ethical decision-making to business executives.

In the sense that we regularly deal with such intangibles as trust, reputation—those abstract values that quantitative-minded executives have some difficulty with—we are bringing squishy issues from the grey light to bright light, forcing them into the black-and-white. We remind executives of the chasm between reality or facts and perceptions, and why failure to bridge this gap feeds public scepticism, legitimises criticism and erodes trust.

It is here that the question of ethics comes full circle. This isn't a game of rules and regulations but one more of perceptions. Denied the opportunity to wiggle away—either by financial types citing the cost, or legal types citing the personal jeopardy or corporate liability of candor—all of the CEOs I have ever met will make a moral choice. Instinctively they know there is nothing more precious than integrity—even when it is very expensive to protect.

. . .

I am not given to farewell addresses. But in my 40 years as counsellor—11 years at the corporate table—I found one word that was as powerful and as persuasive as Mr. Kohlberg's eloquence. This one word could—and did—offset pages of legal and financial arguments.

Whenever I thought we were edging toward some impropriety I evoked this word . . . it was CREDIBILITY.

Today, our own credibility as Public Relations counsel is on the line!

CODE OF PROFESSIONAL STANDARDS FOR THE PRACTICE OF PUBLIC RELATIONS: PUBLIC RELATIONS SOCIETY OF AMERICA

This Code was adopted by the PRSA Assembly in 1988. It replaces a Code of Ethics in force since 1950 and revised in 1954, 1959, 1963, 1977, and 1983. For information on the Code and enforcement procedures, please call the Board of Ethics Chairman through PRSA Headquarters. Reprinted with permission.

Declaration of Principles

Members of the Public Relations Society of America base their professional principles on the fundamental value and dignity of the individual, holding that the free exercise of human rights, especially freedom of speech, freedom of assembly, and freedom of the press, is essential to the practice of public relations.

In serving the interests of clients and employers, we dedicate ourselves to the goals of better communication, understanding, and cooperation among the diverse individuals, groups, and institutions of society, and of equal opportunity of employment in the public relations profession.

To conduct ourselves professionally, with truth, accuracy, fairness, and responsibility to the public;

To improve our individual competence and advance the knowledge and proficiency of the profession through continuing research and education;

And to adhere to the articles of the Code of Professional Standards for the Practice of Public Relations as adopted by the governing Assembly of the Society.

Code of Professional Standards for the Practice of Public Relations

These articles have been adopted by the Public Relations Society of America to promote and maintain high standards of public service and ethical conduct among its members.

1. A member shall conduct his or her professional life in accordance with the **public interest**.

2. A member shall exemplify high standards of **honesty and integrity** while carrying out dual obligations to a client or employer and to the democratic process.

3. A member shall **deal fairly** with the public, with past or present clients or employers, and with fellow practitioners, giving due respect to the ideal of free inquiry and to the opinions of others.

4. A member shall adhere to the highest standards of **accuracy and truth**, avoiding extravagant claims or unfair comparisons and giving credit for ideas and words borrowed from others.

5. A member shall not knowingly disseminate **false or misleading information** and shall act promptly to correct erroneous communications for which he or she is responsible.

6. A member shall not engage in any practice which has the purpose of **corrupting** the integrity of channels of communications or the processes of government.

7. A member shall be prepared to **identify publicly** the name of the client or employer on whose behalf any public communication is made.

8. A member shall not use any individual or organization professing to serve or represent an announced cause, or professing to be independent or unbiased, but actually serving another or **undisclosed interest**.

9. A member shall not **guarantee the achievement** of specified results beyond the member's direct control.

10. A member shall **not represent conflicting** or competing interests without the express consent of those concerned, given after a full disclosure of the facts.

11. A member shall not place himself or herself in a position where the member's **personal interest is or may be in conflict** with an obligation to an employer, or client, or others, without full disclosure of such interests to all involved.

12. A member shall **not accept fees, commissions, gifts or any other consideration** from anyone except clients or employers for whom services are performed without their express consent, given after full disclosure of the facts.

13. A member shall scrupulously safeguard

the **confidences and privacy rights** of present, former, and prospective clients or employers.

14. A member shall not intentionally **damage the professional reputation** or practice of another practitioner.

15. If a member has evidence that another member has been guilty of unethical, illegal, or unfair practices, including those in violation of this Code, the member is obligated to present the information promptly to the proper authorities of the Society for action in accordance with the procedure set forth in Article XII of the Bylaws.

16. A member called as a witness in a proceeding for enforcement of this Code is obligated to appear, unless excused for sufficient reason by the judicial panel.

17. A member shall, as soon as possible, sever relations with any organization or individual if such relationship requires conduct contrary to the articles of this Code.

Official Interpretations of the Code

Interpretation of Code Paragraph 1, which reads, "A member shall conduct his or her professional life in accord with the public interest."

The public interest is here defined primarily as comprising respect for and enforcement of the rights guaranteed by the Constitution of the United States of America.

Interpretation of Code Paragraph 6, which reads, "A member shall not engage in any practice which has the purpose of corrupting the integrity of channels or communication or the processes of government."

1. Among the practices prohibited by this paragraph are those that tend to place representatives of media or government under any obligation to the member, or the member's employer or client, which is in conflict with their obligations to media or government, such as:

a. the giving of gifts of more than nominal value;

b. any form of payment or compensation to a member of the media in order to obtain preferential or guaranteed news or editorial coverage in the medium;

c. any retainer or fee to a media employee or use of such employee if retained by a client or employer, where the circumstances are not fully disclosed to and accepted by the media employer;

d. providing trips, for media representatives, that are unrelated to legitimate news interest;

e. the use by a member of an investment or loan or advertising commitment made by the member, or the member's client or employer, to obtain preferential or guaranteed coverage in the medium.

2. This Code paragraph does not prohibit hosting media or government representatives at meals, cocktails, or news functions and special events that are occasions for the exchange of news information or views, or the furtherance of understanding, which is part of the public rela-

tions function. Nor does it prohibit the bona fide press event or tour when media or government representatives are given the opportunity for an on-the-spot viewing of a newsworthy product, process, or event in which the media or government representatives have a legitimate interest. What is customary or reasonable hospitality has to be a matter of particular judgment in specific situations. In all of these cases, however, it is, or should be, understood that no preferential treatment or guarantees are expected or implied and that complete independence always is left to the media or government representative.

3.   This paragraph does not prohibit the reasonable giving or lending of sample products or services to media representatives who have a legitimate interest in the products or services.

4.   It is permissible, under Article 6 of the Code, to offer complimentary or discount rates to the media (travel writers, for example) if the rate is for business use and is made available to all writers. Considerable question exists as to the propriety of extending such rates for personal use.

Interpretation of Code Paragraph 9, which reads, "A member shall not guarantee the achievement of specified results beyond the member's direct control."

This Code paragraph, in effect, prohibits misleading a client or employer as to what professional public relations can accomplish. It does not prohibit guarantees of quality or service. But it does prohibit guaranteeing specific results which, by their very nature, cannot be guaranteed because they are not subject to the member's control. As an example, a guarantee that a news release will appear specifically in a particular publication would be prohibited. This paragraph should not be interpreted as prohibiting contingent fees.

Interpretation of Code Paragraph 13, which reads, "A member shall scrupulously safeguard the confidences and privacy rights of present, former, and prospective clients or employers."

    1. This articles does not prohibit a member who has knowledge of client or employer activities that are illegal from making such disclosures to the proper authorities as he or she believes are legally required.

    2. Communications between a practitioner and client/employer are deemed to be confidential under Article 13 of the Code of Professional Standards. However, although practitioner/client/employer communications are considered confidential between the parties, such communications are not privileged against disclosure in a court of law.

    3. In the absence of any contractual arrangement, the client or employer legally owns the rights to papers or materials created for him.

Interpretation of Code Paragraph 14, which reads, "A member shall not intentionally damage the professional reputation or practice of another practitioner."

    1. Blind solicitation, on its face, is not prohibited by the Code. However, if the customer list were improperly obtained, or if the solicitation contained references reflecting adversely on the

quality of current services, a complaint might be justified.

2. This article applies to statements, true or false, or acts, made or undertaken with malice and with the specific purpose of harming the reputation or practice of another member. This article does not prohibit honest employee evaluations or similar reviews, made without malice and as part of ordinary business practice, even though this activity may have a harmful effect.

An Official Interpretation of the Code As It Applies to Political Public Relations

Preamble

In the practice of political public relations, a PRSA member must have professional capabilities to offer an employer or client quite apart from any political relationships of value, and members may serve their employer or client without necessarily having attributed to them the character, reputation, or beliefs of those they serve. It is understood that members may choose to serve only those interests with whose political philosophy they are personally comfortable.

Definition

"Political Public Relations" is defined as those areas of public relations that relate to:

> a. the counseling of political organizations, committees, candidates, or potential candidates for public office; and groups constituted for the purpose of influencing the vote on any ballot issue;
>
> b. the counseling of holders of public office;

c.   the management, or direction, of a political campaign for or against a candidate for political office; or for or against a ballot issue to be determined by voter approval or rejection;

d.   the practice of public relations on behalf of a client or an employer in connection with that client's or employer's relationships with any candidates or holders of public office, with the purpose of influencing legislation or government regulation or treatment of a client or employer, regardless of whether the PRSA member is a recognized lobbyist;

e.   the counseling of government bodies, or segments thereof, either domestic or foreign.

1.   It is the responsibility of PRSA members practicing political public relations, as defined above, to be conversant with the various statutes, local, state, and federal, governing such activities and to adhere to them strictly. This includes, but is not limited to, the various local, state, and federal laws, court decisions, and official interpretations governing lobbying, political contributions, disclosure, elections, libel, slander, and the like. In carrying out this responsibility, members shall seek appropriate counseling whenever necessary.

2.   It is also the responsibility of the members to abide by PRSA's Code of Professional Standards.

3.   Members shall represent clients or employers in good faith, and while partisan advocacy on behalf of a candidate or public issue may be expected, members shall act in accord with the public interest and adhere to truth and accuracy

and to generally accepted standards of good taste.

4. Members shall not issue descriptive material or any advertising or publicity information or participate in the preparation or use thereof that is not signed by responsible persons or is false, misleading, or unlabeled as to its source, and are obligated to use care to avoid dissemination of any such material.

5. Members have an obligation to clients to disclose what remuneration beyond their fees they expect to receive as a result of their relationship, such as commissions for media advertising, printing, and the like, and should not accept such extra payment without their client's consent.

6. Members shall not improperly use their positions to encourage additional future employment or compensation. It is understood that successful campaign directors or managers, because of the performance of their duties and the working relationship that develops, may well continue to assist and counsel, for pay, the successful candidate.

7. Members shall voluntarily disclose to employers or clients the identity of other employers or clients with whom they are currently associated, and whose interests might be affected favorably or unfavorably by their political representation.

8. Members shall respect the confidentiality of information pertaining to employers or clients past, present, and potential, even after the rela-

tionships cease, avoiding future associations wherein inside information is sought that would give a desired advantage over a member's previous clients.

9. In avoiding practices that might tend to corrupt the processes of government, members shall not make undisclosed gifts of cash or other valuable considerations that are designed to influence specific decisions of voters, legislators, or public officials on public matters. A business lunch or dinner, or other comparable expenditure made in the course of communicating a point of view or public position, would not constitute such a violation. Nor, for example, would a plant visit designed and financed to provide useful background information to an interested legislator or candidate.

10. Nothing herein should be construed as prohibiting members from making legal, properly disclosed contributions to the candidates, party, or referenda issues of their choice.

11. Members shall not, through use of information known to be false or misleading, conveyed directly or through a third party, intentionally injure the public reputation of an opposing interest.

An Official Interpretation of the Code As It Applies to Financial Public Relations

This interpretation of the Society Code as it applies to financial public relations was originally adopted in 1963 and amended in 1972, 1977, 1983 and 1988 by action of the PRSA Board of Directors. "Financial public relations" is defined as "that area of public relations which relates to the dissemination of information that affects the understanding of stockholders and investors generally concerning the financial position and prospects of a company, and includes among its objectives the improvement of relations between corporations and their stockholders." The interpretation was prepared in 1963 by the Society's Financial Relations Committee, working with the Securities and Exchange Commission and with the advice of the Society's legal counsel. It is rooted directly in the Code with the full force of the Code behind it, and a violation of any of the following paragraphs is subject to the same procedures and penalties as violation of the Code.

1. It is the responsibility of PRSA members who practice financial public relations to be thoroughly familiar with and understand the rules and regulations of the SEC and the laws it administers, as well as other laws, rules, and regulations affecting financial public relations, and to act in accordance with their letter and spirit. In carrying out this responsibility, members shall also seek legal counsel, when appropriate, on matters concerning financial public relations.

2. Members shall adhere to the general policy of making full and timely disclosure of corporate information on behalf of clients or employers. The information disclosed shall be accurate, clear, and understandable. The purpose of such disclosure is to provide the investing public with all material information affecting security values or influencing investment decisions. In complying with the duty of full and timely disclosure, members shall present all material facts, including those adverse to the company. They shall exercise care to ascertain the facts and to disseminate only information they believe to be accurate. They shall not knowingly omit information, the omission of which might make a re-

lease false or misleading. Under no circumstances shall members participate in any activity designed to mislead or manipulate the price of a company's securities.

3. Members shall publicly disclose or release information promptly so as to avoid the possibility of any use of the information by any insider or third party. To that end, members shall make every effort to comply with the spirit and intent of the timely-disclosure policies of the stock exchanges, NASD, and the SEC. Material information shall be made available on an equal basis.

4. Members shall not disclose confidential information the disclosure of which might be adverse to a valid corporate purpose or interest and whose disclosure is not required by the timely-disclosure provisions of the law. During any such period of nondisclosure members shall not directly or indirectly (a) communicate the confidential information to any other person or (b) buy or sell or in any other way deal in the company's securities where the confidential information may materially affect the market for the security when disclosed. Material information shall be disclosed publicly as soon as its confidential status has terminated or the requirement of timely disclosure takes effect.

5. During the registration period, members shall not engage in practices designed to precondition the market for such securities. During registration, the issuance of forecasts, projections, predictions about sales and earnings, or opinions concerning security values or other aspects of the future performance of the company, shall be in accordance with current SEC regula-

tions and statements of policy. In the case of companies whose securities are publicly held, the normal flow of factual information to shareholders and the investing public shall continue during the registration period.

6. Where members have any reason to doubt that projections have an adequate basis in fact, they shall satisfy themselves as to the adequacy of the projections prior to disseminating them.

7. Acting in concert with clients or employers, members shall act promptly to correct false or misleading information or rumors concerning clients' or employers' securities or business whenever they have reason to believe such information or rumors are materially affecting investor attitudes.

8. Members shall not issue descriptive materials designed or written in such a fashion as to appear to be, contrary to fact, an independent third-party endorsement or recommendation of a company or a security. Whenever members issue material for clients or employers, either in their own names or in the names of someone other than the clients or employers, they shall disclose in large type and in a prominent position on the face of the material the source of such material and the existence of the issuer's client or employer relationship.

9. Members shall not use inside information for personal gain. However, this is not intended to prohibit members from making bona fide investments in their company's or client's securities insofar as they can make such investments

without the benefit of material inside information.

10. Members shall not accept compensation that would place them in a position of conflict, with their duty to a client, employer, or the investing public. Members shall not accept stock options from clients or employers nor accept securities as compensation at a price below market price except as part of an overall plan for corporate employees.

11. Members shall act so as to maintain the integrity of channels of public communication. They shall not pay or permit to be paid to any publication or other communications medium any consideration in exchange for publicizing a company, except through clearly recognizable paid advertising.

12. Members shall in general be guided by the PRSA Declaration of Principles and the Code of Professional Standards for the Practice of Public Relations of which this is an official interpretation.

CODE OF ETHICS OF THE INTERNATIONAL ASSOCIATION OF BUSINESS COMMUNICATORS*

The IABC Code of Ethics has been developed to provide IABC members and other communication professionals with guidelines of professional behavior and standards of ethical practice. The Code will be reviewed and revised as necessary by the Ethics Committee and the Executive Board.

Any IABC member who wishes advice and guidance regarding its interpretation and/or application may write or phone IABC headquarters. Questions will be routed to the Executive Board member responsible for the Code.

Communication and Information Dissemination

1. *Communication professionals will uphold the credibility and dignity of their profession by encouraging the practice of honest, candid and timely communication.*

---

*The following Code of Ethics of the International Association of Business Communicators is reprinted with permission of the IABC.

The highest standards of professionalism will be upheld in all communication. Communicators should encourage frequent communication and messages that are honest in their content, candid, accurate and appropriate to the needs of the organization and its audiences.

2. *Professional communicators will not use any information that has been generated or appropriately acquired by a business for another business without permission. Further, communicators should attempt to identify the source of information to be used.*

When one is changing employers, information developed at the previous position will not be used without permission from that employer. Acts of plagiarism and copyright infringement are illegal acts; material in the public domain should have its source attributed, if possible. If an organization grants permission to use its information and requests public acknowledgment, it will be made in a place appropriate to the material used. The material will be used only for the purpose for which permission was granted.

Standards of Conduct

3. *Communication professionals will abide by the spirit and letter of all laws and regulations governing their professional activities.*

All international, national and local laws and regulations must be observed, with particular attention to those pertaining to communication, such as copyright law. Industry and organizational regulations will also be observed.

4. *Communication professionals will not condone any illegal or unethical act related to their*

professional activity, their organization and its business or the public environment in which it operates.

It is the personal responsibility of professional communicators to act honestly, fairly and with integrity at all times in all professional activities. Looking the other way while others act illegally tacitly condones such acts whether or not the communicator has committed them. The communicator should speak with the individual involved, his or her supervisor or appropriate authorities—depending on the context of the situation and one's own ethical judgment.

Confidentiality/ Disclosure

5. *Communication professionals will respect the confidentiality and right-to-privacy of all individuals, employers, clients and customers.*

Communicators must determine the ethical balance between right-to-privacy and need-to-know. Unless the situation involves illegal or grossly unethical acts, confidences should be maintained. If there is a conflict between right-to-privacy and need-to-know, a communicator should first talk with the source and negotiate the need for the information to be communicated.

6. *Communication professionals will not use any confidential information gained as a result of professional activity for personal benefit or for that of others.*

Confidential information can be used to give inside advantage to stock transactions, gain favors from outsiders, assist a competing company for whom one is going to work, assist companies in developing a marketing advantage, achieve a publishing advantage or otherwise act to the detriment of an organization. Such information must remain confidential during and after one's employment period.

Professionalism

7. *Communication professionals should uphold IABC's standards for ethical conduct in all professional activity, and should use IABC and its designation of accreditation (ABC) only for purposes that are authorized and fairly represent the organization and its professional standards.*

IABC recognizes the need for professional integrity within any organization, including the association. Members should acknowledge that their actions reflect on themselves, their organizations and their profession.

Raymond Simon, professor emeritus of public relations at Utica College of Syracuse University, is a veteran public relations educator and consultant with more than four decades of experience in the field. Considered one of the nation's most prolific public relations authors, Professor Simon has written five public relations and publicity writing textbooks. These have gone through ten editions and been used in classrooms at more than 150 colleges and universities in public relations courses and programs.

Professor Simon is an accredited member of the Public Relations Society of America and the recipient of that group's Distinguished Teacher of the Year award. He is author of the Society's second national accreditation examination. Readers of the *Public Relations News* voted him "one of the world's 40 PR leaders" and in its 14th annual *Survey of the Profession* the *pr reporter* named him to be "among the 17 most respected experts in public relations specialties."

Professor Simon is currently Executive Director of the Raymond Simon Institute for Public Relations at Utica College.

Frank Winston Wylie, professor emeritus of public relations and former chairman of the journalism division at California State University, Long Beach, is also a veteran public relations practitioner and educator with more than four decades of experience in the field. This has included work in every major phase of public relations activities in corporate, non-profit, and government organizations, with responsibility for the administration of department and branch offices as well as multi-million dollar budgets.

Professor Wylie is a former national president of the Public Relations Society of America and was recently elected one of 26 Charter Fellows of that organization. He has served as a member of the Accrediting Council on Education in Journalism and Mass Communication and has lectured at more than 50 U.S. colleges and universities.

Professor Wylie has made numerous public relations presentations to a wide variety of organizations: the American Library Association Conference; key note presentation, the American Cancer Society Leadership Conference; the national conference of the Public Relations Student Society of America; and keynote addresses on ethics and public relations to the Association of American Medical Colleges and The Conference Board.

TITLES OF INTEREST IN
ADVERTISING, SALES PROMOTION, AND PUBLIC RELATIONS

For further information or a current catalog, write:
NTC Business Books
a division of *NTC Publishing Group*
4255 West Touhy Avenue
NTC Lincolnwood, Illinois 60646-1975 U.S.A.